Urban Education in America

Urban Education in America

Problems and Prospects

RAYMOND C. HUMMEL
University of Pittsburgh

JOHN M. NAGLE
University of Oregon

New York
OXFORD UNIVERSITY PRESS
London Toronto 1973

Copyright © 1973 by Oxford University Press, Inc.

Library of Congress Catalogue Card Number: 73-76910

Printed in the United States of America

To Beth,
for her care,
understanding,
and patience

Such poverty as we have in our cities degrades the poor and infects with its degradation the whole neighorhood in which they live. And whatever can degrade a neighborhood can degrade a country, a continent, and finally the whole civilized world, which is only a large neighborhood.

George Bernard Shaw

It is the very nature of life to strive to continue in being. Since this continuance can be secured only by constant renewals, life is a self-renewing process. What nutrition and reproduction are to psychological life, education is to social life.

John Dewey

The chief function of the city is to convert power into form, energy into culture, dead matter into the living symbols of art, biological reproduction into social creativity. The positive functions of the city cannot be performed without creating new institutional arrangements, capable of coping with the vast energies modern man now commands: arrangements just as bold as those that originally transformed the overgrown village and its stronghold into the nucleated, highly organized city.

Lewis Mumford

Preface

In the golden age of the early decades of this century—so goes the myth of the melting pot—city schools assimilated the children of the immigrant masses and made them into literate, loyal, employable Americans. Our images of those days are like scenes in a silent cinema: faded photographs of wan, cheerless faces in dingy classrooms. Our hearts are not discomfited; the pathos is past, distant. History tells us that things worked out for those children and for their children as well; the city school was—so the myth might continue—their pathway to better times and places.

Today's educators have much to learn from the experience of that era, as the lively histories of Lawrence Cremin[1] and of Sol Cohen[2] attest. They also have much to unlearn, if Colin Greer is correct.[3] He argues that, in truth, city schools failed miserably with those immigrant children. They left their dull, forbidding classrooms as soon as they could qualify for employment, usually before the age of fourteen; only 7 per cent graduated from secondary school in 1900, and fewer than 10 per cent in 1915. The children of the immigrant poor were Americanized not in schools, but in factories and union halls. Only as they and their children achieved economic stability and a middle-class ethos did schools become relevant places for them.

To revise the melting-pot myth is to freshen our perspective on the current "urban crisis" in education. The implication of the myth is that the children of today's nonwhite and other rural immigrants are more recalcitrant, less ready for schooling than their European predecessors. There are important distinctions between these groups, which this book will delineate. But to dispose of the myth may at least do away with the invidious assumption that current immigrants are less capable of being educated and morally less worthy of entering the American mainstream. The most obvious difference in educational status between the two immigrant groups is that the labor market of 1910 offered employment to those who left school whereas the current one does not. The mandate to educate failing or unwilling adolescents, which imposes the gravest single burden on contemporary urban schools, was largely unknown to schools at the turn of the century.

New perspectives are needed, perspectives that will encompass not only our schools and our history but also our urban institutions, their interrelationships, how they are to operate, and to what ends. Schools in the city have been literally breaking down; their efforts to instruct and influence children have continued to fail; pupils, teachers, parents, and administrators, maneuvering for advantage, are looking for support to coalitions of their own. High school students perceive less and less worth saving about the school, and thus have little to lose by disrupting it. Teachers have organized to promote their collective self-interests no less militantly than have students. Parents are less impressed by professional distance and less worried about what might happen to their children if they ask teachers hostile questions. But the perspectives of all concerned remain fragmentary.

We are all myopic. A bewildered educational and political leadership rides out one urban crisis after another as it gropes for ways to restore order. The institutional structure that sustained the traditional order of urban schools has been eroded drastically by larger urban trends since World War II. A fresh wave of immigrants, this time from rural America, has brought new ways and new problems to the life of large cities. Inner-city schools have been inundated with children whom the schools lack the resources, the techniques, and, in a troubling sense, even the will to teach. Political and fiscal anomalies in urban government have made it enormously difficult for big-city schools to obtain the support necessary to carry out even their traditional instructional tasks, much less assume responsibility for racial integration and for treatment of the whole catalogue of social ills found in a twentieth-century city. Yet both their traditional tasks and their new social responsibilities are ineluctable; urban schools will simply have to learn to deal effectively with both.

The goal of this book is to provide readers—parents, teachers, administrators, school board members, and the general public—with a systematic and comprehensive view of the condition of urban education in the 1970's. The book neither condemns nor defends city school systems. Rather, it surveys them broadly and objectively—noting trends, identifying problems, analyzing causes, and projecting futures. Its perspectives have been influenced by educational history, by research and practice in public schools, and by the recent voluminous flow of writings about urban conditions. Throughout the study, an effort has been made to look beyond symptoms and to discern what there is about a city—particularly about a modern urban setting that is significant to its public schools.

Although our primary interest is in urban education, we have not wanted, even for analytic purposes, to look at urban school systems in isolation from the larger urban milieu. Thus, underlying our analysis are the following premises: first, an urban school system is one of many interdependent social subsystems in a city, and second, the larger social system which we identify as a city has an integrity of its own. Therefore, discussion of the conditions and problems of urban schools requires attention not only to the schools *per se*, but also to the total urban setting and to their interactions with other subsystems in that setting.

Although many of the problems of urban schools derive from internal faults of organization and administration, their most critical problems, we believe, are rooted in their larger urban setting: residential patterns distorted by racial and socioeconomic segregation; meager transportation facilities which cramp the movement of city residents among home, school, job, and recreation; and a labor market that offers inner-city pupils the prospect of unemployment or underemployment in menial jobs and convinces them that schooling is mostly irrelevant. The big-city school has become an arena in which a wide array of social problems are displayed and enacted. Social needs and pathologies which in the past were related only indirectly to the educational process are now being assigned to the public schools for treatment.

These new expectations of city schools are to some degree unrealistic and unfair. Yet city educators cannot continue to project their failures, as their predecessors did in the earlier decades, onto "bad homes" and other conditions. The public is increasingly insistent that the schools work from "where it's at," that they endeavor to reach and teach all children, black and white, able and handicapped, to the limits of their potential. Big-city public schools have thus been recruited during the past decade or so to function as a central institution in urban development and reform. The problems of urban education are coalescing more than ever with those of urban life. It is becoming increasingly clear that we cannot have good public schools in bad cities, nor are we likely to have good cities without developing good urban schools.

For the purposes of this study, the topic "urban education" has been limited by focusing principally, although not exclusively, on the public elementary and secondary school systems in the nation's fifty largest central cities.[4] Each of these cities has a population in excess of a quarter of a million and a public-school enrollment that exceeds 50,000 students. Each is at the heart of a major metropolitan area, surrounded by suburban communities which vary widely in their history, socioeconomic character, and relations with the central city. And each has had to cope in recent years with serious problems resulting from population change, racial tension, economic decline, physical decay, bureaucratic complexity, and an increasing demand for social services. Throughout the study, therefore, the terms "big-city schools" and "urban school systems" are used to refer primarily to the school districts in these fifty large central cities, rather than to districts in their surrounding suburbs or satellite cities.

It is convenient to focus a discussion of urban education on happenings in these city schools, since that is where the nation's problems of urban education are most acute. Geographically, of course, an urban setting includes not only a central city, but also its suburbs, satellite cities, and exurbs; an urban setting includes, in sum, an entire metropolitan region. Inescapably, school districts in all the nation's approximately 250 major metropolitan areas—city districts first, but those in the suburbs soon thereafter—will face many of the same social problems that now embroil the largest urban school systems. Although differing in magnitude, the issues and the social dynamics will be similar. In a certain sense, therefore, big-city schools can be regarded as observation posts or social laboratories in which to study the dysfunctions in our educational systems of today and tomorrow. Urbanologists of the nineteenth century envisioned this role for public schools; it is, in fact, an assumption underlying the analysis in this book.

Throughout the book's preparation, several factors have influenced, if not actually limited, its substantive development. First, the conditions surrounding urban education are rapidly changing, making it difficult to gather information that is both valid and timely. The issues of integration and compensatory education illustrate well the flux of urban education. The 1954 U. S. Supreme Court decision made racial integration in schools a national mandate. During the 1960's, however, the pressure to integrate was accompanied, and somewhat diminished, by the hope of instituting compensatory education programs. Then the pendulum began to swing again, as efforts in compensatory education proved disappointing and as judicial rulings and Office of Education tactics increased pressure on Southern schools and on de facto segregated Northern schools to integrate. And now lately, public antipathy to large-scale busing and to court-imposed integration of students seems once again to be causing a swing of the pendulum. Similar shifts of attitude and of policy have occurred with regard to the decentralization of large urban school districts, the staffing of schools with noncertificated personnel, and the role of community groups in making public school policy. As a result, efforts to analyze and report these conditions become a little like playing tag.

A second factor influencing the study is the insufficiency and incomparability of basic data on public school systems. The Research Council of the Great Cities Program for School Improvement is, as its name implies, solely concerned with the largest city school systems in the United States, and so it generates data primarily for in-house use rather than for comparing urban and nonurban school systems. Data gathered by state and federal agencies and by private researchers typically have not been concerned with urban schools *per se*. It is thus often difficult to derive from the available data comparable statistics that are specifically relevant to a study of urban schools.

Third, the approach of this study is synoptic rather than particular. Its subject is urban education, not the public schools of Portland or Pittsburgh. The aim is to portray the conditions of education in urban settings generally rather than details specific to Los Angeles or Chicago. It is hoped that such a synopsis will both encourage further study and enable the reader to deal more effectively with the problems of education in particular urban settings.

Fourth and finally, on a subject that has ramifications throughout all of modern life, this book offers the perspective of only two authors. Several good anthologies on urban education containing a wider range of information and points of view already have been published. A number of single-author books that have appeared treat certain aspects of urban education intensively; for example, Abraham Bernstein's work, *The Education of Urban Populations*, is witty and urbane on problems of curriculum and instruction.[5] By contrast, this book attempts to be both singular in its point of view and comprehensive in its treatment. As a source book, it may be used both for overview and for detailed study of particular topics.

Frequently in studies such as this, problem-identification and prescription-writing become so badly confused as to offer solutions to problems that have not themselves been adequately defined. Throughout this book, an effort has been made to avoid intertwining designative and prescriptive modes of inquiry. For the most part, recommendations—"what might be done"—have been incorporated only in the final chapter of the book; the remainder is primarily a study of the current state of urban education in the United States.

By way of introduction, Chapter 1 presents a series of vignettes on the urban scene and urban schools. All are reports of actual events; some are given verbatim as originally published; others have been condensed or rewritten. Taken together, they form a cross section of the problems with which urban school systems are currently besieged. In a certain sense, the remainder of the book is a commentary on these vignettes. As a framework for that commentary, Chapter 2 analyzes the systemic character of a public school district and highlights some of its interactions with a complex social, political, and economic environment.

The next five chapters examine the urban school in its urban setting. Chapter 3 focuses on the city itself, on its historical role in education, its status in an increasingly secular and urban society, and its major social and economic burdens in the 1970. With this as a kind of prelude, particular conditions in urban school systems are then examined. Chapter 4 deals with the general character of big-city school districts, their size and scope, Chapter 5 with the personnel involved—students, teachers, administrators, and board members—Chapter 6 with the organization of urban school systems, and Chapter 7 with their financial status.

Finally, Chapter 8 and 9 consider the social and educational conditions likely to obtain in urban settings over the next few decades, and their implications for the future of public education in the nation's largest cities.

March 1973   R. C. H. / J. M. N.

Acknowledgments

The authors have lived in and been fascinated by cities all their lives. We attended city schools and later worked in them as professional educators. The idea of writing this book was sparked, quite unintentionally, by the lectures of Professor Ryland Crary on urban education at the University of Pittsburgh in 1968.

It would be impossible, of course, to acknowledge the assistance of all who contributed to the book. We are particularly grateful, however, to have had available, during its three years of preparation, the resources of the University of Oregon, the University of Pittsburgh, the Center for the Advanced Study of Educational Administration (CASEA), and the Learning Research and Development Center (LRDC). In addition, we wish to acknowledge personally the competent help of Connie Hixson, librarian for CASEA, and of Lynda Alpine Pinson, Jackie Fountain, Carla Borkosky, Sandra Boggs, Darlyne Jacobson, and Beth Nagle for their expert typing and proofreading.

Contents

I Introduction and Framework for Analysis

1 The Problems of Urban Schools   3

2 The Urban School as a Social Organization   23

A Historical Perspective on Urban Schools   26
A Structural Perspective on Urban Schools   37

II Urban Schools in Their Social Setting

3 The City as an Educational Setting   45

From Village to City   47
The Division of Labor and Specialization of Work   50
Industrial Expansion   53
Urban Expansion   54
Secularization   65
The Character of Contemporary American Cities   69
The Burdens of Contemporary American Cities   71
The Changing Character of Migrants to Cities   72

4   Urban Schools: Their Size and Scope   82

The Enormous Size of Urban School Systems   83
The Ultimate Urban School System: The New York City Public
    Schools   86
A Paramount Characteristic of Urban School Enrollments: Racial
    and Socioeconomic Segregation   88
Principal Factors in the Racial and Socioeconomic Segregation of
    Urban Students   89
Racial Segregation in Urban School Enrollments   102
Socioeconomic Segregation in Urban School Enrollments   109

5   The People in Urban Schools   111

The Student   111
Urban Children and the Mass Media   113
Educational Disadvantage of the Urban Child   115
The Teachers   117
The Policymakers   133
The Administrators   138

6   The Organization of Urban Schools   143

Defining the Role of Urban Schools   145
The Character of Bureaucracy in Urban Schools   154
Resistance of Urban School Systems to Change   160

7   The Financial Condition of Urban Schools   168

Urban Expenditures: Mammoth and Becoming More So   170
Urban Expenditures Compared with National, State, and Suburban
    Levels   173
Factors Behind the Financial Crunch in Urban Education   180
In Conclusion   202

III Prospects For Urban Education

8 Trends and Probable Outcomes   207

Trends in Public School Enrollments in Large Central Cities   207
The Prospects for Industry and Employment in Urban
    Centers   212
The Prospects for Education, Employment, and Residential
    Integration of Nonwhites   219
The Prospects for Reconstructing Ghettos and Their Urban
    Settings   227
The Prospects for Metropolitanism in Urban Settings   234

9 Toward a Strategy for Urban School Reform   245

Developing a Methodology for Urban School Reform   246
Achieving Perspective on Urban School Reform   252

In Retrospect   279
Notes   281
Index   295

List of Tables

Chapter 3

3–1   Urban–Rural Distribution of the Population of the United States Between 1790 and 1970   57

3–2   Percentage of Change Between 1950 and 1970 in Total Population of Twenty-nine Selected States   59

3–3   Number and Proportion of the Total Work Force in the United States Engaged in Farming Between 1900 and 1970   60

3–4   Urban–Suburban Distribution of the Population in Metropolitan Areas of the United States in 1950, 1960, and 1970   61

3–5   Comparative Percentage of Change Between 1960 and 1970 in Total Population of Twenty-nine Selected Large Central Cities and Their Respective Suburbs   63

3–6   Percentage of Change Between 1950 and 1970 in Negro Population of the United States; Geographic Distribution of Negroes in 1970   75

3–7   Percentage of Change Between 1960 and 1970 in Total, White, and Negro Population in Sixteen Selected Large Central Cities   76

3–8   Proportion of Negroes in Total Population of Sixteen Selected Large Central Cities in 1950, 1960, and 1970   77

3–9   Disparities in the Social and Economic Characteristics of Central City and Suburban Populations in the United States in 1969 and 1970   80

Chapter 4

4–1   Comparative Enrollment, Staffing, and Expenditure Estimates for Public School Districts in the United States in 1970; by Selected Geographic Areas   84

4–2   Comparative Enrollment, Staffing, High School Graduates, and Expenditure Estimates for Fifteen Selected Large Central City School Districts in 1970   85

4–3   Selected Information on the New York City Public Schools for the 1968–69 School Year   87

4–4   Nonpublic School Enrollment Between 1950 and 1970 as a Percentage of the Total School Enrollment in the United States in Grades K–12   91

4–5   Geographic Distribution of Public and Nonpublic School Students in the United States, 1970   92

4–6   Comparative Percentages of Nonpublic School Students in the Central City and Suburban Regions of Fifteen Major Metropolitan Areas of the United States, 1960   94

4–7   Percentages of Negroes and Whites Enrolled in Nonpublic Schools in Central Cities, Suburbs, and Nonmetropolitan Areas of the United States in 1970; Comparative Percentages of Negroes Enrolled in Public Schools in Those Same Areas   96

4–8   Racial Composition of the Student Enrollment in 1966–67 in Sixteen Selected Large Central City School Districts   103

4–9   Changes in Enrollment Between 1950 and 1960 in Fifteen City School Districts   104

4–10 Changes Prior to 1965 in the Degree of Racial Segregation in Elementary School Enrollments in Ten Central City School Districts   107

Chapter 5

5–1   Increases Between 1965 and 1970 in the Size of Teaching Staffs in Fifteen Selected Large Central City School Districts   118

5–2   Level of Educational Preparation of Classroom Teachers in 1967   121

5–3   Number of Classroom Teachers with Less than a Standard Teaching Certificate in Ten Selected Central City School Districts in 1963 through 1969   122

5–4   Problems Identified as Most Important in 1968 by Teachers in Urban, Suburban, and Rural Schools   127

5–5   Teachers' Salaries and the Cost of Living in Sixteen U.S. Central Cities, 1959–1969   128

5–6   Selected Comparisons of Teacher Salaries with Other Salaries and Costs in 1969–70 in Twelve Cities   131

5–7   School Boards in Twenty-two Large Central City School Districts in 1969: Method of Selection, Term of Office, and Number of Members   134

5–8   School Boards in Twenty-two Large Central City School Districts: Pupil Enrollment, Number of Official Meetings, and Rate of Compensation for Board Members, 1968–69   136

Chapter 7

7–1   Increase Between 1960 and 1970 in Estimated Total Expenditures by Fifteen Selected Large Central City School Districts   171

7–2   Increase Between 1960 and 1970 in Estimated Current Expenditures per Pupil in Fifteen Selected Large Central City School Districts   172

7–3   Estimated Current Expenditures per Pupil Between 1960 and 1970 in Fifteen Selected Large Central City School Districts, Expressed as a Percentage of the National Average   174

7–4   Historical Review Between 1921 and 1970 of Estimated Current Expenditures per Pupil in the United States and in Four Selected Large Central City School Districts, Expressed as a Percentage of the National Average   175

7–5   Historical Review Between 1929 and 1970 of Estimated Current Expenditures per Pupil in Fourteen Central City School Districts, Expressed as a Percentage of Their Respective State Averages   176

7–6   Measures of Tax Effort in 1962 in Central Cities and Suburbs of the Nation's Twenty-two Largest Metropolitan Areas   188

7–7   Municipal Overburden as Indicated by the Comparative Percentages of Property Taxes Used for Noneducational Purposes in Ten Central Cities and in Other Local Governments Within Respective States   190

7–8   An Inadequately Growing Tax Base: Changes During a Recent Five-Year Period in per Pupil Taxable Assessed Valuation in Fourteen Selected Large Central Cities   191

7–9   An Inadequately Growing Tax Base: Estimates of Per Capita Value of Taxable Property in Fifteen Selected Large Central Cities in 1930 and 1960   193

7–10   Ratios of Assessed Valuation to Full-Market Valuation in
        Fifteen Selected Large Central Cities in 1930 and 1960;
        Assessment Ratios in 1962 on Residential Housing Only   196

Chapter 8
8–1   Nonwhite Percentage of School-Age Population in Fifteen
        Selected Large Central Cities of the United States in 1960
        209

8–2   Actual and Projected Employment in the United States
        Between 1960 and 1975, by Major Occupational Group   216

8–3   Actual and Projected Employment in the United States Be-
        tween 1960 and 1975, by Type of Industry   217

8–4   A Growing Urban Negro Middle Class: Changes Between
        1960 and 1970 in Occupational Distribution of Male Ne-
        groes Residing in All Metropolitan Areas of the United
        States   221

8–5   A Growing Urban Negro Middle Class: Increases Between
        1960 and 1970 in Level of Education of Negroes Residing in
        All Metropolitan Areas of the United States.   222

8–6   A Growing Urban Negro Middle Class: Increases Between
        1959 and 1969 in the Annual Income Levels of Negroes Re-
        siding in All Metropolitan Areas of the United States.   222

8–7   Estimated Percentage of White and Negro Households Lo-
        cated in 1967 in Integrated and Segregated Neighborhoods
        in the United States   224–25

I Introduction and Framework for Analysis

1 The Problems of Urban Schools

This Is It

For five months we lived under the threats of a teacher walk-out occasioned in part by rivalry of two major teacher organizations. . . . Teams of investigators from the Department of Health, Education, and Welfare visited schools, collected data, and interviewed community groups to determine if our school system was complying with the Civil Rights Act and not discriminating against Negroes and Mexican-Americans. . . . Students became restless because "soul food" was not served in cafeterias. . . . Community groups demanded involvement in the operation of local schools. . . . The Civil Liberties Union objected to "Silent Night" and the display of the crèche at Christmas time. . . . Agitation from civil rights groups and suburban liberals and political activist clergy continued because integration was not proceeding fast enough. . . . It became evident that badly needed construction projects might not be realized because of escalation of costs. . . . Teachers criticized plans to develop pilot programs in modular scheduling and differentiated staffing. . . . Threaded through some of these were suggestions and petitions that the Superintendent should go. . . . A student walkout on the morning of the funeral of Martin Luther King precipitated a chain of events that led to several nights of rioting and curfews.[1]

These were a few of the events during a single school year in one of the nation's largest urban school systems.

A Changing Demography

In 1950, the population of Pittsburgh exceeded 675,000 people. Ten years later, the city's total population had declined by 10 per cent, whereas its nonwhite population had actually increased in both proportion and total number. Throughout the last decade, these trends continued unabated: the city lost nearly 40 per cent of its young adults, the "young marrieds" with their preschool and early school-age children, and its public school enrollment is now more than 40 per cent Negro.

The average school building in Pittsburgh was built more than fifty-five years ago. Because the newest secondary school buildings in the district were opened more than forty years ago, its high schools are not only racially segregated, but crowded and seriously lacking in the facilities and sites necessary for an adequate educational program for grades nine through twelve.

Like many other major cities in the United States, Pittsburgh has a large nonpublic school system: 75,000 children attend its public schools, but another 46,000 youngsters are enrolled in parochial schools—most of which are Catholic. Moreover, while these two vast school systems operate side by side, the city is completely surrounded by independent political subdivisions whose school districts are totally unrelated to the city school system. And, to date, there has been little tendency in either city or suburbs to initiate or extend inter-city cooperation in elementary and secondary school programs.[2]

Of major cities in the United States, Washington, D.C., may be the most accurate harbinger of urban trends. Expenditures in Washington have been about average for a large city; but neither these nor administrative measures designed to favor the city's remaining white and middle-class residents have succeeded in maintaining a stable population. So many white residents of Washington have fled to the suburbs or enrolled their children in private or parochial schools that the proportion of white students in Washington public schools, which was 55 per cent before the Supreme Court's desegregation decision in 1954, had declined by 1972 to less than 10 per cent. Moreover, the city itself has a substantial Negro majority, and more than 50 per cent of the children in its public schools now come from families below the poverty level.

Dr. Henley's Cry for Help

Almost plaintively, Acting Superintendent Benjamin J. Henley told the school board the other night that "our chief function is instruction. Even if we don't do it very well, we can't do it in the environment we have now." Dr. Henley was talking about the thefts and vandalism that deprive the schools of specialized equipment on which many educational courses depend. He was talking about the dropouts who hang around the schools for want of anything to do other than to disrupt school programs. He was talking about the decline in discipline within some schools, prompting teacher protests and producing lurid testimony on Capitol Hill. He was talking about the distribution of narcotics to school children.

The school system has resisted pressure to call for the assignment of policemen or special security guards through all school buildings, although there is increasing recognition that it may come to that if nothing comes of other efforts to establish a better instructional environment. Already, policemen are being assigned during regular school hours to some schools. Other schools have gotten over their traditional reluctance to call for outside police help when trouble develops. Budget requests are being made for alarm systems and night watchmen to protect typewriters, audio-visual equipment, and specialized laboratory materials during hours when schools are closed.

Unquestionably, the problem cannot be solved indefinitely by making the schools into the little fortress enclaves, walled off from the communities they are supposed to serve. Dr. Henley is right that the community must share responsibility with the schools for the atmosphere within. He is less precise on how to secure the needed community support, other than to go out and ask for it. He put it this way: "The community knows about the dope. The community knows about the dangerous weapons. The total community will have to bring its total pressure to bear if we are going to have safe schools and safe streets and stamp out the unhealthy places children frequent during the day."

Clearly, it is a problem well beyond the schools—one that involves parent groups as well as the police, City Hall as well as the courts, and even Capitol Hill which will need to provide the funds. Dr. Henley's candor in acknowledging the problem is to be commended. What is needed now is initiative—from the Mayor as well as interested citizens—to get something done.[3]

School Boards and Their Clients

In February 1969 the Organization of Concerned Citizens and two of its leaders were barred by court order from disrupting future meetings of the Pittsburgh Board of Education. An injunction issued by a judge of the Court of Common Pleas forbade the protesters from "shouting, talking, clamoring, clapping, or making any loud or disturbing noises at board meetings." They were also prohibited from sponsoring any demonstrations at board meetings or otherwise disturbing the orderly conduct of school board business.

Since the prior spring, the Concerned Citizens—a racially mixed, loosely organized coalition of about fifty persons—had sought opportunities to take part in the deliberations of the school board at its monthly business sessions. To support their demands, they had conducted a series of noisy demonstrations which had forced the abrupt adjournment of several regular school board meetings in December and January. The ruling judge pointed out that, under pressure from the Concerned Citizens and other groups, the board had not only instituted public hearings one week prior to each business meeting, but had also shifted the time of those hearings from late afternoon to early evening so that more school patrons could attend. Apparently unsatisfied, the Concerned Citizens served notice, soon after the court order, that their pressure on the board to make *all* meetings public would continue.[4]

Academic Sickness in New York

Every day, somewhere in New York City's public school system, at least one teacher is shoved or struck by recalcitrant students; uncounted others are cursed and threatened with beatings. Last week, in the wake of thirteen such student assaults in the past six months, teachers at Bronx Junior High School [#—], where 96 per cent of the students are either Negro or Puerto Rican, finally got fed up. Among other things, they asked Principal [——] and the school board to provide more protection than the single patrolman already on full-time duty there [and to] give them the right to kick abusive students out of class. When school board officials failed to meet the demands, 79 teachers—about 30 of them women—protested by turning in their resignations. After a three-day walkout, they were persuaded to return.

The mass resignation was just the latest painful symptom of the sickness that prevails in the nation's largest and least efficient public school system. To service a student population of more than one million and pay a teacher staff of 54,600, New York next year proposes to spend $1.1 billion [over two billion dollars in 1971–72]—more than is spent by 26 states to operate their entire governments. The budget breaks down to an expenditure of about $1,000 a year per student, roughly $400 above the national average; teacher salaries are among the highest of large U. S. cities. Yet the results are academically deplorable: recent surveys showed that New York students ranked well below national norms in such basic skills as reading and arithmetic. . . .

The fact is that no one has any solution to the problems of New York City's schools. "I think we've done as well as most schools, and God knows we've tried hard—but we just haven't done it," concedes Superintendent Bernard E. Donovan. In trying to prevent de facto segregation, for example, the school board adopted an "open enrollment" plan, providing free buses for Negroes to attend white schools; too few cared to make the trip. They've also tried the "Princeton Plan" of pairing white and Negro schools so that all students in each grade can attend the same school. But white parents objected to sending their children into Negro areas, and physical barriers between white and Negro neighborhoods reduced the number of suitable pairings to a mere eight schools.

The city's United Federation of Teachers, which is the nation's strongest local teachers' organization, seems to have no answer either. It refuses to permit school administrators to shift veteran teachers into slum schools against their will. Beginners are thus thrown into some of the toughest teaching tasks in the nation—and are shaken by the experience. "I'll never forget when I was sent into that class, I had to show those children not how to read but how to open a book," says one recent Vassar graduate. Recalling his first day in a slum school, one teacher says that his only help from the principal was the order: "Keep 'em in the room." He did. He also recalls that it took him three lonely years to learn how to teach them.

School board leaders spend much of their energy coping with segregation problems—even though the bigger issue is the quality of education and teachers' expectation of transmitting it. But even segregation defies solution. . . .[5]

Desegregation—A Continuing, Volatile Issue

In the summer of 1971, scores of schoolboys fanned out through the suburbs of Dallas, ringing doorbells and rounding up signatures on a statement opposing an explosive school desegregation plan. Mexican-Americans accounted for about 8 per cent of the district's enrollment, and less than 4 per cent of the district's black enrollment attended integrated schools. The aim of the plan was to integrate each public school's population on the basis of 60 per cent white and 40 per cent minority-group students. This was to be achieved through a broad-scale busing program that would affect a large portion of the city's 185,000 school children, result in the closing of twelve predominantly black schools, and involve busing some children as far as thirty miles each day.

Within days, opposition to the plan mounted. Meetings were held to protest gerrymandering of present neighborhood boundaries. Fifteen hundred parents crowded a meeting in suburban Dallas, where "Keep the neighborhood school concept" became the rallying cry. Families erected front-yard billboards declaring, "We will not bus." Numerous suits were filed. And the Chicano population in Dallas protested that the plan would result in desegregating black schools almost solely with Mexican-Americans, since they were counted along with whites in setting the district's ethnic ratios.[6]

Narcotics Raid at School

In the fall of 1969 the following Associated Press dispatch appeared in major U.S. newspapers:

A group of schoolchildren lined up outside a Bronx public school, books in hand. They also carried stolen merchandise or lunch money to trade for narcotics.

Police seized seven men Wednesday and charged them with bartering with elementary and high school pupils, trading heroin and cocaine for stolen television sets, radios, clothes, and jewelry.

Evading sentries equipped with walkie-talkies, detectives slugged it out with alleged dope peddlers as hundreds of children screamed and ran for cover.

Police said they seized 75 bags of heroin, four capsules of cocaine, and nearly $250 in cash—in pennies, nickels, dimes, quarters, and dollar bills, the youngsters' lunch money.

Some kids sold narcotics in school and were paid in small doses for their own use, detectives said.

The roundup took place outside Public School 23, the main gathering point for daily exchange, police said. Pupils ranged in age from eight to the mid-teens, including some from Morris

High School, police said. An investigation into a rash of thefts from local stores and apartments turned up the narcotics angle, police said.

Men were observed trading narcotics for merchandise each school morning between 7 and 9 A.M., police said. Detectives staked out the public school Wednesday and watched the kids line up for the trade. Then they moved in.[7]

School-University Collaboration: Hopes and Failure

Occasionally, urban universities have tried to bring their knowledge and expertise to bear on the problems facing big-city school systems. In 1966, New York University attempted a program in one of New York City's junior high schools. Two reports published by the *New York Times*, in 1966 and 1967, tell what happened.

The following appeared in July, 1966:

NYU ADOPTING A SCHOOL
FOR BROOKLYN SLUM STUDY

New York University has adopted a junior high school in the middle of the predominantly Negro Bedford-Stuyvesant area of Brooklyn in an effort to show that a slum neighborhood can be rehabilitated by making the school the center of reform.

University faculty and students will saturate the schools and its immediate community and educate the children, reach out to parents, appoint and train local "community agents," and train adults for better jobs.

At the same time, the work in the demonstration school will be used to revamp teacher training procedures and to recruit high school students from slum neighborhoods for teaching careers.

The Ford Foundation has given the project, called the Clinic for Learning, a grant of $350,000 for two and a half years. The Board of Education is adding $100,000 more for additional staff during the next two years. The project is designed to be studied by other universities and schools across the country.

The school to be helped is Junior High School 57. . . . Situated amid crowded old brownstone houses, it was chosen as "a typical school" in a ghetto area, no better or worse than most other schools in such circumstances.

"At first, we ran into some real skepticism on the part of the public school educators, but by now everyone is fired with enthusiasm," said Dr. John C. Robertson, professor of secondary education at NYU's School of Education and director of the clinic.

"This will give a tremendous boost to our teacher morale," said Lewis P. Schwartz, principal of the school. "Suddenly we see goals that can be attained." . . .[8]

Just over a year later, the following progress report appeared:

NYU CLINIC STALLED IN
TRYING TO IMPROVE SCHOOL

Signs of boredom, a sullen snapping of bubble gum, an occasional sharp scuffle, and the weary, hectoring voices of defeated teachers are typical classroom sounds at Whitelaw Reid Junior High School, in the heart of Brooklyn's Bedford-Stuyvesant area.

It is this restlessness, and what a New York University professor calls the "bureaucratic rigidity" of the school system, rather than more lurid lapses of student conduct—violence in the hallways, glue sniffing, pregnancy among the girls—that have defeated efforts of the NYU School of Education to radically change the school.

"We got the hell kicked out of us by the situation," said Professor John C. Robertson, director of the University's "Clinic for Learning" at Junior High School 57. . . . The project, begun last year, was financed by a $350,000 grant from the Ford Foundation and $100,000 from the Board of Education.

"We've abandoned our efforts to change the school," Professor Robertson said. "Our staff has been through a shattering experience. It's a defeat for the university and for the school system." . . .

Professor Robertson did not blame the 1,200 children, of whom 70 per cent are Negro and about 28 per cent Puerto Rican. How could they be attentive, he asked, if the curriculum and the teaching had no relevance to their lives? And he wasn't blaming the parents.

He was critical of the administration. He said the principal, Lewis P. Schwartz, cited "administrative difficulties" for not implementing the clinic's proposals. The teachers also were resistant, he said, being "preconditioned to what the system demands of them." . . .

It was quiet downstairs in the principal's office. "You couldn't sit here last year," said Mr. Schwartz, explaining that last semester the din had spread throughout the school.

He blamed the clinic staff. A year ago, he said, he accepted the experiment with enthusiasm. He thought the infusion of undergraduate students, researchers, and experts would give "a tremendous boost to our teacher morale."

The school needed help. By the Board of Education's standardized achievement tests, J.H.S. 57 was one of the worst in the city. Of 118 junior high schools, it ranked 104 in reading achievement. And reading retardation was disastrous for students seeking jobs.

But now Mr. Schwartz says he is completely disenchanted with the clinic. The staff had encouraged an air of permissiveness, he said, and classroom discipline last year had broken down. This year there has been "a tightening of procedures"—students can no longer roam about at will—but he is convinced that "the university doesn't have all the answers." He wishes the clinic would go away, the sooner the better. . . .[9]

Vandalism, Unrest, Fear

Crisply and dispassionately, the Dean of Students spoke to the student body over the public address system. He stood inside a glass cubicle, close to the microphone, and his words rang noisily through the corridors: "The girl involved in yesterday's incident is not hurt. . . . Rumors that she is dead or dying are totally unfounded. . . . The area is under surveillance by the police. . . . All students are to go directly home after their last class. . . . I repeat, all students . . ."

A small Negro girl, books cradled against her chest, stopped a visitor just outside the Principal's office and said ominously, "You go in there, Mister, and they'll tell you a lot of stories. They'll make a good impression. But don't believe them, Mister. This place is going to explode."

Moments later, the Principal eased back into his chair. "I agree that many things here need improvement," he said, choosing his words slowly, "but many things are as good as they are at other schools. This is no more a problem school than any other in the district or than many in the city."

The school, a sprawling, three-story building, has educated thousands of children from the city's low-income neighborhoods, and for more than a decade it has done so with little interference from parents. Now, however, the parents are pressing strongly for reforms in educational and disciplinary procedures. The school's administration, especially the Principal, views this agitation as something close to a conspiracy. "It's a planned campaign for community control," asserts the Principal, a man with closely cropped hair and silver-rimmed glasses. "And now the parents are beginning to bring outsiders in. They ask us a lot of questions, and whenever we meet, tensions develop."

These tensions, and an atmosphere of mutual suspicion in which rumors fly unchecked, have filtered down through the 1100-member student body, which is 100 per cent nonwhite and two-thirds black. For instance, a recent fight between two boys—one Negro and the other Puerto Rican—was not quelled in the shop class where it began. It grew as friends stepped in, and took on a racial character when 200 students spilled out into the street after school, gathering in angry knots under the nearby overpass of a major expressway. Miraculously, a riot was averted, but persistent rumors that a girl had been injured kept the school on the edge of a crisis for days.

The most readily accessible instruments for expressing student unrest are the fire alarms. According to one of the school's assistant principals, they now sound two or three times a day. The problem has become so severe that the administration has coated the handles of the alarms with a mixture of vaseline and a fluorescent substance that remains invisible until struck by ultraviolet rays. When an alarm is sounded during a class period, suspects are rounded up and examined under a lamp called a Spectroline. If a luminescent glow appears, the offender is disciplined and sometimes temporarily suspended.

Vandalism, too, plagues the school. So many windows have been broken lately that the empty panes are being filled with nonbreakable transparent plastic. So much clothing has been stolen from the coatrooms that many students carry their coats with them throughout the day. Weekend burglaries have become so common —including a series of thefts in which all thirty-three typewriters from the typing classroom disappeared—that an expensive alert system, which automatically telephones the local police precinct station and plays a recorded call for assistance, is being installed.

One morning in early January, a student arrived at school at ten in the morning. It was not noticed at the time, according to the Principal, that "his signature was shaky." Half an hour later, however, the student collapsed in a classroom. Several needles were found in his pockets, and an eyedropper in one of his socks. The boy was taken to a hospital and revived, but the diagnosis—"alcoholic intoxication"—was made public too late, and seemed too suspect, to prevent rumors that hard narcotics had spread to the school. The use of marijuana in restrooms and on stairwells had been suspected for some time and was finally beginning to come out into the open. This latest incident immediately mobilized the school's Parents Association, which met the following night and drafted a letter to school district officials condemning what was termed "the intolerable miseducation and mistreatment of our children at this school." The Association charged supervisors with the physical abuse of students and called for the closing of the school.

A copy of the Association's letter, which was freely distributed, fell into the hands of the school's principal, and its contents infuriated him. "They twist everything around," he argued, pulling a copy of the letter from his breast pocket. "The question is how far the school should go in establishing control. Control is necessary for teachers to teach. The parents ask you for strict discipline, but then when you apply it, they're against you!"[10]

One Tactic to Maintain Order

At the beginning of the 1971–72 school year an Associated Press dispatch indicated that a 50 per cent increase in acts of vandalism and a 30 per cent increase in reported assault cases in the Portland, Oregon, schools had led to more stringent rules and regulations on student behavior. Unprovoked assault on another student or teacher, for instance, would now result in mandatory expulsion from school. In addition, the district's high school principals were told by their superintendent that they would be dismissed if they failed to enforce effectively the new school regulations.[11]

RATES HAVE SOARED
ALONG WITH DAMAGE IN CITIES

In recent years, insurance companies have become increasingly selective and chary when underwriting urban school systems. The record of school property destruction resulting during school disorders in major urban districts is not one to send insurance agents and their company chiefs to bed with visions of easy profits dancing in their heads. . . .

The fact is that school destruction and vandalism is increasing at a dramatically accelerated rate. In the first six months of 1969, the Philadelphia public schools suffered theft and vandalism losses of $1.5 million. Insurance companies have indicated that they will write policies against this kind of loss, but, as the president of the Philadelphia School Board declares, "I would assume the cost would be prohibitive." Insurance agents agree it would indeed. . . . Baltimore's school system suffered damage in 1968 of up to half a million dollars from deliberately set fires in school buildings. . . . The cost of fire insurance for the Atlanta school system jumped from $60,000 to $200,000 in 1968. . . . And

San Francisco was charged a premium increase in 1968 of almost 50 per cent for just fire insurance and extended coverage. . . .

When urban school systems seek to renew their old policies or buy new ones, they find that not only premiums but also "deductibles" are steadily increasing. The head of the School Insurance Department of Los Angeles, which carries liability and property damage insurance totaling $10 million each year, claims that "There is no doubt that social unrest and related problems have caused difficulty in obtaining insurance." He adds that in Los Angeles almost all school insurance policies include "riot and civil disturbance" clauses that cancel coverage unless special premiums are paid in areas of frequent trouble. . . . Until a year ago Milwaukee did not insure its school system against fire, paying instead for damages from a special "fire insurance fund." When the Board decided last year to insure against fire with commercial insurance, the Board abruptly discovered that "many insurance carriers wouldn't even talk to us."[12]

The Fiscal Squeeze Tightens

In November 1968 the school board in Youngstown, Ohio—its coffers almost empty—sent more than 27,000 school children home and locked up the schools for the rest of the calendar year. The district simply lacked the money to carry on any longer. The school board declared that it had run out of money because tax rates, which had not been increased in five years, were simply too low to operate the district's schools, and the last six school levy proposals had all been rejected by Youngstown voters. Since the previous summer the board had been forced to borrow $1.5 million from local banks, but now even those banks refused the school district further credit.

Three months later, the president of the Philadelphia school board announced that public schools would have to close on April 5 instead of June 20 unless emergency funds to make up a deficit in the school budget could be found immediately. Similarly, in Los Angeles the school board threatened to close schools unless the state supplied more money. This threat had been precipitated by the refusal of Los Angeles voters to pass three school proposals in the spring of 1969, including a 49-cent tax boost. In both cases, the state legislatures did come across with sufficient funds to keep the schools open, but school services in Los Angeles were sharply curtailed, and the staff was considerably trimmed during the remainder of the 1968–69 school year.

Throughout the 1969–70 school year, this fiscal squeeze in public education continued, particularly in the nation's urban school districts, wherever the public simply did not come across with the kind of money necessary to operate its schools. By the fall of 1969, it was clear that a "taxpayers' revolt" was growing throughout the country, even in areas where public support for education had always before been high. The San Diego Unified School District lost its first bond election in thirty years with the defeat of a $91.3 million measure intended, among other uses, to improve school buildings declared unsafe in the event of an earthquake. In the entire state of Ohio, only twelve out of twenty-five bond issues were approved in the summer and early fall of 1969, and in Columbus specifically, voters rejected a $63.8-million bond issue by a three-to-one margin—the first time in thirty years that such a proposal had been defeated in the city.

BOSTON DISTRICT ABANDONS

BUSING OF BLACKS, WHITES

The Boston School Committee has voted three to two to abandon a controversial plan to bus some black pupils to predominantly white neighborhoods and whites to a new school in a black neighborhood.

The plan had been defied by the parents—both black and white —of about half the pupils involved. The decision to scrap the plan, announced at a public meeting Tuesday night, was applauded by most of the 400 parents present.

The transfer program was instituted at the beginning of this school year to meet the requirements of a Massachusetts law designed to end racial imbalance in the schools. No alternative plan was proposed by the school committee to achieve balance.

Abandonment of the plan places in jeopardy some $21.3 million in state funds that had been earmarked for the Boston school budget.

School officials said that under the plan, the new Joseph Lee School, in a black neighborhood, should have opened with 585 white children and 520 black children. The school was attended Tuesday by 257 white and 815 black pupils.

Since the start of the school year, approximately 225 white children have continued attending neighborhood schools, and at least 227 black children have been attending the Lee school, although not officially in the district.

White opponents claimed the transfer endangered the safety of the children because the Lee school is in a high crime area.[13]

Teacher Demands

In 1968, the teachers' union in one large American city threatened to strike at the beginning of the school year—despite the existence of a state law which made illegal any work stoppage by a public employee. In support of its strike threat, the union presented to the city's public school board nineteen demands or "major strike issues." These nineteen "issues" suggest clearly the tenor of relations between urban school teachers and urban school boards, as well as the magnitude of demands made today by teachers' unions on school systems which are often fiscally unable to meet those demands.

1. A signed contract in which the board recognizes the union as the sole bargaining agent for the city's school teachers.
2. Salary increases ranging from $1000 to $3000 annually.
3. Full hospital coverage for teachers and dependents.
4. Severance pay for teachers.
5. Fully paid life insurance for teachers.
6. School district underwriting for summer teacher scholarships.
7. Daily preparation periods for teachers.
8. Expansion of the special education program and increased pay for teachers of special education.

9. An elementary school lunch program.
10. A recreation program to open school playgrounds at night and during the summer.
11. A steep reduction in class size.
12. Increased supervision in school hallways and neighborhoods.
13. Special in-school classrooms for students termed disruptive.
14. Removal of restrictions against public participation in school board meetings.
15. No reprisals against teachers involved in a strike.
16. Agreement to invoke provisions of the so-called teacher "amnesty" bill signed earlier in the month by the state legislature and permitting payment of withheld salary increases and increments to those teachers who went on strike the previous year despite the existence of a law making strikes by public employees illegal.
17. All school time lost due to the strike be made up at the end of the school year.
18. Agreement that any additional money which became available above the cost of contract provisions would be a matter for new negotiations between the union and the board.
19. Financial reimbursement for teachers who must prepare their class lesson plans on their own time.[14]

A New Tactic

In a desperate attempt to teach state legislators about the plight of Philadelphia's schools, the city school board in the spring of 1968 invited them to take a personal look at the classrooms. Shaken and dismayed after a day's excursion, one legislator said that the school he visited was terrible and that the principal admitted the children were not learning. The Vice-President of the school board replied, "There are about sixty-seven other schools just like that. What do you think we have been talking about?"

The visits were one tactic in a drive to save the schools from the bankruptcy predicted by the school board by the middle of the next school year.[15]

The Learning Environment

The noise of shifting desks is one of the students' favorite weapons, an extremely upsetting sound. When they are bored they use it to disrupt the class; who can tell the accidental shift from the intentional? A full-scale rearrangement of the seats would produce painful cacophony. Why move desks anyway in a room which is virtually eventless, almost square? This room demands row organizations. (Anyway, rows are a good way of splitting up the class—for organization purposes.)

The room has a quota of desks, not children. There is no space to do anything with the ten to twelve extra desks. These desks complete the rows, reinforce them, make them look better.

Imagine the room, for a moment, without the students' desks and chairs. *There is nothing there.* The room has no character at all. Those rows of desks *do* mean a great deal.

Going out into the hall is a tremendous relief. The space has direction, goals, and meaningful objects in it. It is cool and comfortable. It changes levels. Best of all, you are alone, independent, free of the matrix. The children linger in the halls.

Back in the classroom, everything is harsh, plain, and regular. Any crookedness in the rows of seats is annoying. Anything out of place seems indecent. The urge to be orderly is very strong, but it is impossible to satisfy. The desks are too small for the books, the closets too small for the supplies. Paper, books, and supplies are stacked everywhere. There is no other place to store them. Although the room is not small, anything extra is an intrusion. The work of teaching gradually gives way to keeping the room in order.

Some order, some tidiness, some sense of where things ought to be, is necessary; but the order demanded by the strict, spare geometry of rows and hard walls cannot be maintained by flesh-and-blood children. If the desks *must* be in rows, they *should* be fastened down.

The room continually assaults the senses. The eyes see nothing but hard things, glazed brick, slate blackboard, rough plaster ceiling, metal radiators, vinyl and terrazzo floors, chain-link fencing on glass and aluminum windows, brick and asphalt outside. The softest surface in the room is the wood in the desk tops.

These hard surfaces reflect and intensify high-frequency noises: chalk scratches on the blackboard, desks and chairs grind along the floor, feet scrape, desk tops slam, raucous bells and P. A. systems shout. Even the scratching of pencil on paper can be heard.

Two children sitting together make whispers which carry across the room. They cannot be ignored, the most innocent aside is a disturbance. It asks too much of the student to shout out everything and pay attention to what he is doing. Voices become harsh and strident. All treble and no bass, they seem childish and shrill. The speaker feels foolish and uncomfortable without quite knowing why. He sounds insecure. Everybody sounds insecure.[16]

The Failure of Expansive Reform

The Pittsburgh Board of Public Education has voted to abandon its Great High Schools program. The plan called for five super high schools to replace seventeen existing structures, all of them more than forty years old. An enrollment of 5,000 to 6,000 was planned for each of the big high schools, to be constructed at a cost of $50 million each. They were to provide opportunities for innovations in curriculum and instruction and solve the problems of citywide integration.

Board members opposing the program gave a number of reasons for doing so, including high costs, public opposition, and the fear that the Great High Schools would introduce integration at too late a stage in the educational process. There was also the fear that the necessary school bonds to finance the project could not be sold. Some of the $21.9 million spent on land acquisition, consulting and architects' fees may be salvaged by reselling the land, but much of the money will have to be considered lost.[17]

REPLACEMENTS HARD TO FIND

The black-power and student-power tugs-of-war testing many American public schools are driving out teachers and administrators in alarming numbers—and scaring off potential recruits. Unless peace is restored, some educators warn, critical shortages of qualified personnel may follow in the years ahead. The problem is most pronounced in New York, hardest hit by school strife. But similar problems in other major American cities suggest a problem of national dimensions. Some school officials tend to soft-pedal the existence of any such problem. But others in the field, particularly leaders of school-employee unions, discuss it freely—and in urgent terms.

In New York, resignations and retirements of teachers and administrators jumped sharply in 1968 compared with the previous five years, reports the Council of Supervisory Associations, the school administrators' union. Resignations climbed more than 50 per cent during embattled 1968 alone. Retirements—many of them early retirements—rose more than 20 per cent.

Nationally, the exodus of experienced school personnel from troubled urban schools has become "a very difficult problem." . . . Hard evidence is scarce . . . because people often do not disclose why they resign or retire. But the feeling that emerges in city after city is that teachers and administrators increasingly want to escape the social tension at many urban schools. Besides New York . . . the problem has surfaced in such cities as Washington, Detroit, and St. Louis. In Philadelphia . . . the president of the teachers' union said, "Community hostility toward teachers is one reason why 5,200 vacancies opened during a recent 20-month period in the school system's staff of 12,500 teachers.[18]

INNER-CITY GRADS UNEMPLOYED

Only 5 per cent of the graduates of inner-city high schools are placed in colleges, jobs, or job-training programs by fall, while 50 per cent of the dropouts scheduled to be graduated with the same class have found employment. This startling revelation comes from Detroit's volunteer placement corps, an organization devoted to finding colleges and jobs for youngsters who stay in school after graduation. Mrs. Carole Williams, Director of the Placement Corps, says the inner-city schools do not teach these youngsters job skills, so they seek jobs as unskilled workers—jobs that have already been grabbed by the dropouts. In effect, they have been betrayed by the myth that said they should stay in school.[19]

2 The Urban School as a Social Organization

A spate of recent books reporting the experiences of innovative teachers in city schools has fired up public antagonism toward urban education and raised serious questions about whether urban schools can or even should be preserved.[1] In their indictments, the authors of these books stress the blindness and injustice of the system, the bland cruelty of some teachers and administrators, and the insidious damage being done to children. Having been frustrated in their efforts to change such conditions, most of these authors have since exiled themselves from city school classrooms. But their accounts remain to trouble us, for much of what they assert can be confirmed by an alert observer in any city school. Children are often subjected to indignities; learning suffers; imagination is stifled; hope dies. And school authorities are often oblivious to these outcomes. One can readily share the indignation of such critics, and their desire, along with that of concerned parents and community groups, to change schools radically and fast.

Other observers of the urban scene argue for more modest and deliberate strategies of school reform. Robert Havighurst, for in-

stance, characterizes critics such as Paul Goodman, Edgar Friedenburg, Nat Hentoff, John Holt, Jonathan Kozol, and Herbert Kohl
as "anarchists," in the sense that "they do not like rules and institutions set up by society to regulate the conduct and development
of its members."[2] Havighurst respects the passionate concern and
much of the logic of anarchist criticism, but complains that it fails
to propose programs that can actually be incorporated into public
schools. However interesting their experiments, these critics typically do not assess sufficiently either the resources needed or the
political obstacles that must be overcome to accomplish constructive and lasting reforms. Havighurst distinguishes these "anarchists" from "activists" who recognize the complex institutional
structure of schools and address themselves to changing it as rapidly and extensively as conditions permit, but without totally destroying it.

Havighurst is hopeful that the Establishment itself can produce
responsive innovations. He asks, "How bad is education in our big
cities? Does a dispassionate examination of the facts justify such
widely publicized statements and slogans as 'our children are
dying,' 'requiem for urban education,' 'the end of the common
school,' 'death at an early age,' all applied to the work of the public schools in large cities?"[3] Havighurst contends that many critics,
and the mass media generally, make out a one-sided case against
urban education. He cites the superior average reading scores
among children in 300 of New York City's 650 elementary schools,
and the existence of "good schools" in every large city. He notes
that, although 15 per cent of the children in public schools are
doing poorly, these youngsters typically come from the homes of
parents in the bottom quarter of the population in terms of income, educational level, and occupational status; the other 85 per
cent, Havighurst says, are doing well in school according to standards of judgment applied by most Americans to public education.
There are schools in trouble, and naturally there are rough spots in
any school. But Havighurst finds the conditions in urban schools
in the early 1970's to be far from the desperate state portrayed by
their relentless critics.

We argue neither a radical nor a conservative position toward issues of urban education. Nor are we content simply to steer down the middle of the road. Our purpose is not to campaign for a particular strategy of reform, but rather to clarify through information and analysis the most salient problems facing urban schools in the 1970's and the possibilities for a meaningful resolution. The central issues related to educating an increasingly urban population are simply not yet well enough defined to allow anyone to declare with certainty which strategies are most appropriate for which problems. The news media and the critics of schools perhaps already have recounted enough incidents to suggest where the problems lie. A critical need now is to describe and define the essential problems in ways that will facilitate the planning of suitable reforms of school programs and organizations. If perspective is to be gained, such description and definition are necessary even in instances where no substantial early reforms seem feasible.

Efforts to reform institutions require, moreover, not only the revision or dissolution of existing structures, but also the creation of new structures, and these are not produced in a spontaneous outburst. Radical, overnight revision or elimination of present school structures might well produce, as revolutions often do, overall and long-term effects just as bad as those they were intended to remove. As Melvin Webber suggests, institutional reform requires considerable attention not just to "the manifest problems," but to the "less visible underlying issues" as well.

> The pragmatic traditions in American political life have led us to attack the manifest problems of the moment with heavy commitment, but to avoid the longer-term confrontation of underlying issues. . . . We have yet to implant a counter-tradition in America that, by exploring the future, would inform a national development policy. . . . It is sobering that no sociologist predicted the magnitude of the Negro Revolt, that no pre-war urbanist anticipated the postwar development patterns in American cities, and that, most troubling of all, no one has yet written systematic alternative futures seeking to chart the possible course of events in these fields.

As one consequence of our political traditions and our inadequate theory, we tend to overreact to events of the day. When a curve turns upward, we expect that it will go off the top of the chart; when it turns down, we despair that it will fall off the bottom. . . . We had thought our public school system was unexcelled, until Sputnik shocked us into wholesale reform. We believed that suburban development was going to provide decent homes for all, and now we believe that nothing short of immediate reconstruction of the old cities can save them from disaster. . . .

But it will be an unfortunate mistake, another repetition of our traditional propensities, if we pour our resources into the manifest problems without also dealing with the less visible underlying issues. A deep swell is shaping those curves on our month-to-month charts—a large historical change that may reshape the character of urban society in the developed world. This, too, must command our attention, for the coming changes may so inhibit future social mobility that our present short-run, ameliorative programs could prove ineffective in retrospect. If so, we had better try to anticipate those changes and then modify our action programs to conform.[4]

Urban schools may be regarded as social subsystems which interact regularly with other urban subsystems and which operate daily within the larger social system of an urban milieu. In addition, urban schools have a particular history of earlier decisions that profoundly affect their current state. An adequate framework for understanding urban schools must therefore take cognizance of both their historic and their systemic character.

A Historical Perspective on Urban Schools

There are several reasons for developing a perspective on the history of urban education before attempting to interrupt that history with deliberate reforms. First, it is useful to see a social problem at a distance; perspective often minimizes the impulse to resort to piecemeal solutions. Most past efforts to solve educational problems, as we have already noted, have been piecemeal, a kind of "muddling through," like British foreign policy prior to World War II. For example, under Title I of the 1965 Elementary and Secondary Education Act, many school districts used federal money simply to pay reading teachers for overtime work in an effort to raise the reading scores of youngsters who were at or below average level, even though there was little systematic evidence that this tactic—amounting essentially to "more of the same"—significantly affected their reading competence.

Second, a historical perspective may show that a problem or method we first thought unique has a long chain of historical antecedents. For example, in the last century substantial effort was made to develop individualized instruction and open classrooms. Even then educational reformers were concerned about reaching and teaching youngsters who were new to the city, and they strived, as do contemporary educators, to make school curricula relevant to employment conditions in an urban economy. Third, a historical perspective enables one to see urban schools for the social inventions they are. Fallible human decisions, not inevitable natural forces, have created schools as they are. All their features are the product of deliberate human design or have been incorporated into schools on the back of piecemeal organizational arrangements. It can be argued, moreover, that the basic design and operating principles of urban schools have really not changed substantially since they were formulated in the late nineteenth century. Innumerable revisions in practice and constant debate over method and organization have taken place, but the status of the student and his experience with authority, procedure, space, and time—the conditions which give his life in school a personal meaning—are not much different today from what they were at the turn of the century. Perhaps critically related to student and teacher unrest in urban schools today is the persistence of anachronism in the structure of schools, the roles of teachers, students, and administrators, the interactions between school and community, and the sanctions relied upon to motivate performance and enforce order.

Fourth, a historical perspective provides a check against making invalid comparisons between past and present. There is, for example, an important, but often ignored, difference between the student composition of urban schools now and at the turn of the century. Then, the city public school was essentially an elementary school; fewer than 7 per cent of the nation's school-age population completed secondary school. There was no relevant classification for dropouts; a high percentage of those who left city schools did so as early as the fifth or sixth grade, since they could readily find employment in the vast market for unskilled industrial labor. The masses of city youngsters who constituted a burden for urban schools seventy years ago, therefore, were less than thirteen years of age. By contrast, over 90 per cent of those who currently complete urban elementary schools enter high school, and of those over 65 per cent complete their secondary school programs. This represents a considerable demographic change in urban school enrollments during a half-century. Although primary-grade classrooms still present teachers with serious problems, the difficulties of imposing discipline on adolescents, and their growing demand that curricula be relevant to their interests, increase the burden on urban schools by a quantum leap.

It will be useful to illustrate how policies and programs dating to an earlier era have affected current conditions in large urban school systems.

A Commitment to Mass Education

The supreme achievement of such nineteenth-century reformers as Horace Mann was the development of the common school and the winning of a political commitment by nearly every state in the union to a system of universal education. This commitment underlies not only the hopes for public education, but perhaps its major current problems as well. Public education is, in fact, a synonym for mass education. Consequently, any proposed alternative to the common school must be judged according to how well it serves the nation's commitment to universal education. This means that it must not only contribute to educating all the children of all the people, but must qualify for support from local, state, and federal governments.

Raymond Callahan suggests that educators ought to have taken a realistic look at what was expected of the schools in the early decades of this century—and then threatened to close their doors.[5] Abraham Flexner's 1910 report on medical schools provoked a crisis of this kind in the field of medicine: the required professional training was made lengthy and exacting, schools that could not meet standards were closed, and rigorous entrance requirements were imposed. By reducing or failing to expand the number of available physicians in the country, and at the same time upgrading the qualifications for admission to medical school, the medical profession was able to achieve tremendous autonomy (and a more than salutary income!) for its practitioners. If, by a similar process, the American public had been compelled to consider the real cost of educating all children in an industrial society—especially that of educating and remunerating capable teachers—it might well have made a decision quite other than to commit the nation to mass education. This material commitment seems still to be vague, poorly understood, and perhaps even dubious: American taxpayers are more inclined, for example, to go into debt for consumer goods than for the costs of public education.

The Delusion of Political Separation

Lawrence Cremin, in his classic study of the origins of progressive education, depicts some of the conditions in urban schools in 1890:

> In the cities, problems of sky-rocketing enrollment were compounded by a host of other issues. In school buildings, badly lighted, poorly heated, frequently unsanitary and bursting at the seams, young immigrants from a dozen different countries swelled the tide of newly arriving farm children. Superintendents spoke hopefully of reducing class size to 60 per teacher, but the

hope was most often a pious one. . . . As school budgets
mounted, politicians were quick to recognize one more lucrative
source of extra income. . . . Responsibilities being difficult to
define, corruption reared its ugly—if familiar—head. Teaching and
administrative posts were bought and sold; school buildings—like
city halls and public bath houses—suddenly became very expensive to build; and politics pervaded everything from the assignment of textbook contracts to the appointment of school
superintendents.[6]

Such conditions drove educational reformers in the late nineteenth
century to engage in political action, particularly at the municipal
level. Although they succeeded in eventually wresting the administration of public schools from the direct control of politicians, this
success led to the myth that the public schools were and always
would be entirely free from politics. As Cremin maintains, and as
recent events confirm, it is self-deluding to argue that the nation's
public schools must resist political involvement. As evidence,
Cremin points to the scope and intensity of political action that
brought about the reform of the public schools. Similarly, Sol Cohen's study of the Public Education Association shows the extent
of the political activity in support of the New York City schools
during the first half of this century.[7]

Since public schools in the United States are by definition controlled by the public, and since disagreement is inevitable about
what they should do and about how they should do it, they cannot
but become involved in the controversy intrinsic to the political
process. Ironically, the reformers of city schools at the turn of the
century may have succeeded too well in their political battles; the
monolithic school organization they produced has for years resisted
further efforts at reform, often in the face of savage criticism and
political pressure.

An Emphasis on Social Order

No matter how radical their proposals might have been considered in their time, educational reformers of the nineteenth century

were hardly political radicals by present standards. However they may have differed concerning the democratic creed, they were like-minded in their belief that a prime purpose of education was to sustain the existing social order. Cremin notes, for instance, the positive assurances given by Horace Mann to businessmen of the pre–Civil War era that the common school and universal education "would preserve order, extend wealth, and secure property."[8]

But Cremin names William Torrey Harris, twice United States Commissioner of Education before the end of the nineteenth century, as the person most responsible for shaping the American public school into the social institution it has become. A Hegelian philosopher, Harris saw as the function of the school the teaching of morality and citizenship to the masses and the inculcation of self-discipline. Harris's power as a philosopher and spokesman for public education was further enhanced by his skill as an administrator. He consolidated into common practice the administration of graded schools, with their regular examinations, attendance reports, salary schedules, maintenance, and supervision. In whatever Harris did, according to Cremin, the primary emphasis was "on order rather than freedom, on work rather than play, on effort rather than interest, on prescription rather than election, on the regularity, silence, and industry that 'preserve and save our civil order.' "[9]

Harris believed that education, institutionalized as a social science, would "lead the child to freedom by leading him away from his primitive self."[10] We have become more aware, since Nietzsche and Freud, of the risks and the often devastating results of a socialization process that deliberately attempts to estrange a child from his own images of himself and the world. Reform efforts sparked by progressive educators and psychoanalysts have done much to reaffirm in schools a respect for the child as a human being, and to modify the grim concern for order and discipline implicit in the design of urban schools. Yet a one-sided emphasis on rational self-discipline and on orderly, conforming behavior is intrinsic to school life. It is sobering to conjecture how much of the current student unrest at all levels in American education is actually resistance to an educational process designed to "lead the child . . . away from his primitive self."

The Orientation to Industrialism in American Society

Since the social order that Harris wished to preserve was that of an emerging urban-industrial society, the cooptation of schools to serve its purposes has been dominant for over a century.[11] Schooling, as a consequence, is still viewed primarily as a preparation for becoming a productive worker in an industrialized economy.

One of the less obvious results of this emphasis has been its deleterious effect on the development of the common school. In order to sort out students according to their aptitudes for work, the school has been required to abandon the single, comprehensive curriculum of Horace Mann's common school for the differentiation of curriculum tracks according to aptitude levels. Even though it makes better pedagogical sense to differentiate among groups or among individual students than to prescribe the same learning experiences for all of them, the subsequent differentiation of rewards according to levels of achievement has tended to create a kind of meritocracy, in which a child's educational as well as occupational future is determined largely by his level of aptitude at point of entry.

The assignment of students to different curricular tracks on the basis of "measured aptitude" may be justified as a response to individual differences in ability. However, no school has yet demonstrated that it can compensate adequately for differences in family income and social class, or for differences among students in the quality of their early learning experiences and, thus, in their readiness for formal instruction at the time they enter school. As students are "promoted" from lower to higher grades, the effects of their initial learning abilities and handicaps simply accumulate and the performance gap between "ready" and "unready" students steadily widens. These effects are further compounded when students are assigned on the basis of aptitude measures to different curricular tracks, for inevitably students on the faster track are favored in the performance expectations of teachers, in the quality of instruction received, and in the intellectual stimulation of their fellow students.

Successful middle-class families readily support the differentiation of curricular offerings and educational services, for their children typically start school with bestowed advantages that function much as if they were inherited. For obverse reasons, many leaders in the black community and other minority groups vehemently oppose the use of class-biased psychological and educational tests to assess the educational potential of their children and the academic tracking that follows. By designing programs primarily to screen students and then socialize them according to the needs of an urban-industrial labor force, the nation's urban schools in particular have fostered an elite in which membership depends considerably on learning experiences that consistently reinforce the attitudes and values of the white middle class.

Whether a student enters the job market directly after high school or joins the majority of his classmates who go on to college or some other post-secondary school institution, the principle of using the school as an agency for manpower screening and placement remains the same. The historical connection here needs to be understood by educational reformers, for it actually compounds, under the guise of expanding educational opportunities, the educational disadvantage that has already been compounded by racial and economic discrimination.

The Cult of Efficiency in School Administration

A business-oriented ideology has permeated American cultural life for over a century. Much of what we do either for survival or for fun calls for negotiation with commercial enterprises and the minimizing of costs while maximizing benefits. For years, this ideology has permeated public education as well. Callahan, in his noteworthy study of the social influences that have shaped the administration of public schools, discovered among school administrators a surprising vulnerability to the influence of a business ideology. He was dismayed, for example, to discover how many decisions school administrators tended to make not because they were educationally sound, but because they were expeditious—that is, they saved money, or they protected the administrator's job.

Historically, the position of school administrator became well defined only at the turn of the century, and was strongly influenced by the developing field of "scientific management." As we have suggested, William Torrey Harris appears to have been mainly responsible for making that position the analogue of the industrial manager. A business-oriented desire to "turn out the finest product at the lowest costs" dominated educational decision-making throughout the early decades of this century. When it came time for school boards to vote on budgets and taxes, the emphasis was almost always on "lowest costs."

All this Callahan regards as a tragedy for public education. He argues that the pattern of recruiting and training prospective school administrators and of socializing them in their position was contrary to the kind of educational leadership that was needed. Over the years, "school executives" shunned that role and settled instead for the routines of a manager. Rarely qualified to make meaningful decisions about curriculum and instruction or to attend to the essential educational issues, they usually allowed themselves to become bogged down in purely fiscal matters, the minutiae of record-keeping, and a futile effort to protect schools from their constituents through milk-and-honey public relations campaigns. As a result, many public school administrators today lack the kind of statesmanship needed to deal with the complex social and educational problems confronting public schools in general and urban schools in particular.

An Authoritarian Ethos

Early twentieth-century theorists of America's new urban-industrial society, Social Darwinists like Herbert Spencer and his disciples, "expounded an optimistic creed of efficiency and control" and a sincere belief in scientific progress.[12] For them and many others, science was at once a growing inventory of inviolate truths and a substitute for religion.

Scientific investigation and discovery during the last century have not progressed as Spencer and his colleagues envisioned. The events of two world wars and a toll of 100 million lives claimed by warfare since their time have discredited a simple evolutionary view of social progress. Moreover, we now realize that to be knowledgeable, even scientifically, requires a willingness to live with uncertainty and to draw merely tentative inferences from what we observe. Although today's social scientists share Spencer's predilection for making inventories of available information, they are considerably more sensitive in recognizing that their most confident beliefs may be discredited by new discoveries or simply by the march of events.

Reformers like Spencer wished sincerely to make a better life for all, but their assumptions about human nature were basically "elitist." With their ultimate concern for maintaining social control through well-designed institutions, they regarded the urban school as a sociological laboratory and themselves as "social engineers."

Consequently, the philosophy of Spencer and the administrative innovations of Harris combined to build an educational institution in which an authoritarian ethos found natural expression. Today's schools still reflect this tradition, both in the relations between teachers and students and in those among professional staff members. In large city school systems, interpersonal relationships are highly bureaucratized and linear, proceeding downward from a board of education through a central office and thence to individual schools, their building principals, and finally to teachers and students in their classrooms.

Although the principal of each school building typically has considerable autonomy in assigning teachers and scheduling pupils, a good deal of what he does in the development of the curriculum and the adoption of innovations is conditioned by a sensitivity to the authority of the central office. In many decisions—on textbook adoptions, in-service training, building improvement, equipment purchase, pupil personnel services, and so forth—the building principal in a large urban district has relatively little autonomy.

Thus conditioned by the authority structure in his district, an urban school principal understandably delegates authority only grudgingly and on condition that it will be revoked if "misused" by teachers or teacher committees. Similarly, teachers and principals have rarely been willing to delegate responsibility to students. Edgar Friedenburg has observed, for example, that student government and much of student-administered activity in schools are mostly façade.[13]

Summary

Educational planners at the turn of the century regarded the development of a rationally operated institution as a most important goal. Their strategy for developing and operating a school was essentially that of social engineering. Their model of an educational organization and its management was a "closed system" in which rational decision-making and authoritarian control might be imposed on all the variables. They conceived the educational process primarily as one of conditioning. And the social philosophy that decreed which behavior was proper and which attitudes were valid was essentially elitist, determined in large measure by a business ideology and by the requirements of an urban-industrial society.

It can be argued persuasively that the ideology of the nineteenth century still pervades the administrative and social structure of the nation's public schools. Moreover, the effects of this ideology are particularly evident in large central city school systems, partly because size alone requires echelons of administrators and rationalized procedures, but also because the stress of social change in large cities tends to show up the anachronism of their design and operation. If problems of the kind described in Chapter One are to be dealt with effectively, significant changes will have to be made in the structure and practice of urban schools. The extent and charac-

ter of their problems suggest that big-city schools are not only failing to contribute to the transformation of urban life, as posited by
the educational philosophies on which they are based, but that
their antiquated practices and professions may actually be blocking
that transformation.

A Structural Perspective on Urban Schools

Just as urban schools may be regarded as the historical product
of a chain of decisions made at an earlier time, they may also be
regarded as social systems organized to achieve particular goals
within the larger social system of a community or nation.

The relatively new concept of a social system has become very
important in social science theory. In any hierarchy of systems,
such as the one articulated by Kenneth Boulding, social systems
are among the most complex. As Boulding notes, ". . . it is convenient for some purposes to distinguish the individual human as a
system from the social systems which surround him, and in this
sense social organizations may be said to constitute another level of
organization. The unit of such systems is not perhaps the person—
the individual human as such—but the 'role'—that part of the
person which is concerned with the organization or situation in
question, and it is tempting to define social organizations, or almost any social system, as a set of roles tied together with channels
of communication."[14] The complexity of social systems is a consequence of their depending so greatly on "the content and meaning
of messages, the nature and dimensions of value systems, the tran-
scription of images into an historical record, the subtle symboliza-
tions of art, music, and poetry, and the complex gamut of human
emotion."[15]

Any social system can thus be viewed as a set of roles and con-
stellations of roles devised to achieve a particular social goal or to
meet a particular social need. In this sense, therefore, a school or
school district can be viewed as a deliberately arranged set of roles
—student, teacher, administrator, and so forth—devised to give to

both children and adults competencies and values which they are not likely to develop as reliably and efficiently in a less structured setting.

Analysis of a social system focuses, therefore, not on the individual personalities involved but on the tasks to be performed, the positions defined, and the relations among them. Consequently, the analysis of a school as a social system is not typically concerned with whether Miss Jones is a good teacher, but rather with the qualities and the behavior that define a good performance in the role of a teacher; not, that is, with how Miss Jones in particular feels about her pupils or about her principal, but rather with the tasks, positions, authority relationships, organizational units, and so on, which determine how she will act in relation to her principal, her colleagues, her pupils, and those outside the system who enable it to function.

The concept of a social system can be applied to whatever level of organization interests the analyst. Ultimately, as Talcott Parsons argues, an entire nation can be regarded as a relatively self-sufficient social system comprising a wide range of highly interdependent subsystems—economic, political, legal, religious, educational, cultural, and so on.[16] (And so, as Boulding has reminded us recently, can "Spaceship Earth.")

Public school districts, particularly those in large urban areas, must continually face the four critical problems that Parsons says are applicable to any social system: achieving its goals, integrating its activities, adapting to change, and maintaining legitimacy and viability. In urban America, these problems are intensified by the large number of people involved and the resulting complexity of organizational interdependencies. Daniel Levine and Robert Havighurst have identified, for instance, fourteen major social subsystems that provide indispensable services to a metropolitan community:

1. The local government system, which in many metropolitan areas includes an almost unbelievable multiplicity of local units.
2. The public service system, which includes fire departments,

police departments, water departments, and sewage disposal departments.

3. The cultural system, which includes museums, library districts, radio and television stations.

4. The recreation system, which includes park districts as well as sports and recreation associations and enterprises.

5. The social welfare system, which includes youth service agencies, agencies supplying services to the elderly, employment agencies, and family service agencies.

6. The religious system, which includes denominational bodies and church federations as well as churches and congregations.

7. The economic system, which includes individual firms, management associations, labor unions, promotional organizations, and industrial councils.

8. The civic spirit or "social betterment" system, which includes local neighborhoods as well as areawide civic associations.

9. The political system, which includes political parties as well as less stable political coalitions.

10. The "social leisure" system, which includes fraternal organizations, country clubs, and special activity clubs.

11. The health maintenance system, which includes private as well as public agencies and associations.

12. The transportation system, which includes highway and street departments, rapid and mass transit agencies, and railway, air, and bus lines.

13. The communications system, which includes telephone and telegraph companies as well as the mass media.

14. The educational system, with its public and private school districts and its widely assorted collections of institutions supplying all kinds of educational services to meet a wide variety of demands.[17]

To understand urban schools as part of a larger system, therefore, it becomes necessary to take "the large view" of events, to remain cognizant that everything is ultimately related to everything else. Implicitly at least, the discussion that follows is addressed to how urban schools achieve their goals, organize activities, adapt to change, and maintain viability. It is posited, in addition, that public schools are best organized and operated as "open" systems rather than as "closed" systems and that the nineteenth-century design of schools as "closed" systems produced an anomaly that still persists in most large urban school districts. The rationale for this position is straightforward. As a particular kind of "service" organization, a public school system is highly dependent on the other social systems in which it is embedded and with which it must interact. It can, for instance, claim legitimacy only to the extent that it can meet the educational requirements of society in general and of the immediate community in particular. Yet to meet these requirements, it must simultaneously depend on that community for personnel, technologies, and financial support. To complicate matters, all social systems as well as all their dependent and interdependent relations are in constant flux. To maintain a productive equilibrium between itself and its community, therefore, a school system must be so deliberately organized that it can readily adjust to changing conditions within and outside of its boundaries.

At this point, we can turn most profitably to the theory of organizations recently explicated by James Thompson, writing on "the need to study organizations *in toto* and, for that purpose, the significance of the open systems approach and the certainty/uncertainty dimension."[18] Thompson's working definition of an organization notes the interplay between these two important elements: "We will conceive of complex organizations as open systems, hence indeterminate and faced with uncertainty, but at the same time as subject to criteria of rationality and hence needing determinateness and certainty."[19] This definition seems particularly appropriate for an urban school district. Far more than most other kinds of complex organizations, big-city school districts face, on the one hand, often overwhelming political, social, and economic constraints and contingencies generated by their urban environment and, on the other hand, the need for rationality and certainty as they strive to meet the diverse educational needs of those who comprise that environment.

An organization that is characterized as an open system operates, therefore, in two dimensions: (1) that of the external and impersonal forces that generate and guide its goals and activities; and (2) that of its individual members who work to achieve those goals and carry out those activities. Organizational "uncertainty" is thus a natural result of activity in both these dimensions. This is particularly true of schools, for educational goals and objectives are fluid and subject to continual debate and revision. Rarely can educational goals be defined specifically, and in fact they often may be contradictory. For example, it is generally thought desirable for children to be spontaneous and creative; yet creativity is inhibited by efforts to condition them to obey certain rules and respect certain social symbols, to develop self-discipline and self-control. Just as goals and objectives are always tentative, so too educational procedures, especially those designed to assess whether students are learning the right things and learning them well enough, are impossible to validate in a determinate way. Both goals and procedures must inevitably remain tentative if public schools are to adapt to the changing social and educational needs of a society. One of the greatest challenges to a school system, therefore, is to be able to cope with uncertainty about how children learn and develop, and with uncertainty in the environment of which the school system is a part.

As a system for dealing with problems, an organization must continually subject its activities to criteria of rationality; that is, while encouraging spontaneity and evolutionary change, it must also develop strategies for controlling, averting, or buffering internal and external stresses and dislocations as they arise. The range of these strategies is considerable. An organization may expand its functions, alter its basic design, modify either its ultimate goals or its principal audience, or develop administrative procedures that control both communication and decision-making.

Their concern with systems and their recognition of uncertainty both within and beyond an organization make the theories articulated by Parsons and by Thompson particularly relevant to a study of big-city school systems. Throughout the analysis that follows, attention will be given to three kinds of problems confronting any urban school system: those derived from and exacerbated by the conditions of an urban setting; those having to do with its internal operations; and those related to its interaction with other institutions.

II Urban Schools in Their Social Setting

3 The City as an Educational Setting

We are used to thinking of the city as a place, a large concentration of buildings and streets and people. A city, however, can also be understood as a set of processes, a particular kind of social organization, a particular set of agreements and procedures by which men accomplish certain purposes and, in so doing, generate both new purposes and new ways of achieving those purposes. To varying degrees, all societies transform the natural environment and socialize their members to carry on the necessary work of the society. Cities, however, have transformed man's social environment as well, and in so doing they have transformed man himself.

The critical role of the city in the transformation of men and of societies can in fact be traced to earliest history. As the resources of the ancient city expanded, so did its leisure class and the opportunity for men to act for purposes other than sheer maintenance or survival. From among those with more leisure, especially priests and scribes, there emerged more refined modes of communication, including the art of writing. The development of complex language systems enormously advanced man's ability to conceptualize and to communicate about the "not here and not now," to record his history and to plan his future. Human talents of which the earlier neolithic migrants and villagers had been only faintly aware could now be realized, for, with his increased linguistic facility, man could translate images and dreams into symbols that enabled other men to share them and relate them to their own experiences.

Thus, by affording leisurely thought and communication, the ancient city became a storehouse not only of food and other commodities but of symbols as well, a center not merely for trading goods but for transmitting and exchanging messages. As Lewis Mumford observes, the ancient city became a "magnet" attracting individuals from diverse places who brought their different customs to the city to participate in its work and rituals, in the development of its institutions, and thus in the transformation of their own condition.[1]

To this day, the city remains a switchboard for communication, a magnet for diversity, and a transformer of societies. In any civilizing society—that is, in any society characterized by the development and growth of cities—myth and history are inescapably subject to re-evaluation and transformation as men not only live and work together but also gradually generate new ways of doing so. In nomadic and village-based societies, however, the transmittal of history and myth is accomplished in such a way that each succeeding generation is charged to preserve, even to relive, the past. Villagers thus confront change reluctantly, preferring simply to transmit established beliefs and techniques intact, socializing their young to accept them, emphasizing faith over inquiry. In cities, by contrast, individuals from different backgrounds, engaged in diverse pursuits, confront one another daily and have a concentrated impact on each other's knowledge and beliefs. Moreover, because communication occurs in cities with relative speed and convenience, these confrontations can effect significant changes within an individual's lifetime. Thus a citizen of the city is unlikely to remain comfortable and complacent with his established beliefs and life style. His daily activities inevitably involve him with others who are guided by different histories and values; inexorably he is under pressure to modify his ways of life and his views of both himself and the world around him. Sometimes these transformations take place subtly and unconsciously; other times, they occur as a precipitous conversion.

In more than one sense, therefore—as a magnet attracting diversity, as a center of human communication, and as a transformer of human techniques and values—the city has always been both a geographic setting for the education of man and an active agency in that educational process.

From Village to City

Like schools, cities did not simply happen; they were invented. The original purposes of human settlements were to provide a convenient place for worship, for storing and trading grain and other commodities, and for protection against the vagaries of nature and the designs of other men. Most early settlements had only a fleeting existence. Few grew large enough or endured long enough to become either villages or cities.

The village developed a remarkable continuity in the rearing of children. Relatively unfitted to survive by instinct, man undergoes a longer period of dependence than any other species. He learns to become a competent and responsible human adult through a complex educational process, one that is typically managed by his parents and other caretakers. Prior to the emergence of villages, the development of cooperative human relations and the socialization of youth into responsible adulthood must have been a haphazard process. As the village developed, however, it became a kind of "collective nest" in which to nurture the young, thus affording youngsters the lengthy dependence and playful irresponsibility which is vital to their higher mental development.

The design of the historic neolithic village is still apparent in many parts of the world today. The tenacity of that design is noteworthy, even under such disruptive conditions as those in contemporary Vietnam. The typical neolithic village, according to Mumford, was probably a small cluster of families ranging from six to sixty, each with its own hearth, household goods, and burial plot. There was usually only a rudimentary division of labor, largely on the basis of age and strength rather than of special knowledge or skills.

Continuity of village life was maintained by socialization processes that relied heavily on family history, heroic myths, and moral codes which were treasured and passed from generation to generation. Personal detachment was discouraged; each villager met face to face with his neighbor as he pursued his daily activities. Precedence and authority were based on age alone; consequently, there was an asymmetric, one-way flow of information, ideas, and strictures from the old to the young. Thus conformity, repetition, and patience were basic conditions in a village culture; individuality, innovation, and skepticism were discouraged.

Although some of the structure and functions of the ancient city paralleled those of the neolithic village, most cities were not simply villages grown large. In fact, most villages never became cities, and the centrally organized and ruled city emerged only by degrees. Although the archeological record is still too incomplete to tell a definite story of how and why, between the years 10,000 and 5000 B.C., particular human settlements became cities, the conventional view is that certain favorable conditions for the growth of food and commerce in the river valleys of Egypt and Mesopotamia provided the necessary conditions for some settlements suddenly to "take off," becoming considerably larger and more powerful than their surrounding neighbors. Usually located near waterways and other means of transportation, these settlements became cities when the storing and exchanging of goods and services, especially the keeping of records, became too complex to manage in traditional ways.

Underlying this view of how cities emerged is the assumption that agriculture had developed sufficiently to provide the food surplus that a growing city economy requires. Jane Jacobs, in an intriguing modification of this view, hypothesizes that the earliest cities actually emerged *before* the development of systematic agriculture and the founding of specialized agricultural communities. Agricultural development, she suggests, is really an urban invention: "If my reasoning is correct, it was not agriculture, then, for all its importance, that was the salient invention, or occurrence if you will, of the Neolithic Age. Rather it was the fact of sustained, interdependent, creative city economies that made possible many new kinds of work, agriculture among them."[2]

Jacobs' theory of how and why cities developed is a particular version of economic determinism. According to her theory, a village economy is sparked by the discovery of some particular substance of immediate or prospective value, which rapidly transforms it into an economy based on the exchange of goods and services. In this process it becomes constantly inventive—a critical characteristic of a city economy. In rural and village-based societies, the resistance to change that characterizes their cultural life seems to characterize their economic development as well. Once a level of subsistence has been reached, unless endowed with some special resource or visited by some natural calamity, rural societies typically display little economic inventiveness. By contrast, a vital city economy is continually in flux, creating new areas of supply and demand. It grows and expands either by finding substitutes to replace imported products or by itself manufacturing those products; obversely, it contracts by discontinuing the production of goods and services that are either no longer in demand or available at lower costs as imports.

These are simple principles, but they are vital to the economy and thus to the life of a city. When a government or an association of merchants or workers restricts the development of a new product or obtains artificial support for continuing to produce goods or services that cannot compete with imports, its economy suffers. Often such artificial restrictions or supports can be justified by military necessity, the prevention of unemployment, unfair competition, and the like; but if they are too widespread and too long-standing, they eventually cause an economy to stagnate, giving it a false stability and bringing about its decline. The rise and fall of cities has been viewed in the past mainly as a result of conquest and warfare. Since the Industrial Revolution, however, we have gradually come to recognize the inexorable influence of basic economic processes on the prosperity or the failure of cities and of nations. Thus a city or a nation that imitates the village in adhering to established ways and in restricting economic and cultural change will eventually regress into an oversize village.

The Division of Labor and Specialization of Work

The categorizing of human work into professions, trades, and crafts probably began with the development of cities. Throughout the ages, most men did not work at the same task, confined to a single place, every single day. Even today in village or "uncitified" societies, labor whose timing is not determined by such natural conditions as weather or tides tends to be an unscheduled activity, one that is simply intermingled with other life functions such as religion, play, and sexuality. Reinforced by practices introduced during the Industrial Revolution, however, the "artificial" divisions of human activities into specialized occupations has gradually come to be regarded as the normal way of accomplishing the tasks of a civilized society.

The development of cities stimulated and was stimulated by this division and specialization; it also led to a relevant distinction between *labor* and *work*. As Hannah Arendt makes the distinction, *labor* is that activity of man related to carrying out the biological processes of the human body. It provides the vital necessities required for life itself—food, clothing, and shelter. By contrast, *work* consists of activities related to the artificial world of things, man-made creations that are distinct from man's natural surroundings and his basic biological needs: ". . . labor assures not only individual survival, but the life of the species. Work and its product, the human artifact, bestow a measure of permanence and durability upon the futility of mortal life and the fleeting character of human time."[3] The division and sharing of labor thus defined actually represents a cooperative adding together of the energies of many individuals. The specialization of work, however, requires the co-ordination of varied but particular skills. All human communities seem to have engaged extensively in the division and sharing of labor; only in the city, however, has the assignment of men to specialized occupations been a fundamental economic practice. Without it, in fact, cities could not have emerged and survived.

Evidence abounds that the division of labor and the development of specialized occupations have enabled man vastly to expand his control over his environment. He has been able to use his inventive capacity, not only to ease his labor, but also to fabricate ever more complex tools and instruments with which to provide an ever wider range of goods and services. But civilized men have paid a high price as individuals for this achievement. As one's specialized occupational status became a prime determinant of one's relation to society and of one's sense of identity as a human being, the individual's perspective on life has been narrowed, and his perceptions of "possibility" and of the meaning of life itself have been circumscribed. To Mumford, this sacrifice of perspective on the larger whole is one of the "chronic miscarriages of civilization."[4]

Prior to the Industrial Revolution, with its efforts on a societal scale to increase productivity by specializing work and dividing labor, man through biological evolution had developed a unique ability to adapt to varied environmental conditions. Because he could think and communicate with symbols, he was able to remain in other respects unspecialized, perhaps even somewhat incomplete, in that he was never fully adapted by either instinct or physiology to any single environment. Unlike other animals, whose adaptation depended on their ability to produce specialized biological organs, man was able to adapt by virtue of his complex central nervous system, which enabled him to explore and to invent a wide range of techniques for assuring survival. The division of labor and specialization of work were two such inventions. Since the Industrial Revolution, both have so permeated his daily activities that their grip on his psyche has become almost total.

For example, the belief that jobs are becoming more complex and varied is an illusion fostered by increased educational requirements for entering certain occupations, and by the widespread use of sophisticated equipment such as computers. Even in many specialized occupations, there is a continuing trend to specialize work activities as narrowly as is economically feasible. On perhaps the majority of production and service jobs, workmanship—to use Arendt's distinction—has been mainly replaced by labor. The more production is geared to consumption, the less workmanship is required except in the design of models or prototypes for mass produced merchandise. The ultimate effect is, of course, that the experience of a man at work loses its intrinsic meaning. Workers in industrial societies often complain that their jobs have stripped them of dignity and the sense of personal achievement. Their job satisfactions are then sought in the income, companionship, and fringe benefits afforded by what they are hired to do.

The unintended consequences of assigning specialized activities to children in school are similar to the effect it has on workers. Children in a traditional school setting are required to devote extended periods to tasks whose meaning and purpose may elude them. The orderly division of time, the assignment of prescribed subject areas, units, and sequences, the special roles assigned to school personnel, all simplify organizational problems of dealing with masses of youngsters, and are often justified as tending to instill in children the habits required of adult workers in an industrial society. But they may also impose disabling constraints on the development of a child's intelligence, personality, and self-awareness.

In summary, the rise of industrialism depended considerably on the ability of entrepreneurs to coordinate capital, resources, materials, and workers in large concentrations. Large masses of foreign and rural workers were attracted to the city by the prospects of better jobs and higher income. It was obviously more efficient and less costly to divide their labor and assign them to specialized tasks. In the long run, however, the effects of these strategies of industrialization and specialization on one's sense of worth as a person, and the ability to deal effectively with the world around him may prove exorbitant in their cost.

Industrial Expansion

Needing both a large source of available labor and convenient transportation, most of the industries growing out of the Industrial Revolution took root in the large, established cities of the United States and western Europe. As they expanded, these new industries not only drew on the labor force already residing in cities, but also stimulated the movement of population to the cities from surrounding rural areas. At the same time, improved transportation and the desire of more established nations in Europe to open up new colonial territories abroad encouraged large numbers of Europeans to emigrate from their homelands.

Some of these emigrants settled in large cities; others ventured into newly opened frontier regions in the western United States and in Africa, Australia, and Siberia, thus contributing to the expansion of both industry and agriculture by making possible an enormous increase in both the production of food and the manufacture of goods. After 1800, industrial development led to the mushrooming of urban populations all over the world. According to Mumford, the population of Manchester, England, between 1760 and 1801 increased from 30,000 to 72,000; by 1851 it had risen above 303,000. During the latter half of the 1800's, the rate of urban growth was actually greater in Germany than it was in the United States, despite the vast flow of westward immigration each year.

The steam engine, by providing power for many kinds of facilities in a concentrated space, quickly became the heart of a network of factory buildings surrounded by homes and stores. Factories typically occupied the best sites in American cities, usually along a river or lake whose water could be used for power and as a convenient means of transportation—thus denying recreational areas to the city's inhabitants and leading to the enormous accumulation of industrial waste in the nation's waterways.

In recent decades, technological innovations in production and transportation have enabled many industries to relocate in areas outside the city. Actually, improvements in commuter trolleys and railroads on the one hand, and the poverty and disease prevalent in the slum housing of most developing industrial centers on the other, had begun to stimulate the relocation of city dwellers in substantial numbers as early as the 1880's. The dispersal of factories was facilitated by the expansion of cheap and rapid highway transportation, the development of horizontal assembly lines, and the use of heavy-duty transmission cables for carrying electrical energy over long distances. Truck transportation cut factories loose from the need to be located near a railroad line, and the mass production of the automobile enabled blue- and white-collar workers to commute either to the central city or to new work locations in the suburbs.

Thus industrialism has been the major stimulus in the growth of today's large cities, and has also determined to a large extent the conditions under which city-dwellers live and work. As an effect of industry, cities have increasingly been characterized by highly concentrated populations, multistoried factories, slum housing, lack of adequate municipal services, the exploitation of the many by a few, and all the social ills that ensue when human and environmental needs are made secondary to entrepreneurial profit-making. During the last half century, industrial expansion and changes in methods of production have been a major impetus toward the movement of jobs and people from the central cities and to the surrounding suburbs, and thus to the creation of sprawling metropolitan areas.

Urban Expansion

Future historians may well regard urbanization as the most significant social phenomenon of the twentieth century. The accelerated movement of populations throughout the world from a tribal to a town to a technopolitan culture already has had pervasive effects on every aspect of society. Never have so many people sought so hard to concentrate their lives in so few places.

The extent of this migration and relocation throughout large metropolitan areas has been dismaying in its social, economic, and political effects, the more in view of our inability to control or to adapt to it. Less than a decade ago, one observer wrote, "Now, halfway through the twentieth century, it is apparent that the transition from village to town to city has become a runaway movement in which urbanization, a powerful organizing system which merges small cities with large ones, threatens to destroy the distinctions between small and large places within metropolitan areas."[5]

If urbanization is in fact a "runaway movement," it is one whose dynamics we do not yet fully understand. We are only beginning to understand, for example, the fundamental transformations of the natural environment brought about by urbanization.

Before the Scientific Revolution, the population explosion, and the concentration of mankind in cities, our external environment was what scientists call in an equation a given or a constant. The balance between animal and plant life, the weather, the energy of the sun—i.e., the ecological balance—had gone unchanged for centuries. When a man felled trees to build a house, or shot a deer, or laid rails across the plains, he knew the result of what he was doing because he was slightly changing a constant—the vast pattern of nature—subtracting three from five. There were not enough of him, nor was the power of his science great enough, to upset the ecological balance in which man himself lived.

Now that has changed. When we alter our urban environment, we are not changing a system that has been stable for a great period of time. We are changing an extension of ourselves that is in the process of rapid, complex growth, and about which we have a limited understanding. We spray pesticides and the birds vanish; we build a superhighway and start a riot; we extend charity and break up families; we pass a law to renew our cities and spill slums over the land. Each action we take alters the total system in ways we do not understand and makes the next crash program more immediately necessary and more ultimately hazardous.[6]

By 1970, nearly 75 per cent of the nation's total population of 203.2 million people resided in areas which the U. S. Bureau of the Census classified as "urban"—that is, places having a population in excess of 2,500 inhabitants. More specifically, of every twenty Americans alive in the 1970's, fifteen were residents of an "urban" area; thirteen lived in one of approximately 250 "standard metropolitan statistical areas" (SMSA's),[7] seven lived in an SMSA with a total population in excess of one million people, and three lived in the greater metropolitan area of either New York, Los Angeles, or Chicago.

When we consider the degree to which Americans have converged upon central cities, we get a still clearer picture of how much the United States is already urbanized. In 1970, for example, one out of every four Americans lived in the central city of an SMSA, one out of every seven in a central city with a population greater than half a million people, and one of every fifteen in either New York, Los Angeles, or Chicago.

Comparative figures on population density for the nation as a whole and for its largest cities suggest even more vividly just how concentrated the American population has become. In 1970, the population density of the total United States was only 57 persons per square mile, as compared with the Netherlands, with 970 persons per square mile, or France, with 240 per square mile. But Americans have spread themselves so unevenly across a land mass of 3.6 million square miles that, according to some estimates, nearly 70 per cent of the nation's total population is now concentrated on less than 10 per cent of its total land area. Consequently, metropolitan areas, and particularly the central cities, have such population densities as between 12,000 and 13,000 per square mile in Baltimore, Detroit, St. Louis, and Washington, D.C.; slightly

TABLE 3-1 Urban-Rural Distribution of the Population of the United States Between 1790 and 1970

YEAR	TOTAL POPULATION OF UNITED STATES	PERCENTAGE OF THE NATION'S TOTAL POPULATION CLASSIFIED AS	
		Urban[1]	Rural
1790	3,900,000	5.2	94.8
1810	7,200,000	7.3	92.7
1830	12,900,000	8.7	91.3
1850	23,200,000	15.3	84.7
1870	39,800,000	24.9	75.1
1890	62,900,000	35.1	64.9
1910	92,000,000	45.6	54.4
1930	122,800,000	56.2	43.8
1950	150,500,000	59.2	40.8
1960	178.500,000	62.9	37.1
1970	203,200,000	64.9	35.1

SOURCE: U.S. Department of Commerce, Bureau of the Census, *Statistical Abstract of the United States, 1970; Census of Population, 1970.*

[1] Periodically, the definition of "urban" has been modified; today it includes all populations residing in the nation's approximately 250 Standard Metropolitan Statistical Areas.

over 16,000 per square mile in Chicago, Philadelphia, and San Francisco; and an astounding 75,000 per square mile in the New York City borough of Manhattan.

These figures are in sharp contrast with the geographic distribution at the time of the first national census, when only 5.2 per cent of the total population was urban. The degree and rate of the movement from rural to urban areas in the United States between 1790 and 1970 are shown in Table 3–1. It may be noted that the change in the distribution of the nation's population was most rapid in the hundred years between 1830 and 1930, a reflection of the onset of industrialism and the tremendous influx of European immigrants to America's largest cities.

Urbanization in the United States since 1930, has continued to increase, but at a somewhat slower rate: the proportion of urban residents has risen less than 10 per cent in the last four decades. Even so, nearly 80 per cent of the total population increase in the United States between 1960 and 1970 (in actual figures, 19.1 million out of 24.7 million people) occurred in metropolitan areas. During the decade, the population in metropolitan areas increased by more than 17 per cent, while in nonmetropolitan areas it was increasing by only 8 per cent. Although the rate of increase is now less rapid than before—as is statistically almost inevitable, given the larger base on which it is calculated—urbanization is still being intensified.

Since World War II, the movement of population has been toward the main areas of economic development—the Pacific Coast, the Middle Atlantic states, and the southern rim of the Great Lakes. Although within the last decade there has been a kind of economic rebirth in some areas of the South, with the cultivation of economic resources and the growth of new industries, the movement is still predominantly northward and westward. The nation's center of population is now located somewhere in Illinois. In nearly all areas of the South, the lower Midwest, and Southeast—with the notable exception of Florida and Texas—the growth of population since 1950 has been at a rate considerably less than for the nation as a whole.

Table 3–2 shows the percentage of increase in selected states during the twenty years between 1950 and 1970. It may be noted that twelve of the fifteen states where the percentage of increase exceeded the national average are located either in the West, along the Great Lakes, or on the northern Atlantic seaboard. By 1970, 70 per cent of those living in the Northeast and 74 per cent of those living in the West were in metropolitan areas; in the South, the comparable figure was only 52 per cent. If only the nation's major metropolitan areas—those with an excess of one million persons—are considered, the disparity is even greater: in 1970, 53 per cent of those living in the Northeast and 42 per cent of those living in the West, but only 15 per cent of those living in the South were in major metropolitan areas.

TABLE 3-2   Percentage of Change Between 1950 and 1970 in Total Population of Twenty-nine Selected States

STATE	PER CENT OF CHANGE IN STATE POPULATION BETWEEN 1950 AND 1970	STATE	PER CENT OF CHANGE IN STATE POPULATION BETWEEN 1957 AND 1970
Florida	+143	Indiana	+33
Arizona	+128	Louisiana	+33
California	+83	Illinois	+28
Texas	+74	South Carolina	+24
Colorado	+69	New York	+23
Maryland	+69	Tennessee	+18
Utah	+57	Missouri	+17
Connecticut	+50	Kansas	+16
New Jersey	+50	Nebraska	+15
New Mexico	+43	Kentucky	+10
Washington	+42	Alabama	+10
Georgia	+41	Arkansas	+1
Oregon	+40	Mississippi	+1
Michigan	+39	West Virginia	−15
Ohio	+35		

PERCENTAGE OF CHANGE IN THE ENTIRE UNITED STATES   +34%

SOURCE: U.S. Department of Commerce, Bureau of the Census, *Census of Population, 1970.*

A third movement of population in the United States since World War II has been from the farms to the cities. In the early 1900's, well over a third of the nation's labor force, between ten and eleven million workers, earned a living directly from the land. Greatly increased productivity per farm acre through the use of machinery and improved agricultural techniques has so drastically reduced the need for farm labor that, as Table 3–3 indicates, the proportion has steadily declined during the last seventy years. Between 1900 and 1940, the total number of farmers in the country remained about the same, despite a dramatic increase of 73 per cent in the nation's total population; after 1940, the total number of farmers rapidly declined. By 1970, the total population was

TABLE 3-3 Number and Proportion of the Total Work Force in the United States Engaged in Farming Between 1900 and 1970

YEAR	NUMBER OF WORKERS IN THE NATION'S TOTAL WORK FORCE	NUMBER OF FARMERS IN THE NATION'S TOTAL WORK FORCE	PERCENTAGE OF FARMERS IN THE NATION'S TOTAL WORK FORCE
1900	29,000,000	10,900,000	37.6
1910	37,300,000	11,500,000	30.8
1920	42,200,000	11,400,000	27.0
1930	48,700,000	10,300,000	21.2
1940	51,700,000	9,000,000	17.4
1950	59,600,000	7,400,000	12.4
1960	66,700,000	4,300,000	6.4
1970	78,400,000	3,200,000	4.1

SOURCE: U.S. Department of Commerce, Bureau of the Census, *Historical Statistics of the United States, 1965; Statistical Abstract of the United States, 1970.*

nearly three times greater than in 1900, but the farm labor force was only a third as large.

The result has been an accelerating forced migration by technologically displaced farmers to the nation's urban areas. Between 1960 and 1970, an estimated ten million ex-farmers and their families, nearly 5 per cent of the total population, moved to metropolitan areas. The education and usable skills of these new urban residents were generally insufficient, and many were considered too old, to qualify them for new careers; and nearly all were understandably resentful over the disruption of their life situations. They were thus likely to be added to the ranks of the urban poor and unemployed.

Even more than the tremendous migration of people into the nation's metropolitan areas, the movement of populations *within* those areas, particularly during the last two or three decades, may prove still more crucial to the fate of American cities. For, even as rural and minority groups have migrated toward the central cities, long-time upper- and middle-income residents have been moving

TABLE 3-4   Urban–Suburban Distribution of the Population in Metropolitan Areas of the United States in 1950, 1960, and 1970

DEMOGRAPHIC AREA	1950		1960		1970		CHANGE IN TOTAL POPULATION BETWEEN 1950 AND 1970 (in millions)	PER CENT OF CHANGE IN POPULATION BETWEEN 1950 AND 1970
	TOTAL POPULATION[1] (in millions)	PROPORTION OF METROPOLITAN AREA POPULATION	TOTAL POPULATION (in millions)	PROPORTION OF METROPOLITAN AREA POPULATION	TOTAL POPULATION (in millions)	PROPORTION OF METROPOLITAN AREA POPULATION		
Central cities	52.2	58.5	57.8	51.4	58.6	44.6	+6.4	+12.3
Suburbs	37.0	41.5	54.6	48.6	72.9	55.4	+35.9	+97.1
All major metropolitan areas	89.2	100.0	112.4	100.0	131.5	100.0	+42.3	+47.4
Total United States	150.5		178.5		203.2		+52.7	+35.0

SOURCE: U.S. Department of Commerce, Bureau of the Census, *Census of Population, 1960* and *Census of Population, 1970.*

[1] 1950 data for metropolitan areas are not strictly comparable to the 1970 definition of SMSA's.

away. Except for a few relatively new cities in Texas, Arizona, and California, the population exodus has exceeded the influx in nearly all large central cities.

Table 3–4 indicates the gain by the suburbs and the loss by the central cities. In 1950, nearly six out of every ten residents of metropolitan areas lived in a central city; by 1970, the ratio had been reduced to four out of every ten. The shift in balance occurred early in the 1960's, when for the first time a larger number of people resided in suburbs than in cities. Between 1950 and 1970, the total population of all central cities increased by only 6.4 million, or less than 13 per cent; during the same period of time, the nation's suburban population nearly doubled, rising from 37.0 million to 72.9 million. Between 1950 and 1970, approximately 76 per cent of the nation's total population increase occurred in metropolitan areas; but 80 per cent of this metropolitan increase occurred in the suburbs. During these two decades, in short, the nation's rural areas diminished in population, the suburbs exploded, the central cities grew only very slightly, and the distribution of population in metropolitan areas shifted dramatically.

A consideration of the shift of population between specific central cities and their suburbs during the last decade alone shows how substantial this fourth major population movement has been. Table 3–5 presents data for twenty of the nation's largest central cities, of which the following lost population while their surrounding suburbs were growing rapidly: Cleveland, Chicago, St. Louis, Boston, Detroit, Baltimore, Philadelphia, and even San Francisco. During the decade New York City, a complex of five large boroughs, barely held its own, increasing in population by 1.1 per cent; Manhattan, its most populous borough, actually declined by 10.2 per cent from its 1960 population. Only Dallas, Houston, Columbus, Los Angeles, and San Diego showed a significant increase in central city population; and even in these metropolitan areas, the central cities did not grow nearly as rapidly as their surrounding suburbs.

The apparently irreversible movement to the suburbs, particularly since World War II, has been characterized by one observer as "the civic abdication of the middle classes and their withdrawal into parasitic preserves on the periphery of the city."[8] Although there are many reasons for the withdrawal from cities and the growth of suburbs, not the least has been the easy access by Americans to automobiles and the construction of well over a quarter of a million miles of new highways during the past two decades. Whatever their reasons, each year over 35 million Americans, close to one-fifth of the nation's population, change their residence, over a third of them making what professional carriers define as a long-distance move.

A common motive for changing residence is to own a home

TABLE 3-5 Comparative Percentage of Change Between 1960 and 1970 in Total Population of Twenty-nine Selected Large Central Cities and Their Respective Suburbs

CENTRAL CITY	PER CENT OF CHANGE IN POPULATION OF CENTRAL CITY BETWEEN 1960 AND 1970	PER CENT OF CHANGE IN POPULATION OF SURROUNDING SUBURBS BETWEEN 1960 AND 1970
St. Louis	—17.0	+28.5
Cleveland	—14.3	+27.1
Pittsburgh	—13.9	+4.4
Minneapolis	—10.0	+55.9
Detroit	—9.5	+28.5
Boston	—8.1	+14.7
New Orleans	—5.4	+61.8
Chicago	—5.2	+35.3
Seattle	—4.7	+64.3
Baltimore	—3.5	+34.7
San Francisco	—3.3	+31.9
Philadelphia	—2.7	+20.7
Washington, D.C.	—1.0	+61.9
New York	+1.1	+25.7
Denver	+4.2	+63.7
Los Angeles	+13.6	+20.0
Columbus	+14.5	+32.8
San Diego	+21.6	+43.8
Dallas	+24.2	+61.8
Houston	+31.4	+56.7
In all central cities of U.S. SMSA's	+5.3	+28.2

SOURCE: U.S. Department of Commerce, Bureau of the Census, *Census of Population*, 1970.

where greenery and space are plentiful. In the densely populated environs of a central city, single-family dwellings that offer such attractions are scarce and expensive. In the suburbs, on the other hand, home construction has boomed. During the 1960's, over 13 million new units of private housing were constructed. Home mortgages, guaranteed by federal and state funds, have become relatively easy to obtain, at least for white middle- and working-class

Americans. In addition to the belief that suburban schools are better, some other motives for leaving the city are to escape high crime rates and high taxes and to avoid racial and socioeconomic integration.

Whatever the motives of Americans for moving to the suburbs, one effect on metropolitan areas is to produce, as Cox describes them, "a congeries of fiefdoms and protectorates engaged in the legalized looting of the center city, all the while groping ineffectually with the colossal problems of metropolitan living."[9] And projections of future trends in the United States forecast more of the same. Although the birth rate since 1960 has declined from 24 to less than 18 live births per thousand, the nation's population is expected to continue to increase, at least through the remainder of this century. Analysts in the U.S. Bureau of the Census have made four sets of population projections for between now and the year 2020. Their most conservative estimate indicates that the population of the United States will increase to 226 million by 1980, to 266 million by 2000, and to 299 million by 2020. At the same time, they estimate that the concentration of population in major metropolitan areas will increase from 65 per cent in 1970 to 85 per cent or higher by the turn of the century.

If the nation's total population and the proportion of Americans living in metropolitan areas both continue to increase as predicted, the nation's urban settings will have to accommodate populations during the next three generations that are several times as large as those currently living in them. Demographers project that by the year 2000, the majority of Americans will be massed in one of three megalopoli: "Boswash," extending along the East Coast from Boston to Washington and containing approximately 80 million people; "Chipitts," extending along the Great Lakes from Chicago to Pittsburgh and including approximately 40 million people; and "Sansan," extending along 500 miles of the California coast from San Francisco through Los Angeles to San Diego and containing 45 million people.[10] In addition, they project that the population of Florida, currently just over six million people, will be nearly tripled by migrants from the Northeast and Midwest. If these predictions prove accurate, nearly 200 million people, well over half the population of the United States, will be packed into less than one-tenth of its land area.

Judging from past experience, these projections may prove to be not an exaggeration but an underestimate. In any event, they give evidence of an apparently inexorable sweep toward urbanization in America, and they raise dismaying questions about the future. Will American society adapt itself to the increased density, or will its people become like rats raised experimentally in cramped quarters, suffering physiological changes and the destruction of their normal patterns of food-gathering, mating, and child-rearing?[11]

Two decades ago, Robert Penn Warren made the assertion, now increasingly relevant, that "the world is all of one piece . . . like an enormous spider web, and if you touch it, however lightly, at any point, the vibration ripples to the remotest perimeter."[12] Unless bold, innovative steps are taken to deal simultaneously and systematically with all aspects of urban development—housing, employment, education, mass transit, finances, health—the myriad social problems attendant with urbanization may engulf us in disaster.

Secularization

Superimposed on the rapid urbanization of twentieth-century American society—and that of most other advanced nations—has been a continuing secularization of attitudes and behavior. Ever since the discovery in the sixteenth and seventeenth centuries of the possibility of scientific control of the environment without concern for supernatural forces, Western man has gradually turned away from metaphysical concerns in favor of the here and now.

Harvey Cox describes secularization as "the loosing of the world from religious and quasi-religious understandings of itself, the dispelling of all closed world views, the breaking of all supernatural myths and sacred symbols."[13] As men have become more and more attentive to "this world," they have become essentially skeptical of supernatural explanations, rejecting the patrimonialism of earlier generations, and demanding greater participation in their own government. More and more, they have ceased to regard human values as either eternal or universal; rather, the tendency is to espouse a position of historical relativism, to regard values as man-created and mutable as their relevance is tested in new situations, and to accept the existence of differing, even opposing, beliefs and customs within the same society.

The visible effects of secularization are many: a decline in church membership; the ecumenical movement; the gradual merger of smaller and less well-supported sects; the concern of both courts and the general public with the separation of church and state—all reflecting public disaffection from the norms of traditional religion.

Secularization has also produced a fundamental change in the basic concept of work. More than ever, whether one is a civil servant, a businessman, or a factory employee, work has become segregated from other activities and from the values of one's private life. Technology has effectively freed work from religion. A man rarely does what he does "because it's God's work," but rather because it is what he has been trained to do and because he needs to pay for what he consumes.

Secularization also means that the daily activities of each citizen have become more and more fragmented. One's place of work is now nearly always separate from one's place of residence; one may be involved with several people in different jobs; and one's business associates are seldom one's social companions. To Cox, this fragmentation is disturbing in that urban man "lives in so many different functionally-defined relationships, in which he plays roles not always entirely self-consistent, that he must find ways to isolate at least in part the various circuits from one another."[14]

During the past half century, the values of urban residents have become increasingly materialistic, related to a consumer economy, grounded in the here and now. The media influence him to want "the young look," the new, shiny sports car, glamorous travel, ample money, and to be "where the action is." This materialistic value structure—which frequently leads to a kind of "carnival ethic" and a frittering away of affluence for trivial purposes—has come inevitably into conflict with more traditional values and norms.

George Spindler describes the shift in American values during the past fifty years as a movement from a *traditional* to an *emergent* value system.[15] With the former he associates traditional Puritan morality and all that it connotes: a work-success ethic, individualism, the importance of achievement, a future-time orientation, and an acceptance of the worth of delayed gratification; with the *emergent* value system, Spindler associates sociability and an accompanying denigration of the self-reliant individual, relativism in moral attitudes, tolerance of differences among people and consideration for others, hedonism, and conformity to the norms of the group.

Although Spindler's assessment of the current American scene may be inaccurate in certain respects, there is evidence for the pattern of change he discerns—for example, that since World War II in patterns of child-rearing. Urie Bronfenbrenner, an expert on the American family structure and its patterns of interaction, has observed: "Middle-class parents especially have moved away from the more rigid and strict styles of care and discipline advocated in the early twenties and thirties toward modes of response involving greater tolerance of the child's impulses and desires, freer expression of affection, and increased reliance on 'psychological' methods of discipline, such as reasoning and appeals to guilt, as distinguished from more direct techniques like physical punishment."[16] The implicit relativism of values and the congruence of these parental practices with an *emergent* value system may be noted.

Secularization also has had predictable effects on education. One of the most visible is the intensifying controversy, during the past few decades, over the place of religion in public schools. As American values and behavior have become secularized, most vestiges of sectarian religion have gradually been removed from public school proceedings. Prodded during the past few decades by a series of

Supreme Court decisions, and despite the continuing opposition of traditional religious groups, schools have largely discontinued Bible reading, school prayers, required pledges to the flag, released-time religious instruction, and even baccalaureate services at graduation.

Another visible effect of secularization on public education has been a gradual liberalizing of school curricula and instructional methodologies. Traditionally, both the public and professional educators regarded classical languages, academic subjects, required courses of study, rote learning, corporal punishment, failing grades, and the dismissal of students as normal and desirable features of schools. Today, emphasis has shifted to flexible, nongraded curricula, elective courses, individualized instruction, education for work, and educational programs tailored to the competence and special interests of individual students.

The "opening up" of school curricula and the acceptance of pluralism bring with them a special challenge to public education. When there is a consensus of values among most members of a society, schools have a relatively straightforward responsibility of transmitting those values. But when a society becomes rapidly pluralistic—an inevitable consequence of urbanization and secularization—the role of its public schools becomes more complicated and problematic. Lacking consensus on which knowledge, competencies, and values should be transmitted, schools must thread their way among competing and often conflicting points of view. For instance, some parents may train children to control anger and physical aggression, while others may mostly leave children alone and permit them to act out their anger physically. Should schools simply ignore such differences and avoid the issue by refusing to teach values? Should they support one set of values in preference to another, or should they attempt to teach both without actually endorsing either? These questions and the problems they raise obviously have no simple resolution. If secularization continues, however, and if the value orientations of Americans become ever more pluralistic, the nation's public schools will need continually to engage in delicate negotiations with their clientele.

The Character of Contemporary American Cities

In 1967 Harold Howe, who was then U.S. Commissioner of Education, made this observation: "We will never have first-rate city schools unless we have first-rate cities. . . . It's time educators realize that cities are their business. . . . Educators must start paying attention to some matters we have neglected in the past: to tax policy, to site selection, to multiple use of land and buildings. We should now and then forget about computer-assisted instruction, team teaching, and ungraded classes and dream a bit, not about what kind of city school we want, but about what kind of city we want."[17] Recognizing the inextricable tie between a city and its schools, and the role played by the city itself in the educational process, it behooves us to examine briefly the character of American cities in the 1970's.

The relations among inhabitants of a city are conditioned and complicated by the interplay of massive socioeconomic forces. In an urban tenement, the relations between tenant and landlord are affected by racial tensions, crime, the uneven quality of municipal services, and even the city's tax assessment practices, which may discourage regular maintenance and upkeep of private property. Similarly, the success of a big-city school system is influenced not only by the kind of interaction children have with teachers in the schoolroom, but perhaps even more critically by their daily experience with the city itself.

As a city grows more complex, a new culture, a new way of life, even a new kind of man, comes into existence. Cox has remarked that life in an urban setting has the mobility of a highway cloverleaf and the anonymity of a switchboard,[18] which preserve for the city dweller the freedom to live as anonymously as he wishes and yet see beyond his immediate environs, knowing he can change his situation if he wishes. By the same token, mobility and anonymity make him more tolerant of change, and encourage him to develop a relativistic view toward the values and behavior of others.

To preserve the advantages of anonymity and mobility, the city-dweller typically draws a clear distinction between his public and private existence, carefully guarding primary or organic relationships with family and friends, and striving to maintain those with business associates, neighbors, and merchants at a secondary level. He sets up a kind of "immunization" against persons outside his private life, treating them as agents who perform clearly defined functions. Louis Wirth explains the basis for this uniquely urban distinction as follows:

> Characteristically, urbanites meet one another in highly segmental roles. They are, to be sure, dependent upon more people for the satisfactions of their life-needs than are rural people and thus are associated with a greater number of organized groups, but they are less dependent upon particular persons, and their dependence upon others is confined to a highly fractionalized aspect of the other's round of activity. This is essentially what is meant by saying that the city is characterized by secondary rather than primary contacts. The contacts of the city may indeed be face to face, but they are nevertheless impersonal, superficial, transitory, and segmental. The reserve, the indifference, and the blasé outlook which urbanites manifest in their relationships may thus be regarded as devices for immunizing themselves against the personal claims and expectations of others.[19]

The life style of an urban setting is characterized, as Cox sees it, by pragmatism and profanity.[20] Operating in a purpose-oriented culture where value derives from the attainment of specific ends, urban man considers *doing* to be a primary activity of life and uses *performance* as his ultimate yardstick of progress. Armed with the question, "Will it work?" and using the criteria of utility, feasibility, and economy to judge success, he looks upon life as a series of soluble problems rather than as an inexplicable mystery. In a world where the search for scientific truths and the accumulation of objects of material worth preempt the development of one's humanity, a pragmatic approach to life necessarily follows. Implicit in urban man's pragmatism is a profane "this-world-mindedness," an immersion in the physical problems of life, a tendency to reduce all to operational or functional levels.

Thus, life in an urban milieu, shaped by anonymity and mobility and dominated by pragmatism and profanity, is characterized by considerable social and physical movement, freedom of ethical choice, and rapid change. Each individual has considerable free rein to decide how much emphasis will be given to work as opposed to private life, and thus tends to stimulate further secularization and pluralism. Every city becomes, in effect, three distinct milieux: it is one kind of setting for the residents who give it continuity, another for the daily commuters who live in its suburbs, and still another for the migrants who have either just arrived or are passing through.

The Burdens of Contemporary American Cities

But the amenities of urban life are not equally accessible to all residents. For many, the simple necessities of life must take priority. The events of the past decade have made Americans more aware of economic disparities in the cities, and of the conditions that have aggravated them to the point of crisis: the abandonment of businesses and services; the retreat to the suburbs by the white middle class; the rush of immigrants into the vacuum; the expansion of slums and blight as real estate profiteers capitalize on the newcomers' helplessness; the extraordinary rise in city tax rates, caused at least in part by the increased cost of providing public services; the rapid aging of urban buildings; the deficits caused by a declining tax base, and the devastating spiral of inflation; the pollution of the environment; the rise in drug addiction, poverty, and urban crime; the demands placed on social agencies by the unemployed and unemployable, the sick and poor, the frustrated and alienated; the overtaxing of such municipal services as police and fire protection, electrical power, recreational facilities, and garbage disposal; and the paralysis of city government in the face of all these conditions.[21]

Here, once again, the systemic interdependence of the urban spiderweb becomes vividly apparent. A century of experience has not solved the problems of the central city, or even produced a clear definition of those problems. The public dialogue about the problems of city schools reveals a confusion of causes with symptoms and effects. Above all, the burden of large cities is that a disproportion of their residents is poor and exploited. And it is likewise the burden of urban education that, as city officials so often complain, "We are left with the old, the young, the poor, and the black."

The Changing Character of Migrants to Cities

That those individuals who are economically able to do so have moved first from the less to the more desirable sections of a city and then eventually to the developing suburbs around the city is, of course, inevitable. During the late 1800's and the early 1900's, the movement of the affluent away from the central cities was more than matched by an influx of immigrants from abroad. The newcomers readily found jobs in the developing urban industries, and began the process of socialization to the American way of life. For nearly a century, European immigrants—first those from Germany and Ireland, and after them Italians, Slavs, and Jews—largely comprised the minority population of the nation's largest cities. To some extent, their assimilation into the life of the city depended on their ability and readiness to exchange their native cultural patterns for those of their new surroundings; but they came in such numbers, and brought with them such strong ethnic ties, that they were able to retain many of their traditions.

Throughout the twentieth century, many of the descendants of these early European immigrants have still maintained their older cultural identity; some, indeed, still live in the same neighborhoods in which their grandparents settled on arriving from the old country. Since World War II, however, the vast majority of these descendants have joined the mass migration to the suburbs, and have been gradually replaced by Negroes from the cotton fields of the South, poor whites from Appalachia, and less large but still sig-

nificant numbers of Puerto Ricans, American Indians, and Mexican-Americans. Today, as a result, the nation's minority groups are
concentrated heavily in central cities. Over 70 per cent of those of
Mexican ancestry, nearly 60 per cent of the nation's Negroes, and
virtually 100 per cent of those who have migrated to mainland
United States from Puerto Rico live in central cities.

Most of these newcomers to the city have come with serious
socioeconomic handicaps: limited formal education, few developed
skills, a visibly different skin color, comparatively lower aspiration
levels, and little understanding of the complexities of a city environment. Most of these newcomers have arrived in the city, moreover, at a time when its resources for assimilation are at their lowest
ebb. The special problems of minority groups in American cities
today—the conditions that make their struggle to take hold not
only different but acutely more difficult than that of European
immigrants one hundred years ago—can be summarized as follows.

First, technology has eliminated a large part of the market for
unskilled and semiskilled entry work, and most employers offer
few opportunities for entry training. With the increase in the number of job applicants who come with a high school diploma, or
even with college experience, employers have raised formal educational requirements for entry jobs to a level that not only exceeds
the qualifications of most minority persons, but is spurious and un-
reasonable in relation to what is needed to do a particular job.
Second, unlike the European immigrants, a large proportion of
whom were given systematic on-the-job training, and thus were
able eventually to develop a high degree of specialized skill, most
of the new immigrants to the city neither bring specialized occupational skills nor receive training after they arrive.

Third, the effects of slavery and the aftermath of Reconstruction, the long exclusion of Negro males from other than menial
work, and the exploitation for years of Puerto Rican families and
Mexican migrant agricultural workers are often a severe handicap
in adapting to the new conditions of life in a central city. Most of
the early immigrants from Europe came from relatively stable so-

cieties, bringing with them family relationships and church connections that remained strong and cohesive throughout their assimilation to a new life in urban America. Although they experienced conflicts between new and old values—conflicts that undoubtedly jarred both their own socialization and that of their children—they prospered well enough at work and at home to give them confidence.

Fourth, most of the earlier immigrants arrived knowing that generations of their predecessors had worked their way out of poverty by diligence, saving, and perseverance, and believed that they could do likewise. Recent minority-group immigrants have no such conviction. For too long, they have experienced little in the way of reward for hard work, regularity, and frugality; and they have little evidence that the future will be different.

Fifth, discrimination even against qualified Negroes and members of other minority groups, in jobs and housing, have kept to a trickle their movement to the suburbs, even by those who have moved up economically and can afford to move. Although early immigrants to the United States met with often cruel discrimination, they knew that their work was needed, and the opportunities to improve their condition were real and visible. For most urban nonwhites today, however, jobs are scarce and opportunities elusive. Confined ever more densely in central cities and lacking the qualifications to move up or out, they have become the city's captives. Having little social basis for self-esteem, their ambitions and confidence in their society depressed by the continual experience of failure, it is understandable that many are tempted to strike out in anger or to turn inward to the solace of fantasy through alcohol or drugs.

Negroes and Central Cities

Of all urban minorities, Negroes are the most visible, the most numerous, and the fastest growing group. This has not always been so. Prior to the early 1900's, the great majority of American Negroes lived in the rural South. In 1910, 91 per cent of the nation's

TABLE 3-6   Percentage of Change Between 1950 and 1970 in Negro Population of the United States; Geographic Distribution of Negroes in 1970

GEOGRAPHIC REGION	TOTAL NEGRO POPULATION (in millions)			PER CENT OF CHANGE IN NEGRO POPULATION BETWEEN 1950 AND 1970	PROPORTION OF THE NATION'S NEGRO POPULATION IN 1970
	1950[1]	1960	1970		
All U.S.	15.0	18.4	22.7	+51	100
South[2]	10.2	11.3	12.0	+18	53
All major metropolitan areas:	8.8	12.8	16.8	+91	74
Central cities	6.6	9.9	13.1	+99	58
Suburbs	2.2	2.8	3.7	+68	16
Outside major metropolitan areas	6.2	6.1	5.8	—6	26

SOURCE: U.S. Department of Commerce, Bureau of the Census, *The Social and Economic Status of Negroes in the United States, 1970.*

[1] 1950 data for metropolitan areas is not strictly comparable to the 1970 definition of SMSA's.

[2] Includes the states of Alabama, Arkansas, Delaware, Washington, D.C., Florida, Georgia, Kentucky, Louisiana, Mississippi, Maryland, North Carolina, Oklahoma, South Carolina, Tennessee, Texas, Virginia and West Virginia.

nearly ten million Negroes lived there, and only one-quarter of these were in cities of over 2,500 people. In the last half century, however, as Table 3–6 suggests, the geographic distribution of American Negroes has changed remarkably. It will be noted that the nation's total Negro population has more than doubled since 1910; that nearly half of all Negroes now live *outside* the South; that three-quarters of these reside in metropolitan areas; and that six of every seven metropolitan Negroes live today in a central city. In addition, it is noteworthy that the mass movement of Negroes to metropolitan areas has been occurring at an accelerated rate, particularly since 1950; in twenty years, the number of Negroes residing in central cities actually has doubled, rising from 6.6 million to 13.1 million.

TABLE 3-7   Percentage of Change Between 1960 and 1970 in Total, White, and Negro Population in Sixteen Selected Large Central Cities

CENTRAL CITY	PER CENT OF CHANGE IN TOTAL POPULATION BETWEEN 1960 AND 1970	PER CENT OF CHANGE IN WHITE POPULATION BETWEEN 1960 AND 1970	PER CENT OF CHANGE IN NEGRO POPULATION BETWEEN 1960 AND 1970
St. Louis	−17.0	−31.6	+18.6
Cleveland	−14.3	−26.5	+14.8
Cincinnati	−10.0	−17.2	+15.0
Detroit	−9.5	−29.1	+37.0
Boston	−8.1	−16.5	+65.8
Newark	−5.6	−36.7	+50.3
Chicago	−5.2	−18.6	+35.7
Baltimore	−3.6	−21.4	+29.1
Milwaukee	−3.3	−10.4	+68.3
San Francisco	−3.3	−15.4	+29.2
Philadelphia	−2.7	−12.9	+23.5
Oakland	−1.6	−21.1	+49.1
Washington, D.C.	−1.0	−39.4	+30.6
New York	+1.1	−9.3	+53.2
Atlanta	+2.0	−20.0	+36.8
Los Angeles	+13.6	+5.4	+50.4
All central cities	+5.3	−1.2	+32.6
Suburbs of all central cities	+28.2	+27.5	+29.2
All United States	+13.3	+11.8	+20.1

SOURCE: U.S. Department of Commerce, Bureau of the Census, *Census of Population, 1970.*

Equally important has been the unremitting exodus of whites from the cities. Between 1950 and 1970, the total white population in all central cities of the United States actually declined by 200,-000, as the white population in the nation as a whole was increasing by 42.2 million; 33.6 million whites, the equivalent of almost 80 per cent of the total increase in white population, moved into the suburbs around central cities between 1950 and 1970.

TABLE 3-8   Proportion of Negroes in Total Population of Sixteen Selected Large Central Cities in 1950, 1960, and 1970

	PERCENTAGE OF NEGROES IN TOTAL CENTRAL CITY POPULATION			PERCENTAGE DIFFERENCE BETWEEN
CENTRAL CITY	1950	1960	1970	1950 AND 1970
Newark	17.1	34.1	54.2	+37.1
Washington, D.C.	35.0	53.9	71.1	+36.1
Detroit	16.2	28.9	43.7	+27.5
St. Louis	18.0	28.6	40.9	+22.9
Baltimore	23.7	34.7	46.4	+22.7
Oakland	12.4	22.8	34.5	+22.1
Cleveland	16.2	28.6	38.3	+22.1
Chicago	13.6	22.9	32.7	+19.1
Philadelphia	18.2	26.4	33.6	+15.4
Atlanta	36.6	38.3	51.3	+14.7
Cincinnati	15.5	21.6	27.6	+12.1
New York	9.5	14.0	21.2	+11.7
Boston	5.0	9.1	16.3	+11.3
Milwaukee	3.4	8.4	14.7	+11.3
Los Angeles	8.7	13.5	17.9	+9.2
San Francisco	5.6	10.0	13.4	+7.8
All central cities	12.4	16.4	21.8	+9.4
Suburbs of all central cities	5.2	4.4	4.9	—.3
All United States	9.9	10.4	11.3	+1.4

SOURCE: U.S. Department of Commerce, Bureau of the Census, *Census of Population, 1960; Census of Population, 1970.*

The effect upon cities of this dual movement of residents—whites out and blacks in—has been rapid and devastating. As Table 3–7 indicates, in nearly all the nation's largest central cities there was a decline in both the total population and the white population between 1960 and 1970; at the same time, the Negro population increased substantially. Thirteen of the sixteen selected central cities registered a decline in total population during the decade, the largest loss being that in St. Louis. More important, in each of the sixteen cities the white population declined and there was a gain in the number of Negroes, ranging from 15 per cent in Cleveland and Cincinnati to 65 per cent in Boston and Milwaukee. The larger the metropolitan area, the greater the proportion of Negroes residing today in the central city and the greater the proportionate increase since 1950. Table 3–8 presents comparative data for the same sixteen cities and indicates the rapidly changing proportion of Negroes in each. By 1970, more Negroes than whites were residents of Washington, Newark, and Atlanta; and Boston, Detroit, St. Louis and Cleveland were fast becoming predominantly black. The racial segregation of the nation's central cities thus is increasing, with a greater proportion of nonwhites and nonwhite residential neighborhoods than ever in their history.

The Concentration of Poverty in Central Cities

To some degree, the increase in the Negro population of central cities is related to the concentration of poverty. In 1960, more than 56 per cent of the nation's poor—those below the poverty level as defined by the federal government—lived outside metropolitan areas. By 1969, the poor were almost evenly distributed between metropolitan and nonmetropolitan areas,[22] and in metropolitan areas five of every eight poor persons resided in central cities. As a result of this redistribution of the nation's poor, the percentage of central city residents who are poor—close to 15 per cent—is now double the comparable percentage in suburbs. When racial characteristics are considered, the poverty index becomes even more discouraging: in 1969, one out of every ten whites and one out of every four Negroes in the nation's cities was subsisting at or below the poverty level.

As this last statistic suggests, urban Negroes rarely fare as well economically as do urban whites. This disparity, however, is hardly novel; for years, racial discrimination, not only in cities but throughout the country, has resulted in a considerable gap between Negro and white living standards and opportunities for socioeconomic advancement. Subject to prejudice in housing, hiring, and education, many an urban Negro lives continually on the margin of subsistence. The average lifetime income of Negroes is less than that of whites. They typically pay higher rent than whites for a housing unit of the same size. They are less likely than whites to own property and more likely to occupy urban housing units that lack some or all plumbing facilities. Their rate of unemployment is higher than that for whites. They are less well educated and more often illiterate. Even when they are better educated than the average white, they tend to earn less money. Although the gap in averages for urban whites and urban Negroes has been reduced during the past decade, the plight of urban Negroes has not improved nearly so rapidly as they have a right to expect. An extensive study of the social and economic status of Negroes released in 1970 by the U. S. Bureau of the Census, concluded: "During the 1960's, Negroes continued to make substantial economic and social gains and to consolidate advances made in the 1950's in health, education, employment, and income. Despite these gains, Negroes remain behind whites in most social and economic categories."[23]

In nearly every way as Table 3-9 indicates, the populations of the nation's central cities—both black and white—are socially and economically disadvantaged as compared with their counterparts in the suburbs. The cities include a smaller proportion of residents between 20 and 44 years of age, the period when families grow and income is most apt to rise to its maximum; they include a greater proportion of people over 44 years of age, individuals who usually have less interest in schools and are more likely to be living on fixed incomes. Central city populations include more families headed solely by a female than do suburban populations. And because they tend to be less well educated than their suburban neighbors, city populations include a smaller proportion of technical and professional employees and a greater proportion of minimally skilled operatives and service workers; they have higher male unemployment rates; and, no matter how they are analyzed, the income levels there are significantly lower than for comparable populations in the suburbs. Finally, when racial distinctions are drawn, the

TABLE 3-9   Disparities in the Social and Economic Characteristics of Central City and Suburban Populations in the United States in 1969 and 1970

SOCIOECONOMIC CHARACTERISTICS	IN CENTRAL CITIES	IN SURROUNDING SUBURBS
Age:		
Percentage under 20 years of age	35	40
Percentage between 20 and 44 years	31	33
Percentage 45 years and over	34	27
Family Head:		
Percentage of families with male head	85	92
Percentage of families with female head	15	8
Educational Achievement:		
Percentage of adults 26 years of age in 1969 with less than four years of high school	25	19
Percentage of adults 26 years of age in 1969 with four years or more of college	18	19
Income Levels:		
Median annual income for all families	$9,157	$11,003
Central city median income as a percentage of suburban median income	83.2	
Mean annual income for all families	$10,450	$12,348
Central city mean income as a percentage of suburban mean income	84.7	
Income per family member	$2,989	$3,328
Median income for Negro families	$6,794	—
Median income for families with female head	$4,908	—
Percentage of population below poverty level	13.4	6.3
Percentage of unemployed males	4.6	3.6
Percentage of unemployed females	5.0	5.2
Current Occupations of Males:		
Percentage of professional, technical, and managerial workers	26.9	34.1
Percentage of clerical and sales workers	16.5	14.4
Percentage of craftsmen and operatives	39.6	38.8
Percentage of nonfarm and service workers	16.7	11.2
Percentage of farmers and farm laborers	.3	1.5

SOURCE: U.S. Department of Commerce, Bureau of the Census, *Social and Economic Characteristics of the Population in Metropolitan and Nonmetropolitan Areas, 1970 and 1960.*

economic disparity between residents of a central city and of its suburbs is still further aggravated.

Part of the difficulty of comprehending the meaning of the city and the metropolis is the result of living there oneself. For one familiar with its landmarks, accustomed to its happenings, its rhythms and moods, to see metropolis as a structured whole requires a certain detachment, a distrust of the familiar. To obtain a perspective on the metropolis as a historical process, as a total human enterprise, facts and familiarity are not enough.

In Chapters 2 and 3, an effort has been made to give some perspective on urban schools in their urban setting. We hope to give a similar perspective in the chapters that follow, on the schools themselves.

4 Urban Schools: Their Size and Scope

During the past two decades, city schools have suffered acutely from the exodus of economically and socially resourceful residents, the influx of rural and nonwhite indigents, the decline of tax resources in the face of increased demands for social services, and other consequences of accelerated technological and demographic change. Solely by their own efforts, urban school systems can do little either to contain or to relieve these conditions. Public schools are, as Sam Sieber observes, extremely "vulnerable" organizations, sharing "the probability of being subjected to pressures that are incompatible with [their] goals without the capacity to resist."[1]

The problems of the nation's largest urban school systems stem from at least four sources: the impress of the urban setting itself, the influence of particular social institutions—legislatures, state departments of education, professional organizations, and patriotic groups, among others—the internal complexities of their own bureaucratic structure, and their considerable dependence on the good will of constituents for support.

The Enormous Size of Urban School Systems

The most visible—and in some respects the most dysfunctional—characteristic of America's big-city school systems is their sheer magnitude. Measured by the number of pupils enrolled, personnel employed, and amounts of money spent, this magnitude can be demonstrated first of all by considering the status of big-city school districts in the nation as a whole and in its approximately 250 Standard Metropolitan Statistical Areas.

In 1970 there were 52.9 million students enrolled in *all* public and private elementary and secondary schools in the United States. Approximately 87 per cent of these students, more than 45.9 million, were enrolled in one or another of the nation's 17,181 operating public school districts. To accomplish their assigned task, these school districts collectively employed over two million teachers, administrators, and other instructional personnel, and they spent in excess of $44.4 billion.

The comparative statistics in Table 4-1 indicate in detail, the considerable part played by the nation's big-city school systems in this enterprise. In 1970, slightly more than 25 per cent of all youngsters attending public schools in the United States were enrolled in central city school districts; a third of these youngsters attended schools in fifteen of the nation's largest city school systems, and a tenth of them attended the public schools of New York City alone.

To present these data in a slightly different form, out of every one hundred public school youngsters in grades K–12 in 1970: 2 attended schools in New York City; 7 attended schools in the next fourteen largest city school systems; 16 attended schools in the rest of the nation's major central cities; 37 attended schools in the suburban fringes surrounding those central cities; and 38 attended schools located outside major metropolitan areas. As might be expected, the instructional staff employed and money spent in public school districts in each of these geographic areas were, by and large, proportionate with these enrollments.

TABLE 4-1 Comparative Enrollment, Staffing, and Expenditure Estimates for Public School Districts in the United States in 1970, by Selected Geographic Areas

CHARACTERISTICS OF SCHOOL DISTRICTS	ALL U.S. PUBLIC SCHOOLS	PUBLIC SCHOOLS IN NATION'S APPROXIMATELY 250 SMSA's	PUBLIC SCHOOLS IN CENTRAL CITIES OF ALL SMSA's	PUBLIC SCHOOLS IN FIFTEEN CENTRAL CITIES[1]	NEW YORK CITY PUBLIC SCHOOLS
Estimated Enrollment	45,900,000	28,500,000	11,600,000	4,400,000	1,100,000
Percentage of U.S. Total		62.1	25.2	9.6	2.5
Estimated Full-time Instructional Staff	2,039,200	1,408,800	450,800	197,900	61,900
Percentage of U.S. Total		68.9	22.1	9.7	3.4
Estimated Annual Expenditures	$44,400,000,000	$28,800,000,000	$11,900,000,000	$5,000,000,000	$1,600,000,000
Percentage of U.S. Total		64.8	26.8	11.2	3.6
Estimated Number of Operating School Districts[2]	17,181	5,449	250	15	1
Percentage of U.S. Total		31.7	1.5	<.1	<.1

SOURCE: U.S. Department of Commerce, Bureau of the Census, *Statistical Abstract of the United States, 1970; Census of Population, 1970;* Department of Health, Education, and Welfare, Office of Education, *Fall 1970 Statistics of Public Schools.*

[1] These fifteen central cities include Baltimore, Boston, Chicago, Cleveland, Detroit, Houston, Dallas, Los Angeles, Milwaukee, New Orleans, New York, Philadelphia, St. Louis, San Francisco, and Washington, D.C. Data for Detroit are based on the 1968–69 school year; all other data are for the 1970–71 school year.

[2] In 1970, there were 17,995 public school districts in the United States, including 17,181 operating districts and 814 nonoperating districts.

TABLE 4-2   Comparative Enrollment, Staffing, High School Graduates, and Expenditure Estimates for Fifteen Selected Large Central City School Districts in 1970

SCHOOL SYSTEM	FULL-TIME PUPIL ENROLLMENT IN FALL, 1970	NUMBER OF FULL-TIME TEACHERS IN FALL, 1970	NUMBER OF HIGH SCHOOL GRADUATES IN JUNE, 1970	ESTIMATED TOTAL EXPENDITURES FOR 1970–71 SCHOOL YEAR (in millions)
New York	1,120,100	61,913	50,500	$1,637.1
Los Angeles	649,000	28,584	39,489	726.4
Chicago	563,200	25,229	20,735	621.4
Philadelphia	295,900	12,119	13,128	428.7
Detroit	292,900[1]	10,020[1]	NA	205.5[1]
Houston	239,400	9,034	10,991	162.4
Baltimore	192,800	8,547	7,261	206.2
Dallas	160,200	5,903	8,179	131.9
Cleveland	150,800	5,661	7,293	161.6
Washington, D.C.	145,700	7,486	4,980	179.9
Milwaukee	133,000	5,921	7,818	119.7
St. Louis	113,500	4,153	4,084	103.2
New Orleans	109,900	4,549	4,999	88.0
Boston	97,400	4,100	4,110	97.4
San Francisco	90,000	4,712	5,602	132.3
Total	4,353,800	197,931	189,169[2]	$5,001.7

SOURCE: U.S. Department of Health, Education, and Welfare, Office of Education, *Fall 1970 Statistics of Public Schools.*

[1] Data for 1969–70 school year.

[2] Does not include data for Detroit.

To demonstrate in another way the immensity of big-city school systems, we can consider their status in their respective metropolitan areas. In 1970, 28.5 million youngsters attended schools in the 5,400 public school districts located in major metropolitan areas of the country; of these 28.5 million youngsters, slightly more than 40 per cent attended public schools in the central cities of those areas. Thus, although central city school districts constituted in 1970 less than one-twentieth of the public school districts located in the nation's major metropolitan areas, they employed close to a third of the teachers and spent more than two-fifths of the dollars expended for public elementary and secondary education in those metropolitan areas.

Using the data presented in Table 4-2 as a point of departure, we can highlight in several ways the magnitude of the fifteen largest central city school districts in the United States. In 1970 their total student enrollment of over four and one-quarter million exceeded public elementary and secondary school enrollments in every state of the nation except California. More specifically, enrollments in New York, Los Angeles, and Chicago alone each exceeded the enrollments in nearly half the nation's fifty states; and that in San Francisco, the "smallest" of the fifteen big-city school districts, either exceeded or equaled school enrollments in Vermont, Wyoming, and Alaska. The graduating class in any *one* of these fifteen districts typically exceeds the *total* pupil enrollment in over 90 per cent of all public school districts in the United States. The total annual expenditure in these fifteen big-city school districts taken together equals the total expenditure for all public elementary and secondary education in California and in New York, and is between two and three times as great as comparable figures for Illinois, Michigan, New Jersey, Ohio, Pennsylvania, or Texas.

The Ultimate Urban School System:
The New York City Public Schools

In diversity, complexity, and immensity, the New York City public schools may be considered the ultimate urban school system. As Table 4-3 indicates, its enrollment of over 1.1 million pupils in 1968–69 represented over 2 per cent of all public school youngsters in the country and exceeded the total 1970 population in all but five central cities in the United States—New York, Chicago, Los Angeles, Philadelphia, and Detroit.

To educate this mass of students, the New York City school system maintained more than 900 buildings, including 615 elemen-

TABLE 4-3   Selected Information on the New York City Public Schools for the 1968–69 School Year

1. Number of Administrative Units		2. Citywide School Enrollment	
Elementary Schools	615	Pre-Kindergarten	8,784
Junior High–Intermediate		Kindergarten	91,213
Schools	149	Elementary	510,602
Academic High Schools	62	JHS–Intermediate	228,446
Vocational High Schools	28	Academic High School	235,876
Schools for Socially		Vocational High School	40,202
Maladjusted Children	37	Special	6,799
"400" Schools	6		
Schools for the Deaf	2		
Occupational Schools	4		
Total	903	Total	1,121,922

3. Number of Employees Authorized for Day School Instruction (total staff, 109,332)

Pedagogical:		Nonpedagogical:	
Principals, Assistants, and		Clerical and Administra-	
Chairmen	3,677	tive Personnel	5,877
Day-School Teachers	58,982	Paraprofessionals and	
Technicians, Secretaries,		School Aides	20,042
and Others	3,518	School Lunch Employees	11,138
		Custodial Employees	6,098
Total Pedagogical Staff	66,177	Total Nonpedagogical Staff	43,155

4. Total Expense Budget for Board of Education and	
Related City Departments	$1,472,019,313

SOURCE: New York City Public Schools, *Facts and Figures: 1968/69.*

tary schools, 149 junior high–intermediate schools, 90 academic or vocational high schools, and 49 special service schools. It employed some 59,000 regular day-school teachers, over 25,000 regular substitute teachers, more than 4,000 supervisory staff, including principals, administrative assistants, and department chairmen, and an army of noncertificated employees exceeding 43,000 and including clerical and secretarial help, teachers' aides, paraprofessionals, school lunch employees, and custodial helpers. New York regularly employs more full-time classroom teachers than the schools of Los Angeles, Chicago, and Philadelphia combined; its staff of noncertificated employees is larger than the combined teaching staffs of St. Louis, Milwaukee, Houston, Detroit, Baltimore, and Washington, D.C. Finally, the cost of operating the New York City public schools for a single fiscal year exceeded $1.4 billion in 1968–69 and had increased to over $1.7 billion by the 1970–71 school year. Its expenditure was then greater than the combined costs of operating all public schools in the four cities of Los Angeles, Chicago, Philadelphia, and Detroit.

Because of their tremendous size and the complex demands placed on them, the New York City public schools must provide dozens of specialized services for their diverse clientele. For instance, during the 1968–69 school year over 100,000 youngsters were enrolled in special education programs, a figure which exceeds the total public school enrollment in any one of several large cities, including Boston, Atlanta, Indianapolis, Buffalo, Seattle, and San Francisco. As part of these special education services, the district was obliged to maintain either separate schools or extensive programs within schools for youngsters considered to be socially maladjusted, mentally retarded, or physically handicapped. Besides these special education programs, in 1968–69, the school system operated over 3,700 adult classes, some 175 day and evening summer schools at all levels of the curriculum, and nearly 200 recreational programs, including 460 after-school centers, 466 evening community centers, and 53 vacation day camps. To provide these specialized services alone requires a suborganizational unit whose size and staff surely rival the size and staff of nearly every other public school district in the country.[2]

A Paramount Characteristic of Urban School Enrollments: Racial and Socioeconomic Segregation

Far more significant than size, diversity, or the density of neighborhoods from which they are drawn is the extreme segregation of current urban school populations by race and socioeconomic level.

There is evidence that segregation has a negative effect on educational motivation and attainment, and on the way students perceive themselves and others. Moreover, as population migrations to, from, and within metropolitan areas weave new demographic patterns, and as the disproportion of students who are either poor or non-white or both increases in central cities, the social effects of segregation are compounded—extending to the level of particular school buildings and even to particular classrooms, and thus exacerbating the racial and socioeconomic isolation of a particular student's experience.

Principal Factors in the Racial and Socioeconomic Segregation of Urban Students

The major factor underlying this racial and socioeconomic segregation appears to be the trend toward urbanization and the consequent geographic redistribution of ethnic, racial, and economic groups. Other factors that have magnified the segregating effects of urbanization include the operation of nonpublic school systems, the apparent inability of city school systems effectively to control segregation of enrollment, and the influence of federal, state, and local legislation.

The Effects of Urbanization

Racial and socioeconomic segregation of student enrollment within urban public schools has resulted principally from radical shifts of certain groups of Americans since World War II.

This redistribution has been anything but random; it has amounted to a process of sorting out. Roughly speaking, the exodus of population from cities has been responsible for the *socioeconomic* imbalance between them and the suburbs, and the influx of population has led to a *racial* imbalance. Robert Havighurst describes the evolution of a modern-day urban slum as follows:

> As the total population of a megalopolis grows, the slum belt around the central business district becomes thicker. This is the

result not only of the growth in total population but also the concentration of lower-class people in areas of poorest housing,
which are usually in the oldest parts of the city. Those who can
afford to do so move away from the inner city as their economic
circumstances improve. In general, working-class people whose income permits it move out of the slum district and take up residence farther from the center of the city, while people in middle-
class districts of a central city move out to the middle-class suburbs. Thus the ever growing total population divides itself into
a lower-class conglomerate at the center, with successively higher
socioeconomic groups at greater distances and the upper middle-
class and the upper-class largely in the suburbs.[3]

The racial imbalance in major metropolitan areas has developed
primarily during the last two decades as nonwhite minority groups
have rushed to fill the residences in the nation's central cities left
vacant by white, suburb-bound middle- and higher-income families. For nearly a century and a half, European immigrants comprised most of the minority ethnic population of the nation's
largest cities. Since World War II, however, the migration of
tightly knit families from southern and eastern Europe has gradually diminished, and as members of these minority ethnic groups
within the cities have gained a solid economic footing in American
society, they have redistributed themselves geographically in accord
with their new economic status—moving to higher-income areas of
the city and/or to its neighboring suburbs. Masses of America's
newer minorities, mostly nonwhites, have moved into the void,
leaving the central cities with a disproportion of residents who are
nonwhite and an even greater disproportion who are both poor and
nonwhite.

The Influence of Nonpublic School Systems

Between 1950 and the mid-1960's, nonpublic schools—which include both private and parochial institutions—were responsible for
educating a steadily increasing proportion of American youth. As
Table 4-4 indicates, the percentage of students in grades K–12 in

TABLE 4-4 Nonpublic School Enrollment Between 1950 and 1970 as a Percentage of the Total School Enrollment in the United States in Grades K–12

YEAR	PERCENTAGE OF NONPUBLIC SCHOOL STUDENTS IN GRADES K–8	PERCENTAGE OF NONPUBLIC SCHOOL STUDENTS IN GRADES 9–12	PERCENTAGE OF NONPUBLIC SCHOOL STUDENTS IN GRADES K–12
1950	11.8	8.1	10.9
1951	11.7	9.0	11.0
1952	11.9	9.3	11.3
1953	12.6	9.2	11.7
1954	12.7	8.8	11.8
1955	13.4	9.8	12.6
1956	13.9	10.2	13.1
1957	15.9	10.0	14.3
1958	15.9	10.5	14.6
1959	16.1	10.9	14.9
1960	15.2	10.1	14.0
1961	14.7	10.4	13.7
1962	14.9	9.4	13.5
1963	15.3	10.1	13.9
1964	15.6	11.0	14.3
1965	15.3	11.2	14.2
1966	14.5	10.3	13.4
1967	14.1	9.4	12.8
1968	12.9	9.6	12.0
1969	12.3	7.9	11.1
1970	12.1	7.9	10.9

SOURCE: U.S. Department of Commerce, Bureau of the Census, *Current Population Reports: Population Characteristics*. Calculated from reports of fall enrollment surveys.

the nation's nonpublic schools rose from 10.9 per cent in 1950 to 14.3 per cent by 1964, an increase of over 3 per cent. Since 1964, however, the proportion has rapidly declined, owing largely to the severe financial problems of nonpublic schools, particularly parochial schools. By 1970, the percentage of American youth in nonpublic schools was thus again comparable to the 1950 percentage.

Nonpublic elementary schools have fared slightly better than

TABLE 4-5 Geographic Distribution of Public and Nonpublic School Students in the United States, 1970

KIND OF SCHOOL	TOTAL ENROLLMENT IN THE UNITED STATES[1]		TOTAL ENROLLMENT IN CENTRAL CITIES		TOTAL ENROLLMENT IN SUBURBS		TOTAL ENROLLMENT IN NONMETROPOLITAN AREAS	
	Number (in millions)	Percentage of Total	Number (in millions)	Percentage of Total	Number (in millions)	Percentage of Total	Number (in millions)	Percentage of Total
Public	46.5	87.9	11.5	82.8	17.0	86.3	18.0	93.3
Private	6.4	12.1	2.4	17.2	2.7	13.7	1.3	6.7
Totals	52.9	100.0	13.9	100.0	19.7	100.0	19.3	100.0

source: U.S. Department of Commerce, Bureau of the Census, Population Characteristics: School Enrollment, October, 1970.
[1] These data include student enrollment not only in grades K–12, but in nursery schools as well, accounting for the slight disparity between data presented here and in Table 4-4.

nonpublic secondary schools during the past two decades. The prospect that public money may become available to nonpublic schools, that some kind of "voucher" system for financing elementary and secondary education may be adopted, suggests that the percentage of all nonpublic school students in the United States may begin once again to increase. Whether or not any increase takes place, the nation's nonpublic schools can be expected to continue drawing off sizable numbers of potential public school students. Those who support nonpublic schools argue that they save tax dollars and that closing them would mean havoc for public education. Their critics rejoin, however, that, despite initial chaos, sufficient funds and facilities could be found to enroll all children in public schools, and that the selective enrollment in nonpublic schools, which inevitably distorts the demography of a public school, is reason enough to close them. The issue of support for nonpublic schools is far too sensitive and complex to be treated here; but it is important to recognize the effect of relatively large and selective pupil enrollments in nonpublic schools on those in big-city public school systems.

One critical factor in this effect is that nonpublic schools are not distributed randomly throughout the United States, but tend to be concentrated in central cities. In 1970, only 27 per cent of the nation's elementary and secondary school pupils lived in central cities, as compared with 38 per cent of those enrolled in nonpublic schools. As Table 4-5 indicates, the proportion of nonpublic school students in central cities is generally greater than in either the suburbs surrounding those cities or the nation as a whole. In cities, one out of every six youngsters attends a nonpublic school; in suburbs and in the nation, the ratio is closer to one out of eight.

The larger and older a central city, the greater its proportion of nonpublic school pupils is likely to be. Consider the data for 1960 presented in Table 4-6: In ten out of fifteen metropolitan areas, including six of the nation's largest and oldest, the percentage of nonpublic school students in the central cities was higher than in the suburbs surrounding them. These cities included Philadelphia,

Boston, New York, Chicago, and Detroit. In St. Louis, Cleveland, Baltimore, New Orleans, and Washington, D.C., the relatively high percentage of nonpublic school pupils is probably related to the high proportion of Negroes in those cities.

Throughout the 1960's, the disparity between urban and suburban nonpublic school enrollment either remained stable or, in some metropolitan areas, actually increased. In the metropolitan

TABLE 4-6 Comparative Percentages of Nonpublic School Students[1] in the Central City and Suburban Regions of Fifteen Major Metropolitan Areas of the United States, 1960

METROPOLITAN AREA	PERCENTAGE OF STUDENT POPULATION IN THE CENTRAL CITY ATTENDING NONPUBLIC SCHOOLS	PERCENTAGE OF SCHOOL POPULATION IN THE SUBURBS ATTENDING NONPUBLIC SCHOOLS	DEGREE TO WHICH CENTRAL CITY PERCENTAGE EXCEEDS SUBURBAN PERCENTAGE
San Francisco	20	8	+14
Philadelphia	37	24	+13
Boston	27	17	+10
New York	25	16	+9
Chicago	31	24	+7
Detroit	21	16	+5
Houston	10	6	+4
Dallas	9	6	+3
Los Angeles	13	10	+3
Milwaukee	30	27	+3
St. Louis	26	26	0
Cleveland	24	25	−1
Baltimore	17	19	−2
New Orleans	30	33	−3
Washington, D.C.	13	19	−6
United States	24	17	+7

SOURCE: U.S. Department of Commerce, Bureau of the Census, *U.S. Census of Population and Housing, 1960.*

[1] These enrollment data include nursery schools and schools with grades K–12.

areas of Buffalo and Milwaukee in 1968, for instance, "only slightly more than half of the children in school attended public school, as compared with more than two-thirds of the children in the suburbs of the same area."[4] And in 1970, the percentage of nonpublic elementary and secondary school students still exceeded both the national average and the average within the surrounding suburbs for San Francisco, Philadelphia, Boston, New York, Chicago, Cincinnati, Detroit, and Pittsburgh.

This disparity between central city and suburban nonpublic school enrollments has important racial and socioeconomic implications. Students in nonpublic schools tend overwhelmingly to be white and to be mostly from families with middle and higher incomes. The reasons for this are clear. Nearly 95 per cent of all the pupils enrolled in the nation's nonpublic schools are those in Catholic parochial schools; and fewer than 7 per cent of the Negroes in the United States are Catholic. Consequently, except in the few cities where Catholic Negroes tend to congregate—notably Chicago, St. Louis, and New Orleans—the number of Catholic Negroes is simply not sufficient to offset the relatively high number of Catholic whites who elect to attend nonpublic schools. The result is the kind of geographic distribution depicted in Table 4-7. In central cities, Negroes account for less than 11 per cent of the enrollment in nonpublic schools, but they represent 22 per cent of the total population and 33 per cent of the enrollment in the public schools.

The socioeconomic imbalance in a city's nonpublic schools ensues partly from the fact that they charge some tuition, which is paid in addition to the taxes that go to support public schools. Since poor families are less able to afford such a double burden, even when scholarships and tuition exemptions are allowed for, their children are thus less likely to attend nonpublic schools.

The selectivity of urban nonpublic school enrollment therefore sets up a vicious circle: the disproportion of white middle- and upper-income youngsters enrolled in nonpublic schools intensifies the degree of racial and socioeconomic imbalance in urban public

TABLE 4-7 Percentages of Negroes and Whites Enrolled in Nonpublic Schools in Central Cities, Suburbs, and Nonmetropolitan Areas of the United States in 1970; Comparative Percentages of Negroes Enrolled in Public Schools in Those Same Areas

GEOGRAPHIC AREA	TOTAL NONPUBLIC SCHOOL ENROLLMENT OF ALL RACES	PERCENTAGE OF WHITES ENROLLED IN NONPUBLIC SCHOOLS[1]	PERCENTAGE OF NEGROES ENROLLED IN NONPUBLIC SCHOOLS[1]	PERCENTAGE OF NEGROES ENROLLED IN PUBLIC SCHOOLS
Central cities of SMSA's	2,400,000	88.3	10.2	32.5
Suburbs of SMSA's	2,700,000	96.1	2.4	6.2
Nonmetropolitan areas	1,300,000	96.5	2.5	12.0
Total United States	6,400,000	93.4	5.3	14.9

SOURCE: U.S. Department of Commerce, Bureau of the Census, *Population Characteristics: School Enrollment, October, 1970.*
[1] The percentages of Negroes and whites in nonpublic schools do not total 100%, for the reason that the data do not account for all nonwhites in nonpublic schools.

schools, thus inducing still other white middle- and upper-income families to send their children to nonpublic schools or to move to the suburbs, and so on *ad infinitum.* Although other forces behind the exodus of white middle-class children from urban public schools are perhaps stronger, the large number of nonpublic schools in central cities has certainly contributed to it.

The Inability of Urban School Systems to Act Effectively to Reduce Segregation

Some critics point to the failure of urban school systems to modify traditional practices in response to demographic and social change, citing as one example the multiplicity of small, autonomous school district units in most metropolitan areas—nearly 75 in Boston, nearly 100 in Detroit. By the decade of the 1960's, they argue, the political obstacles to consolidation of city with suburban school districts, especially to achieve racial or socioeconomic integration, had become so enormous and explosive as to be insuperable.

Other critics argue that if there had been a real desire to reduce segregation in urban schools, it could have been accomplished through two strategies: first, by doing away with the sacred principle of the neighborhood school; and second, by developing more forward-looking policies for drawing boundaries, assigning pupils, and locating schools. The following is representative of this argument:

> . . . the existence of racial imbalance in public schools testifies to the absence of any effective policy to eliminate segregation. Our measures of segregation reflect "non-decisions," and public policy can reasonably be defined to include non-decisions as well as decisions. The maintenance of neighborhood schools in a city with a segregated housing pattern is a public policy, inasmuch as there is no fiscal technological reason why children need to be assigned to neighborhood schools. The U.S. Civil Rights Commission points out several policy options for school districts wishing to desegregate: the "pairing" or merging of attendance areas of two or more schools; the establishment of central "educational parks" integrating students from throughout the school district; and the closing of predominantly Negro schools and the dispersal of their students among other schools in the community. The only technological innovation these policies call for is the school bus, and since 75 per cent of all public school children in the nation already ride buses, the feasibility of the bus seems beyond question.[5]

In defense of urban school administrations it should be pointed out that in some form all of these strategies for dealing with segregation have been tried by the nation's major urban school systems during the last decade, and none has proved both lasting and effective. Moreover, public sentiment is in such flux that today's solution often becomes tomorrow's problem. In the 1960's, for ex-

ample, busing was viewed by many as a viable solution to the problem of racial and socioeconomic segregation in schools. By the
early 1970's, however, and in particular during the early months of
1972, public opposition to busing rose to a crescendo as a political
issue. In mid-1972, legislation in support of higher education was
delayed in Congress for many weeks by the introduction of amendments to the Higher Education Act designed explicitly to prevent
the use of busing to achieve racial integration in schools. As finally
passed, these amendments delay all busing orders by lower courts
until January 1, 1974, or until all appeals have run their course.
They similarly postpone desegregation orders that do not mention
busing, but that require the transfer of pupils from one school to
another "for the purpose of achieving a balance among students
with respect to race." At this writing, therefore, the foes of busing
appear to have won a victory. But the issue is by no means resolved, and urban school systems will continue to be confronted by
the flux of changing public attitudes toward racial integration in
schools.

The Influence of Legislation

Existing state and federal legislation, either unintentionally or
as a residual effect of earlier decisions, often discourages or impedes
efforts to desegregate schools. For example, the existing tax structure and the laws governing landlord–tenant relations in most
large cities indirectly promote racial and socioeconomic segregation.
Given their common-law origins in the medieval relations between
a lord and his vassals, such laws typically fail to assign mutual
and interdependent rights and responsibilities to the contract-
ing parties. It has been nearly impossible for a tenant to obtain
remedies from his landlord for intolerable conditions in a rented
apartment; according to the law, the landlord has minimal obliga-
tions to the tenant, but the tenant must continue to pay rent so
long as he actually occupies the premises—regardless of whether
he does so willingly or is forced to do so by circumstances. So long
as the tenant continues to pay, the landlord has little incentive to

make improvements. The tightness of the housing market in most cities, moreover, enables the landlord to keep his rents high; and the typical big-city tax structure, which bases taxes on assessed valuation, further discourages the landlord from making improvements that might increase his taxes. Taken together, these conditions—all of which have been deliberately written into legislation for other purposes—simply accelerate the movement to the suburbs by tenants, particularly those who are white and belong to the upper or middle class. The situation worsens when they are replaced by tenants who are poor or who belong to nonwhite minority groups; when these tenants meet with the same legal constraints, they are without the resources and/or the social qualifications to find alternative housing in the suburbs.

A second legal constraint that tends to preserve the existing racial and socioeconomic imbalance in urban school enrollments is the effect of anomalies in the way educational responsibilities are shared among federal, state, and local governments. Legally, the responsibility for education rests with the states; traditionally, state governments have delegated most of that authority to local school districts. As these local school districts became increasingly autonomous, the concept of *local control of education* became an almost unquestioned tenet of the American democratic system. Where individual schools are concerned, this concept seriously impedes efforts to reduce de facto segregation, since it limits those efforts to small geographical areas and it thus permits many instances of extreme segregation to continue without remedy. Short of withdrawing state aid, mandating district reorganization, or legislating racial and socioeconomic integration for all school districts—each of which entails serious political and social risks—state governments have had no adequate remedies for racial and socioeconomic imbalance in schools. Until significant action can be taken at the state level, efforts to desegregate pupil enrollments both among and within existing school districts, urban or otherwise, will depend mainly on the consensus of local populations and their elected representatives.

As of 1972, the prospects for achieving the national goal of maximum school integration were less promising than ever. Political opponents of the realignment of school districts, busing of students, and other deliberate attempts to bring about integrated school enrollments had become organized and militant. The manifest reasons subscribed to by white parents have been that they want their children to attend schools in their own neighborhoods, and that they fear their youngsters will be unsafe and will receive inferior schooling in a racially integrated school. Racial prejudice, however, is a deep and powerful current in this issue. In the early 1970's, this opposition was joined by an unlikely coalition of (1) black political organizations who favored all-black schools as a means of inculcating a more intense consciousness of identity among black children; (2) their white supporters; and (3) black parents who wished simply to protect their children from the strife of an integrating school. The majority of black citizens, however, together with a decreasing minority of whites who were politically liberal, seemed still to subscribe to the goal of maximal school integration and to special strategies such as busing that were designed to achieve it.

A third way in which legislation tends to foster continued school segregation, or at least to discourage efforts to reduce it, has to do with the construction of new buildings. By this means, along with the careful selection of sites, racial and socioeconomic imbalance within a school district can often be reduced, at least temporarily. For decades, however, urban-renewal legislation has offered economic rewards or advantages to a local community for building new schools within urban renewal areas. Although the building of new schools and new housing gives a façade of improvement to an urban renewal area, it does not do away with racial segregation. In fact, the consequence of conventional slum clearance and urban renewal has frequently been to intensify racial homogeneity in city neighborhoods, and thus to increase racial imbalance in the city as a whole.

In somewhat similar fashion, by increasing the federal funds available to ghetto schools, Title I of the Elementary and Secondary Education Act of 1965 in effect reinforced the current levels of segregation in urban schools and discouraged school districts from seriously attempting to reduce those levels. One critic has written of ESEA that "the legislation itself does not absolutely preclude fighting poverty with integration, but it tends in this direction."[6]

Despite these handicaps, some states have enacted strong legislative measures to reduce school segregation.[7] In 1965 Massachusetts took the strongest such action to date by passing a Racial Imbalance Act, which provided that on notification by the state board that one of its schools was racially imbalanced—that is, that it had 50 per cent or more Negro pupils—a local school district was required to file with the board a plan to eliminate the imbalance. If within a reasonable time the district failed to show progress toward achieving the desired level of racial balance, the Massachusetts Commissioner of Education had no choice but to refuse to certify further state school aid for the district. In New York, New Jersey, and Illinois, where general laws guaranteeing equal educational opportunity already exist, the state boards and commissioners of education have construed these laws as a mandate to school districts to begin eliminating racial imbalance through the careful selection of future school sites and the drawing of future school attendance lines. The sanctions available to enforce most of these mandates, however, are typically too weak and too vague to assure their effectiveness.

In sum, little effective state legislation has been enacted either to encourage or to require school districts to deal with the effects of population mobility, housing policy, or nonpublic school enrollments in maintaining racial and socioeconomic segregation of schools. Much of the state legislation currently in force seems either explicitly or implicitly to encourage continuation of present patterns of racial and socioeconomic imbalance. This should not be surprising. State legislatures typically have been dominated, in both number and power of legislators, by rural interests; the people who suffer most from racial and socioeconomic segregation, since they are concentrated in central cities, have had relatively little leverage for influencing those legislatures.

Racial Segregation in Urban School Enrollments

Big-city schools tend to enroll a racially imbalanced portion of the total public school population found in the metropolitan areas of which they are a part. The imbalance extends to individual buildings and even to classroom assignments, which are typically based on student aptitude at point of entry and on standardized achievement testing. During the past thirty years, the percentage of white school-age youngsters living in central cities has steadily declined: it stood at 17 per cent in 1940, 15 per cent in 1950, 12 per cent in 1960, and less than 10 per cent in 1970. For the same three decades, the percentage of nonwhite school-age youngsters living in those same central cities has steadily increased: the figures are 13 per cent in 1940, 18 per cent in 1950, 26 per cent in 1960, and over 30 per cent in 1970. By 1970, eight out of every ten Negro children in the nation's major metropolitan areas lived in the central cities of those metropolitan areas, as compared with only four out of every ten white youngsters.

Equally revealing are the figures on the racial composition of public schools—both elementary and secondary—in sixteen of the nation's largest central cities. Of the sixteen cities listed in Table 4-8, eleven had public school enrollments in 1966–67 that were between one-third and two-thirds nonwhite, and in all but one of the sixteen districts the enrollment was at least one-quarter nonwhite. When elementary school enrollments alone are considered, the degree of racial imbalance becomes even sharper. By the mid-1960's, the enrollment in public elementary schools was more than 60 per cent black in Washington, D.C.; Chester, Pennsylvania; Wilmington, Delaware; Newark; New Orleans; Richmond, Virginia; Baltimore; East St. Louis; St. Louis; Gary, Indiana; and Philadelphia. Given movement of population in metropolitan areas since that time, this list undoubtedly has expanded, and perhaps even doubled.

TABLE 4-8 Racial Composition of Student Enrollment in 1966–67 in Sixteen Selected Large Central City School Districts

SCHOOL DISTRICT	PERCENTAGE OF WHITE STUDENTS ENROLLED	PERCENTAGE OF NONWHITE STUDENTS ENROLLED
Washington, D.C.	9	91
Baltimore	37	63
St. Louis	38	62
Philadelphia	42	58
Detroit	43	57
San Francisco	44	56
Chicago	46	54
Cleveland	47	53
Memphis	49	51
New York	50	50
Pittsburgh	62	38
Buffalo	64	36
Boston	74	26
Los Angeles	75	25
Milwaukee	76	24
San Diego	90	10

SOURCE: Research Council of the Great Cities Program for School Improvement, *Status Report: 1967*.

The rate at which nonwhite pupil enrollment has been increasing in the nation's largest urban school systems is, naturally, not dissimilar to the rate of increase in the total black population of each major city. As indicated in Chapter Three, the number of Negroes living in all central cities nearly doubled between 1950 and 1970, from 6.6 million to 13.1 million. At the same time, the number of whites living in central cities declined by 200,000, with the inevitable result of that between 1950 and 1970 the number of black students in public schools greatly increased.

In the decade between 1950 and 1960, the enrollment of nonwhites in every one of the fifteen city school systems listed in Table 4-9 increased many times faster than did that of whites. In fact, in eight of the cities, nonwhite enrollment doubled while white enrollment actually declined. The enrollment of whites in

TABLE 4-9   Changes in Enrollment Between 1950 and 1960 in Fifteen City
School Districts

SCHOOL DISTRICT	PER CENT OF CHANGE IN TOTAL ENROLLMENT	PER CENT OF CHANGE IN WHITE ENROLLMENT	PER CENT OF CHANGE IN NONWHITE ENROLLMENT
Milwaukee	+47	+36	+327
Los Angeles	+70	+57	+167
Buffalo	+9	−2	+147
San Francisco	+21	+4	+144
Houston	+108	+104	+127
Detroit	+12	−10	+122
Chicago	+22	+3	+120
Cleveland	+24	+2	+119
Boston	−3	−9	+92
Washington, D.C.	+22	−29	+91
Baltimore	+36	−1	+85
New York	+15	+6	+85
St. Louis	+8	−11	+77
Philadelphia	+13	−1	+68
Pittsburgh	+5	−2	+44
United States	+39	+38	+47

SOURCE: U.S. Department of Commerce, Bureau of the Census, *U.S. Census
of Population and Housing, 1960.*

the Detroit public schools, for instance, declined by 10 per cent
during the decade, whereas the enrollment of nonwhites increased
by 122 per cent. This disparity in urban school enrollments continued throughout the 1960's: white student enrollment in central
cities declined by over 3 per cent, whereas nonwhite enrollment increased by over 50 per cent.

The degree of racial imbalance *within* urban districts—both
among buildings in each district and among classrooms in each
building—is indicated in two important national studies conducted by the federal government during the mid-1960's. In 1964,
in response to Section 402 of the Civil Rights Act of 1964, Harold
Howe, then U.S. Commissioner of Education, authorized an extensive survey "concerning the lack of availability of equal educational

opportunities for individuals by reason of race, color, religion or national origin in public educational institutions at all levels in the United States. . . ."[8] A major question to which the survey addressed itself was the extent to which racial and ethnic groups were segregated in the nation's public schools. Data on this and other questions were collected in 1965 and presented in the now famous Coleman Report on *Equality of Educational Opportunity.*

Although the Coleman Report was based on a national survey of school districts that varied considerably in size, its conclusions regarding racial segregation by school buildings are particularly relevant.

> The great majority of American children attend schools that are largely segregated—that is, where almost all of their fellow students are of the same racial background as they are. Among minority groups, Negroes are by far the most segregated. Almost 80 per cent of all white pupils in 1st grade and 12th grade attend schools that are from 90 to 100 per cent white. And 97 per cent at grade 1, and 99 per cent at grade 12, attend schools that are 50 per cent or more white.
>
> For Negro pupils, segregation is more nearly complete in the South (as it is for whites also), but it is extensive also in all the other regions where the Negro population is concentrated: the urban North, Midwest, and West.
>
> More than 65 per cent of all Negro pupils in 1st grade attend schools that are between 90 and 100 per cent Negro. And 87 per cent at grade 1, and 66 per cent at grade 12, attend schools that are 50 per cent or more Negro. In the South, most students attend schools that are 100 per cent white or Negro.[9]

In fact, the data given by the Coleman Report on the degree of racial segregation in the nation's public schools probably underestimated the actual degree of segregation, since it has been noted that a number of large, highly segregated urban systems did not cooperate fully with the Coleman team—including those of Boston, Chicago, Cleveland, Columbus, Cincinnati, Houston, and Los Angeles.[10]

At about the time the Coleman Report was being prepared, a

second survey, focusing more particularly on public schools in the nation's metropolitan areas, was being conducted by the U.S. Commission on Civil Rights. In 1965, President Johnson asked the Commission to "turn its careful attention to the problems of race and education in all parts of the country" and then "to develop a firm foundation of facts on which local and State Governments can build a school system that is color-blind."[11] The Commission was instructed to "determine the extent of racial isolation in the public schools" and, more particularly, in a sample of one hundred city school systems throughout the United States. The final report of the Commission, in 1967, drew the following conclusions:

> The data revealed that the racial isolation in the public schools is extensive and has increased since 1954. School segregation is most severe in the Nation's metropolitan areas where two-thirds of the country's Negro and white populations now live.
>
> There are 1.6 million Negro children and 2.4 million white children enrolled in elementary schools in 75 representative cities studied by the Commission. Of the Negro children, 1.2 million (75 per cent) attend schools where the student bodies are more than 90 per cent Negro. Of the white children, 2 million (83 per cent) are enrolled in schools where the student populations are more than 90 per cent white. Nearly 9 of every 10 Negro children in these 75 cities attend elementary schools where the student bodies range from 50.5 to 100 per cent Negro. The extent of school segregation was not necessarily dependent upon the size of the school system, the proportion of Negroes enrolled, or whether the cities were in the North or the South.[12]

Continuing surveys by the Commission unfortunately indicate that efforts in the nation's largest metropolitan areas to desegregate individual school buildings have made only minimal progress since 1965.

Finally, to supplement these data resulting from national studies, it is useful to examine the incidence of racial segregation by school building in a sample of the nation's largest urban school systems. Table 4-10 indicates the degree to which building-by-building segregation increased prior to 1965 in twelve selected cities. Because

TABLE 4-10 Changes Prior to 1965 in the Degree of Racial Segregation in Elementary School Enrollments in Ten Central City School Districts

SCHOOL DISTRICT	YEAR	PERCENTAGE OF NEGRO STUDENTS IN 90–100% NEGRO SCHOOLS	YEAR	NUMBER NEGRO STUDENTS IN 90–100% NEGRO SCHOOLS	PERCENTAGE OF NEGRO STUDENTS IN 90–100% NEGRO SCHOOLS	INCREASE IN 1965 OVER EARLIER PERCENTAGE
Oakland	1959	7.7	1965	9,043	48.7	+41.0%
Cleveland	1952	57.4	1965	41,034	82.3	+24.9
Milwaukee	1950	51.2	1965	14,344	72.4	+21.2
Pittsburgh	1950	30.4	1965	9,226	49.5	+19.1
San Francisco	1962	11.6	1965	3,031	21.1	+9.5
Philadelphia	1950	63.2	1965	66,052	72.0	+8.8
Cincinnati	1950	43.7	1965	11,155	49.4	+5.7
Detroit	1960	66.9	1965	77,654	72.3	+5.4
Buffalo	1961	80.5	1965	13,106	77.0	−3.5
Indianapolis	1951	83.2	1965	15,426	70.5	−12.7

SOURCE: U.S. Commission on Civil Rights, *Racial Isolation in the Public Schools*, 1967.

the base-line dates range from 1950 to 1963, the data for the twelve cities are not entirely comparable. But they clearly demonstrate the increase in both the total Negro enrollment in each district and the degree of racial segregation in individual schools. In only two of the twelve districts did the degree of segregation decline during the given period of time; even there, the decline was less than 15 per cent. In the other ten cities, the degree of racial segregation among schools increased from 6 per cent in Detroit and Cincinnati to as much as 41 per cent in Oakland and 25 per cent in Cleveland.

One of the major cities not included in Table 4-10 is New York. Recent data on ethnic changes in the New York City public schools show several trends: first, the number of predominantly Negro and Puerto Rican schools (schools with 90 per cent Negro and Puerto Rican enrollment at the elementary level and 85 per cent at the secondary level) continues to increase, whereas the number of predominantly white schools (those with comparable percentages of white youngsters) is on the decline.[13] More specifically, between 1960 and 1965 the number of predominantly white schools declined from 42 to 31 per cent; simultaneously, the number of middle-range schools remained relatively stable at 46 per cent, while the number of predominantly Negro and Puerto Rican schools actually increased from 15 to 23 per cent.

These data reveal that a rather mixed pattern of racial segregation is developing in the New York City public schools. When changes in enrollment among Negroes, Puerto Ricans, and whites are separated out, the pattern becomes even sharper: first, any integration achieved in New York between 1960 and 1965 affected whites more than it did nonwhites; second, despite the increased number of middle-range schools and the decreased number of predominantly white schools in New York, both the percentage of white students and the percentage of Negro students enrolled in schools where students of their own race predominated rose significantly between 1960 and 1965; third, given the demographic changes since 1965, the patterns established prior to 1965 in the New York City public schools have undoubtedly solidified.

The evidence presented in the preceding discussion indicates the extent to which racial imbalance operates both among and within school districts. Specific evidence of racial isolation *within* individual schools—that is, among classrooms—is difficult to obtain, since school officals typically decline to reveal such data. It is possible, nevertheless, to infer that in racially integrated schools the "tracking" of students—placing them in classes on the basis of I.Q. scores, standardized testing, and academic performance—often produces separation not only by scholastic ability, but by race as well.

Socioeconomic Segregation in Urban School Enrollments

Apart from measured intelligence, socioeconomic level is the only consistent variable in all studies of educational attainment. Havighurst found in his intensive study of Chicago public schools, for example, that "the differences among the 21 school districts in Chicago are largely socioeconomic in character, and there are parallel differences in student achievement."[14] Thus it is critical that in urban school enrollments *socioeconomic* imbalance is at least as severe as *racial* imbalance, both between urban and suburban districts and among individual urban school buildings and classrooms. The extent of this stratification in schools can readily be inferred from three primary urban conditions.

First, the population movements associated with urbanization during the past few decades have led to a disproportion of poor people in central cities. In 1970, 15 per cent of central city populations but only 7 per cent of suburban populations, were classified as poor. Central city populations include a higher percentage of families headed by a female. The median of school years completed is lower. As a result, these populations include a smaller proportion of technical and professional employees and a greater proportion of clerical and service workers; the unemployment rate for males is higher, and the median family income is significantly lower, than in adjacent suburban populations.

Second, when racial distinctions are drawn *within* city populations, urban nonwhites, particularly Negroes, are almost always less well off economically than urban whites. At the same time, pupil enrollments in big-city public schools are almost always disproportionately nonwhite.

Third, city neighborhoods are themselves segregated by family income levels and/or race. This fact, and the practice of drawing school attendance lines according to the principle of the neighborhood school, combine to enforce considerable socioeconomic segregation even within the buildings of a city school system. In his study of population migration in the Chicago area since the 1930's and 1940's, Havighurst noted: "To a child growing up in Chicago today, this trend of population means that he is more segregated by family socioeconomic status than he would have been if he had grown up in the Chicago area about 1940. At the earlier time, a child in a Chicago school was more likely to have in his school or class children of quite different family background. At the present, there are slum areas so large that a child living there never sees children from middle-class homes. The middle-class children for the most part live in the suburbs or on the edges of the city."[15]

The sad irony of this situation is that, despite their burdens and handicaps, urban schools are still probably the chief means of help available to children disadvantaged by racial and socioeconomic segregation. It is to the city schools that they must look for education and for hope.

5 The People in Urban Schools

The Student

> . . . the sources of inequality of educational opportunity appear to lie first in the home itself and the cultural influences surrounding the home; then they lie in the school's ineffectiveness to free achievement from the impact of the home and in the school's cultural homogeneity which perpetuates the social influences of the home and its environs.[1]

As people have concentrated in the metropolis, as they have become more mobile and more "secular," the concepts of family and neighborhood have changed markedly. For most people, the traditional extended family has been reduced to a nuclear one with one or two adults in the family unit. Simultaneously, the neighborhood has been transformed into a relatively small and deliberately selected set of friends, most of whom are accessible only by telephone or automobile; only in a few neighborhoods in some large cities are there still occasions for block parties and for intermingling of neighbors on sidewalks and stoops. These changes have had a deep effect on the life experiences of the city child. Writing of neighborhoods in areas under urban renewal, Urie Bronfenbrenner has observed:

Whereas the world in which the child lived before consisted of a diversity of people in a diversity of settings, now for millions of American children the neighborhood is nothing but row upon row of buildings inhabited by strangers. One house, or apartment, is much like another, and so are the people. They all have about the same income and same way of life. And the child doesn't even see much of that, for all the adults in the neighborhood do is come home, have a drink, eat dinner, mow the lawn, watch TV, and sleep. Increasingly often, today's housing projects have no stores, no shops, no services, no adults that work or play. This is a sterile world in which many of our children grow, the "urban renewal" we offer to the families we would rescue from the slums.[2]

Except in rare instances where ethnic or religious ties have served to unite a city block or section of residents, most urban neighborhoods have become increasingly impersonal and devoid of a cohesive spirit and a mutually recognized code of conduct.

Human interactions in urban settings have thus tended to become increasingly superficial, impersonal, transient, and instrumental. Children brought up in such conditions are inevitably deprived of meaningful contact with persons whose competencies and values are different from those of their families. Lacking such opportunities in their formative years, they frequently fail to develop the sensitivities and interpersonal skills essential for success in the schoolroom. Children who are socialized in big-city streets, in particular, discover to their confusion that the behavior that enabled them to survive in the street is denigrated and punished in the classroom. Many urban youngsters, finding the gap between necessary street behavior and the behavior expected in the schoolroom too great to bridge, then immunize themselves psychologically against the school and its professional staff or, as an ultimate step, drop out from school entirely.

For a child, as urbanization transforms both home and neighborhood, it creates a "world out there" that is in constant flux. Change continually affects his circle of neighborhood buddies, the adults he sees on the street, his schoolmates, and sometimes even his family. The degree of flux can be measured as the rate of change in enrollment in most big-city schools, which is dramatically greater in low-income as compared with higher-income neighborhoods. For example, in Manhattan, where the pupil population is predominantly Negro and Puerto Rican, the average mobility rate in one recent year was reported to be 51 per cent; and in three schools in which the enrollment was almost entirely Negro, the turnover rate for a particular year was reported to be 100 per cent.[3]

The major determinant of change in school building enrollments is, of course, the rate of in-migration and out-migration in particular big-city neighborhoods. According to a study of movements of population in Chicago, covering a low-income area, a public-housing area, a middle-income area, and a high-income area over a ten-year period: "Between 1955 and 1965, the enrollment in schools serving the public housing sample increased 97.9 per cent. In the low income area, the increase was 95.8 per cent. This compares to a 12.8 per cent increase in the enrollment in the middle income area and a very stable 1.2 per cent increase in the high income area. To illustrate the rapidity of the low income population mobility, more than half of the ten-year increase in the enrollment of the public housing sample came during a single 12-month period."[4] As might be expected, this relatively high rate of mobility among low-income families is not unrelated to the public school success of their children. There is evidence that the more frequently a child changes schools in the middle of a school year, the greater the chances that he comes from a home environment that is unstable and educationally unsupportive, that he is overage for grade placement, and that he is significantly deficient in such basic academic skills as reading, speaking, and computing.[5]

Urban Children and the Mass Media

The media of mass communication may be influencing the attitudes and values of children even more significantly than do his family, church, and school. If so, this influence is likely to be strongest in an urban setting. In any metropolitan area, the most pervasive and influential of the media is television. Studies conducted several years ago in Chicago by Paul Witty and Paul Kinsella indicated that elementary school students viewed TV an average of twenty hours per week, and high school students an average of thirteen hours per week.[6] A study by Wilbur Schramm revealed that, on the average, one-fifth of a child's waking hours between the ages of three and sixteen are spent looking at television; that is, the average child spends as much time watching television each year as he does going to school.[7]

Despite the apparent success of programs like "Sesame Street" and "The Electric Company," and the hope they offer for educational television, much of what a child sees on television either works at cross purposes to those of school and family or is a misrepresentation of reality. Testimony before numerous federal and state subcommittees in the last decade or so has repeatedly drawn attention to the exploitation of sex, violence, dishonesty, and crime by television programs in such a way as to make them appear desirable and worthy of emulation. Another tendency is to promote what one critic calls "the standard, northern United States urbanized outlook," characterized by middle-class attitudes and value judgments: "Hospitals are well equipped. Society is prepared to and able to come to the rescue in time of the individual crisis. Fair play is important. Judges are sober. Policemen should be evenhanded, calm, and incorruptible, strong, brave, and understanding. Everyone has the right to speak his mind. Lawyers are smart. Everyone is entitled to the best education of which he is capable. The able and diligent will, with a little luck, do well in the world. Alcoholism is a disease. People should be kind to animals and children. Everyone is created equal."[8]

For children who live in the city, this romanticized "urban outlook" is at variance with reality. Life for them is just not like that! And when their teachers attempt to foster a similar outlook, these children of the city, who know it to be otherwise, become justifiably cynical and contemptuous toward schools and teachers.

Educational Disadvantage of the Urban Child

The major criticism of urban schools by educators, students, parents, and community leaders is that they have failed to respond adequately to children who have special learning handicaps and discouragements, or to help children make a connection between formal learning in the classroom and the realities of urban life.

One of these realities is the socioeconomic disadvantage of widespread unemployment, family breakdown, and inadequate housing. In 1950 it was estimated that one child out of every ten attending public schools in the nation's fourteen largest cities could be considered socioeconomically disadvantaged. By 1960 this proportion had increased to one in three, and it is believed that by the early 1970's it had risen to approximately one out of every two.[9] These statistics are particularly significant in view of the assertion that "the single most important determinant of educational achievement is family income."[10] The evidence seems incontrovertible that such factors as poverty, slum housing, unemployment, parents' cultural deprivation, racial discrimination, and the absence of a father are directly related to school attendance, academic achievement, I.Q. scores, pupil retention, and formal educational outcomes.[11]

For most disadvantaged children of the city, home is in a ghetto; whether that ghetto is white or black, it has an imprint on the attitudes, values, and expectations of those who live there. Black ghettos in particular are typically inhabited by people with a heritage of deprivation, frustration, maltreatment, and hopelessness. The ghetto is a dead end. Thus, a ghetto child's image of his parents is frequently one of frustration, conflict, enforced idleness, and despair. In many families, the mother is forced to assume the responsibilities of both parents. There is evidence that children in homes without fathers are more likely to demonstrate "low motivation for achievement, inability to defer immediate for later gratification, low self-esteem, susceptibility to group influence, and juvenile delinquency."[12] Even where both parents are present, relations within ghetto families cannot but be strained by conditions that prevent the father and the mother from obtaining respectable work, income, and social status.

Finally, for people in ghettos the values associated with the Puritan ethic have little or no relevance. Ghetto children observe a system that does not appear to reward honesty, perseverance, and hard work, but rather those in a position to take the greatest advantage of others: absentee landlords who exploit their tenants, narcotics pushers, numbers runners, and storekeepers selling inferior goods at exorbitant prices. The child of the ghetto is thus strongly tempted to adopt "hustling" as a way of life. And because this cruel pattern tends to renew itself from one generation to the next, the cycle of deprivation—social, political, and economic—becomes nearly inevitable.

A big-city school superintendent, Carl Dolce, has written of the ghetto child: "A victim of his environment, the ghetto child begins his school career psychologically, socially, and physically disadvantaged. He is oriented to the present rather than the future, to immediate needs rather than delayed gratification, to the concrete rather than the abstract. He is often handicapped by limited verbal skills, low self-esteem, and a stunted drive toward achievement; by sight, hearing, and dental deficiencies; by hernias, malnutrition, and anemia."[13] A big-city elementary school principal, Samuel Shepard, has described the disadvantaged pupils in urban school systems as

> the many, many children who don't eat any breakfast at all, to say nothing of an adequate lunch; the children who come from families in which there is no father and in which the mother, having to work, keeps the oldest boy or girl out of school half or more of the school year to take care of the pre-school kids; the many children whose families consist of six to ten other children together with parents and even grandparents or aunts and uncles, all living within two or three rooms that provide no privacy and little opportunity for peace and quiet, to say nothing of a place conducive for study.

Children coming from such homes are bound to bring discipline problems to the school—fights, destruction of school property, disrespect for themselves, teachers, the custodial staff, and
even for the principal. The pupils' widespread lack of interest
and poor achievement almost inevitably lower the morale and
enthusiasm of the teacher staff, with the result that the vicious
cycle of apathy, discouragement, and perfunctory effort sets in.[14]

Undoubtedly, the greatest challenge facing big-city school systems today is the need to provide children like those described by
Dolce and Shepard with useful and meaningful educational experiences. If forced to meet this challenge alone, however, urban
schools are doomed to failure, for nearly all socioeconomic disadvantages that affect educational aspiration and achievement are
themselves external to the school.

The Teachers

By 1968, approximately 36 per cent of the nation's public school
teachers were employed in what the National Education Association defined as "urban" school systems; 35 per cent were teaching
in "suburban" school systems, and the remaining 29 per cent in
"rural" systems.[15] Table 5-1 indicates the extent to which teaching
staffs in fifteen of the nation's largest central city school districts
have grown during the past five years.

Historically, because more than half the persons who receive
teaching certificates in June leave teaching within two years,[16]
the nation's total supply of available teachers has been limited and
the competition among better-paying school districts particularly
keen. Only during the past few years have public school enrollments became sufficiently stabilized, and the number of teaching
candidates sufficiently large, to produce a slight oversupply of public school teachers throughout the total United States. For big-city
school systems, however, the current oversupply has only mildly
relieved a perennial staffing problem. As the most recent data in

TABLE 5-1   Increase Between 1965 and 1970 in the Size of Teaching Staffs in Fifteen Selected Large Central City School Districts

| SCHOOL DISTRICT | NUMBER OF FULL-TIME AND PART-TIME CLASSROOM TEACHERS | | | | INCREASE IN TEACHING STAFF BETWEEN 1965 AND 1970 | |
	Fall 1965	Fall 1967	Fall 1969	Fall 1970	Number of Teachers	Percentage
New York	47,388	53,700	60,691	61,913	+14,525	+30.6
Los Angeles	21,575	24,179	30,291	28,584	+7,009	+32.4
Chicago	20,812	22,007	23,046	27,591	+6,779	+32.6
Philadelphia	10,580	11,705	11,965	12,157	+1,577	+14.9
Detroit	10,264	10,399[1]	10,020[1]	NA	NA	NA
Houston	8,230	9,129	8,840	9,034	+804	+9.8
Baltimore	7,114	8,894	9,504	8,547	+1,433	+20.1
Washington, D.C.	5,617	6,415	7,403	7,486	+1,869	+33.3
Milwaukee	4,705	4,778	5,060	5,921	+1,216	+25.8
Dallas	5,401	5,703	5,929	5,903	+502	+9.3
Cleveland	5,338	5,417[1]	6,449	5,694	+356	+6.7
San Francisco	3,676	3,767	4,798	4,712	+1,036	+28.2
New Orleans	3,796	4,272	4,151	4,550	+754	+19.8
St. Louis	3,851	4,158	3,975	4,153	+302	+7.8
Boston	4,060	3,878	4,346	4,107	+47	+1.2

SOURCE: U.S. Department of Health, Education, and Welfare, Office of Education, *Fall 1965, Fall 1967, Fall 1969, and Fall 1970 Statistics of Public Schools.*

[1] Data for the year were not reported to the U.S. Office of Education; the data presented are for the previous school year.

Table 5-1 indicate, total staff needs have begun to level off in urban schools as well, but big-city school systems must wage a battle on two fronts: they must continue to recruit new teachers each year, and they must also attempt to retain the experienced and committed teachers who are the heart of any school staff. The seasoned big-city school teacher often becomes disillusioned after years of service to an institution and a community both of which are either unable or unwilling to show any appreciation. Both experienced and new teachers are likely to be enticed by the advantages of suburban over city schools: smaller class sizes, more and newer equipment and supplies, pleasanter working conditions, newer buildings,[17] higher salaries, and the prospect of teaching youngsters who share the teacher's predominantly middle-class values.

The concern of teachers in urban schools with total pupil-staff ratios is apparently justified by evidence suggesting that these ratios have an important relation to student achievement. When teachers are assisted by nonteaching personnel—teacher aides, lay readers, team teachers, teacher consultants, as well as traditional administrative and supervisory personnel—the learning outcomes for youngsters are significantly higher, even with a large number of learners per teacher.[18]

A report published in 1961 by the Research Council of the Great Cities Program for School Improvement suggested that to attain ideal pupil-staff ratios in large city schools, at least thirteen additional staff members per 1,000 pupils were needed.[19] The need today is no less critical. This earlier figure, moreover, was based only on full-time programs; if it had included the overriding costs of providing part-time special instruction and extensive counseling services, the gap between actual and desired pupil-staff ratios would surely have been even greater.

On the disparity in staffing between urban and suburban school districts, Michael Usdan's investigation covering the Chicago public schools and those of one of its more affluent suburbs concluded: "To staff six elementary schools in a densely populated square mile of Chicago's Southside comparably with Evanston's schools would require 111 additional teachers, an increase of 45 per cent. This increase in only six of Chicago's hundreds of schools would cost some three-quarters of a million dollars. If DuSable High School on Chicago's Southside were to be staffed comparably to New Trier High School which services a number of affluent northern and southern suburbs, an increase of 40 per cent would be needed."[20] Usdan added that "the statistics would be little different for any other Great City vis à vis its more affluent suburbs."

The data in Table 4-1 in the previous chapter bring Usdan's 1964 observations up to date. In 1970, 11.6 million youngsters were enrolled and 450,800 instructional staff members were employed in the central city school systems of the nation's approximately 250 Standard Metropolitan Statistical Areas; the average pupil-staff ratio was approximately twenty-five to one. Suburban schools, by contrast, enrolled about 16.9 million youngsters and employed approximately 958,000 instructional staff members, a pupil-staff ratio of less than eighteen to one. In other words, for every 100 pupils, suburban schools employed six instructional staff members whereas urban schools employed only four.

Nevertheless, big-city public schools usually manage to employ teachers who have more education than the average public-school teacher in the United States and at least as much education as their suburban counterparts. Table 5-2 compares the degree of preparation obtained by those who were teaching in the fall of 1967 in the nation as a whole, in central cities and their surrounding suburbs, and in seventeen of the nation's largest central city school districts. In fifteen of the twenty-five central cities listed, the percentage of teachers with either a master's or doctor's degree exceeded the average both for the nation as a whole and for all suburbs of those central cities.

It may also be noted that in 1967, sizable numbers of teachers who had not yet received a bachelor's degree were working in the public schools of Baltimore, Boston, Cleveland, and Detroit. For years, as Table 5-3 indicates, big-city school districts have been forced to round out their teaching staffs by hiring individuals who have not yet earned a required academic degree, been certified by a state department of education, or received the specialized certificate required for teaching in a particular city. Since 1967, some districts appear to have been able to reduce their dependence on noncertified teaching personnel; others, however, have made little progress in this direction. In Baltimore, for instance, the number of noncertified teachers in the district actually increased between 1964–65 and 1969–70; by 1969, the number of noncertified teachers

TABLE 5-2   Level of Educational Preparation of Classroom Teachers in 1967

SCHOOL DISTRICT	PERCENTAGE OF CLASSROOM TEACHERS			
	Without Bachelor's Degree	With Bachelor's Degree	With Master's Degree	With Doctor's Degree
Chicago	0.0	70.1	29.3	0.6
Denver	0.0	77.4	22.5	0.1
Los Angeles	0.0	76.8	22.9	0.3
Atlanta	0.1	76.6	20.8	2.4
Dallas	0.1	69.2	30.7	0.1
San Diego	0.1	67.7	32.1	0.1
Houston	0.2	69.2	30.6	0.0
Philadelphia	0.6	65.3	33.9	0.1
Kansas City	0.7	58.5	40.7	0.0
San Francisco	1.5	74.3	23.9	0.4
Columbus	1.9	78.5	19.5	0.1
Washington, D.C.	2.9	71.9	24.8	0.5
Milwaukee	3.1	66.6	26.9	3.4
Indianapolis	3.2	50.2	46.3	0.3
Memphis	3.2	79.9	17.0	0.0
Minneapolis	3.2	73.1	23.7	0.0
Cincinnati	3.5	64.7	31.6	0.2
St. Louis	3.8	61.6	34.4	0.3
New York	4.6	62.2	32.8	0.4
Pittsburgh	7.0	55.8	37.1	0.2
New Orleans	7.3	73.3	19.3	0.1
Boston	10.3	45.6	43.5	0.6
Detroit	11.4	53.3	35.0	0.2
Cleveland	12.1	71.6	16.3	0.0
Baltimore	15.9	55.2	28.8	0.1
In all central cities	3.2	67.0	29.5	0.3
In all suburbs	4.0	69.5	26.3	0.2
In all rural areas	9.3	72.1	18.4	0.2
In all U.S.	5.7	69.8	24.2	0.3

SOURCE: U.S. Department of Health, Education, and Welfare, Office of Education, *Statistics of Local Public School Systems*, 1967.

in the Baltimore city schools represented more than 20 per cent of the total teaching staff.

Assuming that large-scale use of teaching personnel without a

TABLE 5-3 Number of Classroom Teachers with Less than a Standard Teaching Certificate in Ten Selected Central City School Districts in 1963 through 1969[1]

SCHOOL DISTRICT	Fall 1963	Fall 1964	Fall 1965	Fall 1966	Fall 1967	Fall 1968	Fall 1969
Baltimore	1358	1410	1618			1939	2005
Boston					30	38	
Chicago					602	7679[2]	
Cleveland	219	133	110				
Detroit	97	257	314	582			
Los Angeles	1350		400	366	421	430	
Milwaukee	40	38				68	
New Orleans	216	177	397	219	367	297	300
Philadelphia	76					176	400
Washington, D.C.	1722	2220	2525	2800	2400	1863	

SOURCE: U.S. Department of Health, Education, and Welfare, Office of Education, *Fall 1964, Fall 1965, Fall 1966, Fall 1967, Fall 1968,* and *Fall 1969 Statistics of Public Schools.*

[1] The spaces indicate either that no data were reported to the U.S. Office of Education or that all teachers had a standard teaching certificate.

[2] Includes teachers who met the requirements of the State of Illinois, but who were not fully certified by the City of Chicago.

baccalaureate degree or a standard teaching certificate lowers the quality of instruction in a school, we can estimate the effect of the practice on instruction. During the 1968–69 school year, the public school districts of Baltimore, Boston, Chicago, Los Angeles, New Orleans, Philadelphia, and Washington employed as teachers a total of nearly 12,500 individuals not fully certified to teach. Estimate that half these individuals taught in secondary schools and met an average of 160 students per day, and that the other half taught at least twenty-five elementary school youngsters a day. In just these eight large central city school districts, over 150,000 elementary school students were taught for most of each day and approximately 1,000,000 secondary school students for part of each day by noncertificated and thus presumably, inadequate teachers. Over a 180-day school year, such numbers accumulate to enormous amounts of pupil instructional time.

Ironies in Teacher Placement

To find an adequate number of qualified teachers is for urban school systems only the beginning of the staffing problem; appropriate assignments must also be made. For a number of reasons, teacher placement in big-city school districts typically results in a high concentration of the youngest, least experienced, and least well qualified teachers in schools with the most disadvantaged students; conversely, schools with the lowest proportion of disadvantaged students are likely to be staffed by teachers with the most experience and the most extensive post-baccalaureate education. In urban schools, therefore, youngsters who most need good teaching are least likely to get it, whereas those able to learn with ordinary help typically enjoy the best teaching available in the district. Where this occurs, the inevitable effect is to widen the gap in performance between youngsters who are socioeconomically disadvantaged and those who are not.

This perverse pattern of staffing can be traced largely to the psychology that pervades much of the teaching profession. Perhaps even more than other "service professionals" such as doctors and lawyers, public school teachers have failed historically to assign the greatest professional value and prestige to assisting those youngsters who have the least skill and the greatest handicaps. Frank Riessman has written, for instance, that most teachers "who work with underprivileged children today find this a most unattractive, unrewarding task. . . . Teachers much prefer to teach 'nice' children in 'nice' schools in 'nice' zones."[21] In general, high professional status in public education tends to be associated with teaching academically successful students in college preparatory programs and in advanced courses, as compared with those less academically able, and those in vocational-technical programs and remedial courses.

This differentiation in status means that as teachers gain experience and seniority in a school district, they tend to transfer *from* schools with high percentages of economically and socially disadvantaged students *to* schools where those from middle- and upper-income families are more numerous. As a result, teaching assign-

ments in big-city school systems become available when experienced
inner-city teachers who have gained seniority transfer to outlying
schools in the city or when, overwhelmed by the working conditions
in a ghetto school, they either move to suburban districts or leave
teaching entirely.

To fill these vacancies, central city school administrators have
been forced to assign either beginning or uncertified teachers to
their most demanding teaching posts. Furthermore, because city
school districts have not always been able to staff their schools
completely, they often have been forced to rely on an inordinate
number of full-time substitute teachers, particularly for ghetto
schools. For example, in 1966 in one major American city, 94 per
cent of the teachers in the city's high-status schools were regularly
assigned; the comparable figure in that city's ghetto schools was
less than 64 per cent.[22]

Given the lower rate of increase in the size of urban school
teaching staffs during recent years, and the growing oversupply of
teachers in particular content areas, this pattern of staff placement
may begin to change to some extent during the next decade. It will
not change fast enough, however, to affect staffing patterns in
urban ghettos as they grow in area and population. That those
urban public schools most in need of experienced and competent
personnel will continue to be staffed by a disproportionate number
of the least qualified, least experienced, and most transient of a
city's public school teachers appears, unfortunately, to be inevitable.

Teacher-Parent Relations in Urban Slum Schools

After a comprehensive study in the mid-1960's of the public
schools of Washington, D.C., A. Harry Passow concluded that
teachers assigned to work with lower-income youngsters in urban
slum schools tend to be "people without any real concern for these
children and with the common stereotype of them as children of
low ability." He added, "Many teachers in slum schools are bewildered and desperate; they feel they cannot reach these children. . . ."[23] Other writers have made similar observations. Kenneth Clark has written that "a key component of the deprivation

which affects ghetto children is that, generally, their teachers do not expect them to learn," that "teachers tend to emphasize discipline rather than learning," and that "apathy seems pervasive" in most urban slum schools.[24]

At the heart of these assertions is the implied criticism that the slum teacher does not work hard enough to build effective working relations with the parents of his students. James Coleman, after an extensive study of educational opportunity in America's public schools, concluded that a pupil's home and family environment actually account for more of the variance in his learning than does his formal scholastic instruction.[25] The traditional response of educators to such conclusions has been to blame the youngsters and their parents for failing to adjust to the school environment. Such blame is irrelevant, and an evasion of an important challenge to educational practice.

There are, unfortunately, many obstacles and few precedents to building constructive parent-teacher relations in slum schools. Traditionally, teachers and parents have met mainly when a child has either failed or misbehaved. Only infrequently have they done so simply out of friendliness or common interest; rarely have teachers and parents in slum schools collaborated in assessing a student's progress or discussing new educational programs. Concerned with professional status and with their own objectives, teachers have typically fostered a superordinate-subordinate relation with parents. Many teachers see education as exclusively the business of educators, and they neither expect nor desire parents or the general public to collaborate in assessing pupils, evaluating schools, or developing new programs.

In sum, attitudes held by many urban school teachers and administrators toward their roles in a school and in its larger community simply intensify the conflict between home and school, particularly in areas that are predominantly Negro and lower-class:

Low-income Negro parents view the schools as formidable, hostile, impregnable, closed structures which are necessary by law, but not by choice. The teachers work in the community, but are not part of the community. Teachers drive to school and leave as soon as the school day is completed. They rarely visit the community and never participate in its activities. The buildings are large; and, after a school day is completed, they are very dark.

These negative institutional attitudes are organizationally implemented through the goals that are established. Most school teachers and officials view their goals as primarily controlling the students and (either directly or indirectly) the parents, then avoiding trouble or embarrassment which might occur as a result of interacting with the parents, socializing, or acculturating parents and students to the middle-class way of life, and lastly teaching the 3 R's.

Low-income parents and students perceive these goals and resent the school officials and teachers for establishing this primary goal. Control is necessary as a form of discipline, but, not an end in itself; socialization is not recognized by most parents as a goal. But, neither control nor socialization are primary goals. Thus the hierarchical arrangement of institutional goals, which the teachers and parents each establish, are in conflict.[26]

Problems of Teachers in Urban Schools

In 1968, the Research Division of the National Education Association conducted a nationwide survey of problems confronting teachers in urban, suburban, and rural school districts. The following were those most often cited: (1) insufficient time for rest and lesson preparation during the school day; (2) excessive class size; (3) insufficient clerical help; (4) inadequate salaries; and (5) inadequate fringe benefits. Each of these was considered by seven of every ten teachers to be one of the most important problems they faced, although—as Table 5-4 suggests—urban, suburban, and rural teachers did not always agree on which problems were most critical.

Among urban teachers, large class size was by far the problem most frequently cited. The data presented earlier on pupil-staff and pupil-teacher ratios suggest that class size tends to be larger in big-city schools than in either suburban or rural schools. There is evidence, however, that differences in class size itself are much less significant to student learning than they were once thought to be, even though the number in a classroom certainly affects discipline,

TABLE 5-4 Problems Identified as Most Important in 1968 by Teachers in Urban, Suburban, and Rural Schools

	PERCENTAGE OF TEACHERS IN SAMPLE WHO REGARDED PROBLEM AS OF "MAJOR" IMPORTANCE		
PROBLEM	In Urban School Districts	In Suburban School Districts	In Rural School Districts
1. Large class size	40.4	33.4	30.6
2. Inadequate salary	34.9	24.5	30.3
3. Lack of public support for schools	27.8	17.4	23.7
4. Inadequate fringe benefits	27.7	22.3	31.3
5. Ineffective grouping of students in classes	24.3	18.2	24.2
6. Classroom management and discipline	23.3	10.8	12.1
7. Inadequate assistance from specialized teachers	22.5	21.0	30.3
8. Ineffective testing and guidance program	21.1	14.2	20.8

SOURCE: National Education Association, NEA Research Bulletin, December, 1968.

the frequency of face-to-face contact between teachers and students, and the possible choices among modes of instruction.

The evidence suggests three conclusions about class size. First, there appears to be no optimal size for maximum student achievement; regardless of how the research data are divided for analytic purposes—by grade level, subject, experimental design—or the time when the research was conducted, the results are inconsistent and provide no firm basis for arguing that class size is significantly correlated with student achievement. Second, "proper class size is a function of many factors, including course objectives, nature of the subject matter, nature of the teaching process used, and teacher understanding and morale, among others."[27] And third, far more important to learning than any fixed ratio of pupils to teacher in a classroom are "the ability of the teacher as a classroom practitioner

TABLE 5-5 Teachers' Salaries and the Cost of Living in Sixteen U.S. Central Cities, 1959–1969

CENTRAL CITY	CITY WORKER'S FAMILY BUDGET	AVERAGE TEACHER SALARY	RATIO OF SALARY TO BUDGET
	Fall 1959[1]	1960	1959–60
Houston	$5,370	$5,027	93.7
Cleveland	6,199	5,993	96.7
Kansas City	5,964	5,777	96.8
Atlanta	5,642	4,935	87.6
Boston	6,317	6,578	104.0
St. Louis	6,266	6,240	99.5
New York	5,970	7,367	123.4
Seattle	6,562	6,121	93.3
Minneapolis	6,181	6,011	97.2
Washington, D.C.	6,147	6,426	104.8
Baltimore	5,718	6,179	108.1
Philadelphia	5,898	6,081	103.1
San Francisco	6,304	7,378	117.1
Chicago	6,567	7,278	110.7
Los Angeles	6,285	7,281	115.7
Detroit	6,072	6,843	112.7
	Spring 1969[2]	1968–69	1968–69
Houston	$9,212	$7,134	77.4
Cleveland	10,453	8,214	78.6
Kansas City	9,943	7,882	79.3
Atlanta	9,233	7,485	81.1
Boston	11,108	9,250	83.3
St. Louis	10,065	8,654	86.0
New York	11,236	9,696	86.3
Seattle	10,485	9,110	86.9
Minneapolis	10,369	9,063	87.4
Washington, D.C.	10,503	9,292	88.5
Baltimore	9,735	8,748	89.9
Philadelphia	10,160	9,295	91.5
San Francisco	10,865	10,088	92.8
Chicago	10,332	9,697	93.9
Los Angeles	10,285	10,038	97.6
Detroit	9,972	10,009	100.4

and his willingness to be flexible in his approach to teaching."[28] Thus, although a reduction in class sizes might well alleviate problems of student discipline for big-city school teachers and thereby enhance their morale, it appears unlikely that merely reducing the size of classes will in itself improve student achievement. What appears to be called for is an amelioration of home environments and of the relations between home and school, a change in teacher attitudes toward students and toward the teaching role, and increased participation by students in planning and assessing their own learning.

The second major problem cited by urban school teachers in the NEA survey was inadequate salaries and fringe benefits. This complaint seems justified; the typical salaries of teachers are barely adequate for surviving financially in any of the nation's major metropolitan areas. Almost without exception, salary schedules in large central city school districts are a handicap in attracting and holding qualified and experienced instructional personnel. Although in most central city school districts the average teacher's salary compares favorably with that paid in their respective metropolitan districts, it does not adequately compensate for the more onerous working conditions—older buildings, poorer equipment and supplies, and more serious and frequent discipline problems. Moreover, the average teacher's salary in most central city districts does not compare well with either the cost of living in a central city or the average salaries paid to other, less well educated city employees.

Table 5-5 compares the cost of living and the average public

SOURCE: U.S. Department of Labor, Bureau of Labor Statistics, *City Worker's Family Budget for a Moderate Standard of Living*; National Educational Association, *Economic Status of Teachers in 1963–64 and Economic Status of the Teaching Profession, 1970–71.*

[1] As defined by the Bureau of Labor Statistics, this 1959 "city worker's family budget" represents the costs for a worker's family to maintain a "modest but adequate" living standard in each of the large central cities listed.

[2] The revised cost of maintaining a "moderate" standard of living for a family consisting of an employed husband, aged 38, a wife not employed outside the home, an 8-year-old girl, and a 13-year-old boy.

school teacher's salary in sixteen large central cities in 1960 and 1969. Despite their militance during the late 1960's and their efforts to force salaries to a respectable level, public-school teachers in each of the sixteen large central cities were actually less well off in 1969 than they had been in 1960. At the beginning of the decade, the average teacher's salary exceeded the cost of living on a "moderate" scale for a family of four in nine of the sixteen cities; moreover, it amounted to at least 95 per cent of that cost in all but three of the remaining cities. By 1969, however, the ratio between an average salary and the cost of living had shifted drastically. Only in Detroit was the average salary still comparable. In eleven of the cities, the ratio had dipped to less than 90 per cent; and in three of these, the average teacher was paid less than four-fifths the cost of living on a "moderate" scale. Some clue as to whether the trend continues downward or has begun to reverse can be gained by examining comparable data for 1966 and then comparing the ratios for each city at the three different points in time. In all sixteen cities, the ratio of average salary to cost of living declined between 1960 and 1966; by contrast, in thirteen of the cities, excluding Cleveland, New York, and San Francisco, the gap began to close after 1966—although not nearly as rapidly as it grew in the early years of the decade.

Table 5-6 gives comparative data on salaries and costs for teachers and others in these same sixteen central cities in 1970. It will be noted that the minimum starting salary for teachers was lower than the average salary for general-duty nurses in seven of the sixteen cities, and substantially lower than the average salary for auto-body repairmen in all sixteen of them. In fact, even when average rather than starting salaries are considered, body repairmen in the sixteen cities made significantly more money than public school teachers in 1970. Given the worsening conditions in urban schools, compared with the generally expanding market for other types of workers in an urban setting between 1960 and 1970, it is hardly any wonder that central city school districts found it increasingly difficult to attract and hold beginning teachers.

TABLE 5-6   Selected Comparisons of Teacher Salaries with Other Salaries and Costs in 1969–70 in Twelve Cities

CENTRAL CITY	PUBLIC SCHOOL TEACHER		ESTIMATED AVERAGE ANNUAL EARNINGS[1]		MAXIMUM SALARY FOR TEACHERS IN 1970	RATIO OF MAXIMUM SALARY FOR TEACHERS TO A "MODERATE" FAMILY BUDGET[2]
	Minimum Starting Salary	Average Salary	General Duty Nurses in Private/Public Hospitals	Body Repairmen in Auto Body Shops		
Cleveland	$7,000	$9,220	$7,700	$11,950	$13,000	110%
Houston	7,020	7,837	NA	11,600	10,060	104
St. Louis	7,200	9,878	7,500	10,500	13,400	127
Philadelphia	7,300	10,000	7,050	9,050	13,800	127
Baltimore	7,500	8,998	7,450	10,600	13,400	127
San Francisco	7,520	10,900	8,800	10,450	15,040	132
Los Angeles	7,590	10,350	8,300	11,600	14,730	136
Boston	7,600	9,300	7,900	9,250	13,500	112
Washington, D.C.	7,800	10,660	8,050	11,850	14,680	133
Chicago	8,000	10,400	7,700	12,000	14,750	133
Detroit	8,277	NA	8,200	15,000	16,500	156
New York	8,450	9,800	8,500	8,700	16,000	132

SOURCE: U.S. Department of Labor, Bureau of Labor Statistics, *Monthly Labor Review*, November 1970; National Education Association, Research Division, *Salary Schedules for Teachers, 1970–71*; U.S. Department of Health, Education, and Welfare, Office of Education, *Digest of Educational Statistics, 1970*.

[1] The average annual earnings of general duty nurses and body repairmen were estimated by the Research Division of National Education Association. For both, a work year of 1950 hours was assumed.

[2] The 1970 "city worker's family budget" is the revised cost of maintaining a "moderate" standard of living for a family consisting of an employed husband, aged 38, a wife not employed outside the home, an 8-year-old girl, and a 13-year-old boy.

The last two columns of data in the table suggest why it is difficult for central city districts to retain their most experienced teachers. In one of the sixteen cities, Houston, the *maximum* teacher's salary in 1970 barely exceeded the cost of a moderate standard of living for a family of four; and in fourteen of the remaining fifteen cities, the maximum teacher's salary was no more than a third again as great as the cost of a moderate standard of living in that city. This hardly provides incentive for teachers to remain with central city school districts for the twelve to fifteen years required to reach maximum salary levels, especially when comparable teaching salaries can be made in the surrounding suburbs where the costs of living are not nearly so high.

Finally, in nearly every major metropolitan area in the country, the very best pay for teachers is not in central cities, but in the more affluent suburbs surrounding them. For example, the school systems in Winnetka, Evanston, Scarsdale, Bronxville, Abington Township, and Grosse Point, all suburbs of major American cities, pay for comparable positions at least a few hundred dollars more per year than do their respective central city school systems.

It is thus hardly surprising that teachers began to be militant in the nation's largest central city school systems. Nor is it surprising that the American Federation of Teachers won its first major victory in the New York City public schools, the largest urban school district in the country, and has continued to expand its influence in nearly every urban center in the United States. Militance by teachers and the growth of teacher organizations have become major variables in public education throughout the country. During the 1960–61 school year, there were only three teachers' strikes; during the 1969–70 school year the number had risen to 180, and the total for the decade topped 500. More than half a million teachers participated in organized strikes during the decade, with a loss of more than five million man-days of instruction.[29] In central cities especially, rivalry between the increasingly militant National Education Association and the American Federation of Teachers, the frequency and magnitude of teacher strikes and work stoppages, and the growing need to resolve differences through collective negotiations, have had disruptive effects on educational processes, on relations among teachers and administrators, and on student learning. There have been indications, as teachers everywhere increasingly subscribe to collective action to improve working conditions, that the NEA and the AFT will develop closer ties and perhaps eventually amalgamate, further strengthening their bargaining positions and increasing their collective power.

The dimensions and dynamics of teacher militance are complex, and have been well documented elsewhere. It need only be observed here that the nation's big-city school systems continue to have serious problems "within the family." Plagued by shortages of qualified staff, they cannot offer either the salaries or the working conditions necessary to persuade enough well-prepared and experienced teachers to remain as career employees. Of those who are employed, some are unqualified, others are ineffective, and nearly all are joining in the demand for improved working conditions and for a greater voice in administrative decision-making.

It is impossible at this point to say whether the current polarizing of school boards and teacher organizations over the issue of collective negotiations is merely a phase in the development of a profession, or a final step in the development of a labor-management relationship. Whatever the ultimate answer, in New York, Chicago, Los Angeles, Detroit, and nearly every other large central city in the United States, militance by teachers and intransigence by school boards have split public school districts into warring factions, to the detriment of administrator-staff and school-community relations, and above all of education for the students themselves.

The Policymakers

As the governing power in a public school district, the citizen school board receives considerable public attention. In an urban setting, where a public school district is one of the most visible and accessible institutions of community life and where its prob-

TABLE 5-7   School Boards in Twenty-two Large Central City School Districts in 1969: Method of Selection, Term of Office, and Number of Members

SCHOOL DISTRICT	METHOD OF SELECTING BOARD MEMBERS	TERM OF OFFICE FOR BOARD MEMBERS	NUMBER OF BOARD MEMBERS
Atlanta	General election	4 years	10
Baltimore	Appointed by Mayor; approved by City Council	6 years	9
Boston	General election	2 years	5
Chicago	Appointed by Mayor; approved by City Council	5 years	11
Cincinnati	General election	4 years	7
Cleveland	General election	4 years	7
Dallas	Special election	*	*
Denver	Special and general elections	6 years	7
Detroit	General election	6 years	7
Indianapolis	General election	4 years	7
Los Angeles	General election	4 years	7
Miami	General election	4 years	7
Milwaukee	General election	6 years	15
Minneapolis	General election	6 years	7
New Orleans	Special and general elections	6 years	5
New York	Appointed by borough presidents	**	**
Philadelphia	Appointed by lower court judges	6 years	15
St. Louis	General election	6 years	12
San Diego	General election	4 years	5
San Francisco	Appointed by Mayor; approved by electorate	5 years	7
Seattle	General election	6 years	7
Washington, D.C.	Special and general elections	4 years	11

* Not reported by the district in response to survey.

** Prior to 1969, the New York City Central School Board was appointed by the Mayor, served for seven years, and consisted of nine members. As of June, 1969, a "special interim board" consisting of five members appointed by the five borough presidents replaced the Central Board for a term of one year. That original term was then extended for another year. In addition to the "special interim board," there are in New York thirty nonsalaried local school boards. The nine members of each local school board, formerly appointed by the Central Board, were elected for the first time at a special election in March, 1970.

lems are multiple, a school board is almost continually embroiled in controversy. Chapter Six will deal with some of the difficulties urban school boards encounter when they try to mediate between the school system and the community. For the moment, let us consider how urban school boards are selected and how they function.

In most of the nation's largest central cities, as Table 5-7 indicates, school boards are elected on a nonpartisan basis. Since members so elected are directly accountable to the public who elected them, theoretically at least they are not subject to pressure by political organizations. At the same time, however, school board elections often attract candidates less interested in schools than in using membership on the school board as a stepping stone to some other elective office. Dallas, Denver, New Orleans, and Washington, D.C., conduct *special* elections to the school board, a practice that has other advantages and disadvantages. On the one hand, voters in a special election know more clearly whom they are voting for and what the candidates stand for; they do not have to decipher a long ballot as in most general elections. On the other hand, few people typically vote in a special election, and those who do often are not a representative sample of the total public; special elections tend to attract elderly voters and only those others who are especially conscientious. So far as the principles of direct accountability and responsibility to the public are concerned, the least desirable method of selecting school board members would seem to be by appointment, as they are in Baltimore, Chicago, and San Francisco (by the mayor), in Philadelphia and Pittsburgh (by lower court judges), and in New York (by the borough presidents).

In recent years the number of big-city school board members who receive compensation for their services has significantly increased. A decade ago, board members in fewer than one out of every five districts were compensated; today, as the data in Table 5-8 indicate, the ratio is closer to one out of three. In 1968–69 board members in thirteen of the nation's largest urban school systems received no compensation. Even in those districts that did compen-

TABLE 5-8   School Boards in Twenty-two Large Central City School Districts: Pupil Enrollment, Number of Official Meetings, and Rate of Compensation for Board Members, 1968–69

SCHOOL DISTRICT	PUPIL ENROLLMENT	NUMBER OF OFFICIAL MEETINGS			RATE OF COMPENSATION FOR BOARD MEMBERS
		Regular	Special	Total	
Atlanta	117,200	12	3	15	President $350/month; others, $300/month
Baltimore	119,700	20	10	30	None
Boston	94,000	23	5	28	None
Chicago	583,100	24	2	26	None
Cincinnati	85,100	22	2	24	None
Cleveland	152,000	24	3	27	$240/year
Dallas	157,300	44[1]	0[1]	44	None[1]
Denver	97,000	9	19	28	None
Detroit	292,100	24	2	26	None
Indianapolis	108,300	24	2	26	None
Los Angeles	732,800	144	44	188	$75/meeting, not to exceed $750/month
Miami	250,900	12	12	24	$2400/year
Milwaukee	130,200	13	2	15	$600/year
Minneapolis	70,000	22	2	24	None
New Orleans	108,000	20	6	26	None
New York	1,122,000	12	11	23	None[2]
Philadelphia	295,200	20	12	32	None
St. Louis	113,000	11	6	17	None
San Diego	170,800	109	4	113	$50/meeting, not to exceed $400/month
San Francisco	136,600	24	6	30	$1200/year
Seattle	93,500	24	3	27	None
Washington, D.C.	148,500	10	37	47	$1200/year

[1] Data are current as of 1966.

[2] After June, 1969, Central Board members received $100 per working day.

sate board members the rate of payment was extremely inconsistent, ranging from less than $1,000 per year in Cleveland and Milwaukee to more than $3,500 in Atlanta, Los Angeles, and San

Diego. There seems to be little correlation between the rate of compensation to board members and the city's population, the enrollment in the district, or the number of official meetings. For example, board members of the Atlanta public schools, where student enrollment amounted to approximately 117,000, met officially only eighteen times, yet each member earned $3,600 a year for his or her services; whereas board members in Detroit, where student enrollment was more than twice as great, met twenty-six times and received no compensation. No matter how many hours of unofficial meetings are attended by most urban school board members, it is unrealistic to expect a policymaking body that meets only a few hours each month to make thoughtful decisions or to be alert in responding to the public it serves.

In their attitudes school boards can almost always be placed near the conservative end of any liberal-to-conservative spectrum, primarily because they tend to represent the well-established sections of a community. Furthermore, most members of public-school boards are white, non-Catholic, and of the middle or upper class. For example, a study in depth of members of the Boston School Committee by William Greenbaum and Joseph Cronin showed most members to have values described by social scientists as "local rather than cosmopolitan, particularistic vs. universalistic, personal vs. professional, I–thou vs. I–it, and traditional–charismatic vs. rational–legal."[30] In his broad analysis of all personnel in public education, George Spindler places board members at the extreme traditional end of a traditional–emergent value continuum, arguing that they generally are "people who have a stake in keeping things as they are, who gained their success within the framework of the traditional value system, and consequently believe it to be good, and who, by virtue of their age, grew up and acquired their value sets during a period of time when American culture was presumably more tradition-oriented than it is today."[31] This disposition toward the status quo often leads to a serious gap between an urban school system's policymaking body and those who are dissatisfied with its performance and administrative procedures.

This gap is often aggravated by the content of school board meetings in most of the nation's largest central cities, where the topics debated are often only remotely related to the experience of students. In fact, Greenbaum and Cronin discovered during their two-year study of the Boston School Committee that its deliberations dealt more often with the employment of adults than with the education of children.[32] The School Committee voted on 1,618 matters during the two years; of those issues only sixty-four, or 4 per cent, dealt directly with educational policy; of the sixty-four, only three were initiated by members of the committee, and only one of these three was initiated without prior pressure from either teacher or community groups. Greenbaum and Cronin concluded that ". . . many school board members simply do not care about placing major emphasis on education, vis-à-vis emphasis on politics and employment."

Many reasons lie behind this apparent lack of interest in educational issues. A major one is that as urban school districts have increased in size and complexity, and as policy decisions, particularly those related to instruction, have demanded increasingly specialized knowledge, urban school boards have had to lean more and more heavily on the expertise of staff specialists. Most boards thus have gradually delegated to their staffs increasing responsibility for making critical policy decisions, while the boards themselves have become essentially monitors for the public and mediators only in time of conflict and crisis. From the perspective of representative democratic government, this has been an unfortunate, though inevitable, development in the role of a lay school board. As will become clearer in Chapter 6, a major effect of this gradual withdrawal of big-city school boards has been to increase substantially the power in each district of the professional bureaucracy and of special interest groups.

The Administrators

As a vocation, educational administration has had a very short history. Nevertheless, the role of a public school administrator has already undergone several major changes; it has been perceived successively as that of educational superman, technical manager, democratic leader, and applied social scientist.[33] The image of educational superman was espoused early in the twentieth century by Elwood P. Cubberley, who argued that public schools ought to play a prominent role in American society. Noting that the schools were responsible for assimilating the immigrant, training the worker, abolishing illiteracy, providing vocational guidance, and creating national standards of health and morality, Cubberley argued that to guarantee fulfillment of these responsibilities, a school administrator inevitably has to be all things to all people: "His is the office 'up to which and down from which authority, direction, and information flow.' He is 'the organizer and director of the work of the schools in all their various phases. . . .' He is 'the executive office of the school board and also its eyes, and ears, and brains.' He is 'the supervisor of the instruction in the schools, and also the leader, adviser, inspirer, and friend of the teachers.' "[34]

During the 1920's, the public school administrator became a technical manager whose primary task was to promote efficiency in school programs. As the principles and practices of scientific management began to be developed in other areas of public administration, a public school administrator was expected to apply such concepts as division of labor, unity of control, economic analysis, accountability, and specialization by purpose, process, and clientele.

During the 1930's, somewhat in reaction against the scientific management school, the human relations approach to management became prominent. Stimulated by the work of Chester Barnard[35] and by the often-cited Hawthorne experiments of F. I. Roethlisberger and W. J. Dickson,[36] training programs for school administrators began to de-emphasize a purely economic approach to managing schools in favor of such concepts as "statesmanship" and "democracy" in school administration. The essential norms now became social concern, public inspiration, and the active involvement of teachers, parents, and pupils in the educational decision-making process.

The most recent definition of the occupational role of a school administrator, developed in the late 1950's and 1960's and still influential today, is the view of the public school administrator as a social scientist. He is expected to be conversant with the basic concepts of sociology, psychology, political science, economics, anthropology, and organizational theory as well as with the traditional concerns of school administration, and to monitor, analyze, and influence individual and group behavior in terms of those theories.

Unfortunately, as Luvern Cunningham and Raphael Nystrand have observed, the impact of these four images or role expectations for a public school administrator has been much more cumulative than successive. This is particularly evident in current educational programs designed to prepare future school administrators.

> Although we now perceive the administrator as an applied behavioral scientist and urge students to become capable students of behavioral science, we have not put aside altogether the images of the educational superman, technical expert, and democratic leader. We have developed instead a very crowded curriculum which, in too many cases, conveys a composite image of the administrator who is all-knowing, well-versed in all details of administering schools, and able to use behavioral science "principles" to manipulate others under the guise of encouraging participation.[37]

As is becoming clear, especially in the nation's urban school systems, it is inhuman and unrealistic to expect one human being to be simultaneously an educational superman, a technical manager, a democratic leader, and an applied social scientist. In fact, many individuals who have typically been recruited to educational administration seem unable to play any of these roles effectively:

> The era when sufficient qualifications for success as a school administrator were sound judgment, a pleasant personality, and some knowledge of finance, construction, and curriculum is rapidly passing. Contemporary administrators are confronted and perplexed by increasing social demands upon schools, diverse and

broadly-based challenges to existing structures of authority, difficulties associated with managing and changing large bureaucratic organizations, and a host of technical and pedagogical alternatives. The world of the public school administrator has changed considerably in recent years, and it is apparent that there is a shortage of individuals who possess the skills necessary to succeed in this new setting.[38]

Unfortunately, this shortage of skilled administrative personnel has its most negative repercussions in large central city school systems where the problems of organization and management often elude human belief and competence. An extensive study of contemporary public school administrators was made by Keith Goldhammer *et al.* during the mid-1960's, designed "to analyze and categorize those problems which school superintendents perceive as basic to the effective operation of their schools."[39] Although the interview sample included superintendents from rural and suburban as well as urban school settings, most of the problems they identified are relevant to big-city school administrators. These problems include the following: (1) the demand by parents and students that schools be accountable for the outcomes of their instructional programs; (2) increased self-criticism among educators and a growing demand for broad involvement in decisions regarding the school's role; (3) local, state, and federal pressures that reduce the independence of school districts; (4) teacher militancy and the growing bent toward "unionism"; (5) the shortage of qualified teachers; (6) the need to develop curricula attuned to the particular needs of the district; (7) the definition and evaluation of quality education for all socioeconomic groups; (8) the identification of the proper political role of administrators in the community; (9) the need for decentralization of decision-making; (10) racial problems; (11) educating the culturally deprived child; and (12) the inadequacy of present revenues.

As the Goldhammer study concludes, ". . . the problems appear to arise from relatively few sources. They arise from the major social dislocations affecting American society; from the rapid social changes affecting American communities which impose changes upon the schools; from cultural changes which necessitate new role definitions for educational administrators; from individual characteristics of superintendents; and, seemingly, from the persistence of traditional modes of organizational behavior and governmental structures and practices."[40]

Faced with the need to make an immense number of decisions each day, most urban school administrators lack the time and opportunity to study problems carefully before they act. Moreover, their social backgrounds and career experiences often have failed to sensitize them to urban conditions, especially to the changing life styles and social expectations of central city residents. In examining the biographies of eleven big-city school superintendents listed in Who's Who, Robert Crain and David Street found that about two-thirds were from small cities or rural America, began their teaching in small towns, and had little administrative experience prior to their superintendencies in large city school systems; none of the eleven had attended a first-rate undergraduate college, and only one had finished graduate school before beginning his career.[41] For most, their prior experience was unlikely to qualify them for innovative leadership of a complex urban institution.

6 The Organization of Urban Schools

Prior to the technological revolution of recent decades, extensive formal education for most Americans was more a luxury than a necessity. The life chances and the personal value orientations of the typical American were determined largely by home, church, and occupation—especially the occupation of his father. Within the past three decades, however, the relation of education to occupational status has caused the school to displace the church and to rival the home as a main determinant of life chances and the formation of values. The extended family has shrunk to a nuclear one, whose authority has been dissipated by television, peer influences, and the many distractions attendant on high geographic and social mobility. Likewise, the influence of religion has been vitiated by the growth of science and the spread of skepticism and secular values.

Thus, although they lack direct political power and are not organized to bring about social change, the nation's public schools have been subjected by the march of events to intensified public pressure and scrutiny. School leaders have been forced to respond to such interests as those of labor unions, federal agencies, and community groups. This is particularly true in large central cities. Between these interest groups and the schools themselves, however, stands the "system," whose invisible but powerful influence shapes and maintains a city's public schools. Urban school systems are so complex that no one can fully understand how they function; yet, they remain the instrumentality of learning experience, to which billions of dollars are committed each year for the purchase of time, services, space, equipment, and supplies. The struggle for control among interests with a stake in the system—students, parents, teachers, administrators, politicians, and taxpayers—is thus inevitable.

Locked playground gates, bureaucratic routines and paperwork, and formal relations with parents and students represent efforts by the system to insulate and protect itself from the community; at the same time, public meetings, citizens' committees, school board and tax elections are part of the effort by the patrons to influence its operation. Meanwhile, another struggle for influence also takes place *within* the system. Formalized hiring practices and supervisory procedures, strikes and sanctions, and a maze of in-house rituals and privileges are among the tactics used.

To function at all, urban school systems must adapt to a variety of pressures—or, to borrow a concept from organizational sociologists, the delivery structure of a school system must be made congruent with its demand structure. A demand placed on the system can be met effectively only if that demand is consistent with the system's goals, capacity, and capability. A public school system, for instance, cannot exempt its teachers from the penalty for disregarding a state law that prohibits strikes by public employees. Nor can a state-controlled public school system legally permit any of its schools to be controlled, staffed, and operated by any one community group.

The delivery structures of large urban school systems and their capability of meeting the demands made on them will be examined in this chapter as follows: (1) the definition of a desirable role for public schools in an urban setting; (2) the outmoded myths of the unitary community and political separation as guidelines for operation; (3) the bureaucratic structure of large urban school systems; and (4) their inherent resistance to change, as fostered by red tape, professional intransigence, lack of incentive, and inadequate procedures for program planning and evaluation.

The chapter that follows will complete this treatment of big-city schools with an account of their financial condition. To some observers, particularly those who are part of the system itself, a lack of adequate resources underlies almost all the other problems of urban education; to others, however, it appears more like a convenient excuse for maintaining the status quo.

Defining the Role of Urban Schools

The role and functions of a social institution in its social setting are always subject to revision as social needs and conditions change. The task of defining the role of institutions in an urban setting is complex because of their many interdependent and often conflicting relationships.

Fourteen metropolitan subsystems identified by Levine and Havighurst were listed in Chapter 2.[1] Each of these subsystems has its own goals and activities, none of them either unique or totally in harmony with those of the other subsystems. At times they may actually compete or conflict with one another. The ability of a city school system to achieve racial integration, for example, may be undercut by a decision of the department of housing to concentrate low-income residents in densely populated public projects. Or the department of public works may build roads and parking facilities that encourage increased use of automobiles even while the environmental authorities warn of air pollution.

In defining the goals and activities of an urban school system, therefore, reference must be made to the goals and activities of other metropolitan subsystems. The managers of a school system must take cognizance, for example, of residential and industrial construction under way, even though they may have little influence on those activities, as well as of employment patterns and of legal decisions affecting racial and/or socioeconomic segregation, since the schools will inevitably be affected by them.

This is not the only problem, as John Goodlad discovered in his survey of over one hundred schools clustered in and around the major cities of thirteen states: "Neither principals nor teachers were able to articulate clearly just what they thought to be most important for their schools to accomplish. And neither group was very clear on changes that should be effected in the near future."[2] This is probably true of most school personnel across the country. Except in an academic way, most public school educators in America have not grappled seriously in their day-to-day activities with the basic questions of education: what kind of human being do we intend to produce, and what kind of schooling is most desirable for the purpose?

The answers to questions such as these are not, of course, to be found in a day. They have profound philosophical, psychological, and social implications. Yet to the extent that public schools fail to acknowledge these questions, their own legitimacy as a social institution and educational agency is in danger of being lost. Continued vagueness of purpose will inevitably mean further loss of public support, and even the prospect that in the 1970's they will have lost whatever purpose they once had.

The problem of defining the role for big-city public schools is, of course, especially acute. Should urban schools continue to reflect their urban milieu, or do they have a responsibility to change it? Can and should a public school system espouse a particular set of values? Can and should it be simultaneously a *social* and an *educational* institution? For example, do urban schools have as much responsibility for bringing about racial integration as for maximizing each child's educational opportunities?

Havighurst has defined two possible models for the role of an urban school system.[3] Although not mutually exclusive in all respects, they are sufficiently different as to provide a point of departure in thinking about urban education. Havighurst calls one the "four-walls school," the other the "urban community school." The first takes as its highest priority the education of each child to the best of its ability, regardless of origins, color, intelligence, or handicaps; this means good schools, well equipped and well staffed. The aim of the "four-walls school" is educational efficiency and economy—the most effective use of taxpayer dollars. And because it regards the community and the social setting, especially their potential conflicts, as a threat to its essential purpose, the "four-walls school" requires that the boundaries between the school and its milieu be maintained and controlled.

The "urban community school," on the other hand, is based on the principle that neither school nor community can survive without the other, and that a supportive relationship requires extensive interaction between the two. This second model takes its cues from the dynamics of the urban crisis. The educator actively encourages the participation of citizens and community groups in solving problems and in planning educational programs. He accepts "the frustration of working with people who themselves are confused and uncertain about the schools, believing that the only way to solve the problems of the city is to work on a give-and-take basis with citizens and community organizations."[4] The distinction here is, of course, between a *closed* and an *open* system, between one that attempts to isolate itself from external forces and one whose activities are designed to respond to systems outside itself. In some respects, the face-off in urban education today is between those who espouse the concept of a closed, "four-walls" school and those—to be found mainly outside existing school systems—whose preference is for a more open, "urban community" school.

With these two models in mind, we can now examine the characteristics of an urban school system that tend to reduce its capacity to meet new and changing demands.

As is true of other social institutions, urban school systems continue to adhere to philosophies of operation that are no longer appropriate—once viable principles that have become myths, or what

John Kenneth Galbraith labels "conventional wisdom." Two myths that exert the most deleterious influence in big-city school systems are those of the unitary community and of political separation.

The Myth of the Unitary Community

In the early development of the nation's big-city school systems, a salient characteristic was their adherence to principles of egalitarian democracy. They operated on the assumption, that their primary task was to provide all youngsters with the same educational experiences, and that by so doing they would assure every child of an adequate education. Historically, insistence on these principles helped urban schools to resist pressures for privileged treatment to particular political or ethnic interests. The common school, the high school that followed, and still more recently the junior and community college, were all established as public service agencies for equalizing the life chances of all who attend them.

The concern for equality was gradually transformed, however, to an emphasis on "sameness." Public schools generally have been organized and administered to serve the student population in a nondifferentiated, standardized fashion. School programs have rarely been introduced until they could be made available to all students in the city. Ostensibly, resources have been distributed among all the schools in a district on the basis of such objective criteria as the square footage of classrooms and average daily attendance. Even the architectural design of urban school buildings has seemed to reflect this desire to guarantee equality through similarity, as witness the indelible image of most urban school buildings: impenetrable, multistoried, dirty-brick, surrounded by asphalt and chain-like fences.

It has long been feared that if public schools accommodated to differences among students and social groups, they would, as one observer has put it, cultivate "group and class differences in the twig-bending stage which would lead to deeper socioeconomic cleavages in the adult community."[5] Consequently, equality of educational opportunity has traditionally been measured in terms of input (dollars spent for education) rather than output (measures of pupil achievement). Any increased allocation of resources to schools in one area of a city has typically aroused noisy opposition from other areas—even though the increase would be unlikely to diminish the quality of education provided for students in those other areas. (Ironically, as the next chapter will indicate, despite the arguments for equal educational opportunity *within* districts, there has been little reduction of disparities in resources allocated *across* school districts, particularly across urban and suburban districts.)

Underlying the historical drive for egalitarian democracy in public education and the accompanying fear of differentiated treatment of children has been the myth of the unitary community. The city, according to that myth, is a consensual, organic body whose equilibrium is threatened by encounters between opposing interests and classes. Such mechanisms, therefore, as universal education, nonpartisan local government, at-large elections, and civil service procedures are assumed to be necessary for achieving and sustaining a common way of life. In relation to the school system, the myth of the unitary community argues as follows:

> . . . the city is a unity for purposes of the school program. That is, regardless of ethnic, racial, religious, economic, or political differences and group conflicts in other arenas of urban life, education need not, and should not if it could, recognize or legitimize those differences. Education is a process that must not be differentiated according to section or class. Learning is the same phenomenon, or should be, in every neighborhood. Physical facilities and personnel should be allocated without regard to whatever group conflicts might exist in the community.[6]

During the past few decades, the myth of the unitary community has been increasingly discredited by the rapid emergence of a pluralistic and secular society. The nation's large cities have always functioned to some degree as a melting pot, helping immigrants— first those from Europe and now, more recently, those from the nation's rural regions—to qualify for work in an industrial society, and promoting in them a loyalty to the American political system. Urban populations continue in important ways, however, to be heterogeneous; members of different social and ethnic groups differ markedly in their appearance, habits, and values. These differences may be accepted as inevitable, and can also be regarded as desirable, perhaps even essential to the vitality of an urban society.

Despite such cleavages among social and ethnic groups, many urban school systems continue to operate as though the unitary community and egalitarian democracy were both actualities. For example, strategies for individualizing instruction, when they are attempted at all, are intended mainly to help a child progress through a standardized curriculum; except in isolated experiments, no youngster is offered an educational experience unique in both content and process, one tailored to a particular need or learning style. Typically, urban school systems hire teachers to fill any of a range of positions in the district rather than because they have the competencies for a particular school or classroom; typically also, urban school systems promote administrators "through the ranks" —from teacher to counselor to vice-principal to principal to district office—and they transfer them among schools as if there were no important distinctions among these occupational roles or among the administrative requirements of individual schools.

The future of urban education crucially depends on the ability of big-city schools to dispel the myth of the unitary community and modify the traditional interpretation of equal educational opportunity. To bring about this development, the general public will first have to be persuaded that genuine equality of opportunity may require *different* as well as *unequal* expenditures and treatment in public schools, and the people who run urban school systems will then have to operate accordingly. The introduction of compensatory education programs for "disadvantaged children" has done much to speed both developments; considerable efforts have been made by the schools, with at least tentative support by the public, to provide "have-not" children with both *more* and *better* formal education than is provided to their better-situated classmates. Regardless of the degree to which these compensatory education programs have failed to fulfill early hopes for them, their very initiation has served to challenge the historic assumptions underlying the myth of the unitary community and the meaning of equal education.

The Myth of Political Separation

Generally speaking, the nation's urban school systems enjoy formal autonomy and political freedom, although it should be remembered that they achieved such immunity only after a half century of vigorous political efforts climaxing in the early decades of this century. The only formal procedure through which public schools are directly accountable to an urban community is through the regular election of school board members; and in cities where board members are appointed rather than elected, even this formality is denied. State regulations, although legion, are typically so loose and general as to leave ample room for board members, teachers, and administrators to act with little trepidation. Like all public school systems, those in cities are dependent on the general public and their local governments for financing; but once a budget has been approved, they enjoy considerable freedom to decide how funds will be allocated within a particular school. Until recently, moreover, the personnel in an urban school had rarely, if ever, been held accountable for the educational outcome of those expenditures. Finally, bureaucratic procedures add to the autonomy of urban school districts by dissipating and depersonalizing the thrust of grievances brought by parents, pupils, and taxpayers.

In part, therefore, the political autonomy of urban school systems derives from their organizational character, but in large part this autonomy is the outcome of years of effort by professional educators to insulate urban school systems from the community—to build a "four-walls school"—by repeating the persuasive but spurious assertion that public education must be kept "free of politics." In practice, this usually means keeping urban schools free from the influence of noneducators, be they government officials, community leaders, or mere parents.

The most insistent argument for insulating public education from political influences consists of citing the day when politicians —particularly those in the cities—ran public school systems purely on the basis of patronage, and the inequities that result when schools cater to the special interests of racial, religious, or ethnic groups. The benefits to teachers of tenure and standardized salary schedules are emphasized. But the larger questions of political reality and accountability are ignored. In short, advocates of political separation evoke the myth of the school system itself as a unitary community.

Over the years, the attempt to separate schools from politics has been a mixed blessing for American education. Protected from the inroads of political patronage and encouraged to develop programs on the basis of educational needs, educators in big-city school systems have actually had considerable opportunity to design good schools and to promote their development. Whatever the constraints imposed by inadequate funding, gigantic size, and student turmoil, the procedures for minimizing the influence of municipal politics have afforded urban school personnel a modicum of freedom to operate and even to bring about innovations.

On the other hand, the insulation of educators and of urban schools from politics has made them increasingly unresponsive to valid political demands. The organizational interests of urban schoolmen have been permitted to remain primarily internal, with the result that most of them have become ensnared in a contradiction: claiming the status and prerogatives of professionals, they have behaved as bureaucrats dedicated to maintaining the system in its current state. When children fail to learn, urban teachers and administrators have been quick to find fault, not with the system, but with the children and their families. For instance, a survey by the U.S. Office of Education of building principals in the New York City public schools noted: "If there are failures, the blame is always on others, never on the principals or the school system they represent. Children come from 'disorganized and emotionally damaging homes.' They do not 'respond' to what has worked in the past for middle-class children."[7] As a group, urban school personnel have made only minimal efforts to come to grips with the factors they blame. In their relative freedom from political constraints, they generally have been allowed by the public and by municipal governments to maintain a system that protects them remarkably from the dissatisfaction of their constituents.

The era of political autonomy and insulation of urban schools may, however, soon be over. Disenchantment with the nation's public schools, above all those in large cities, is growing. Students, teachers, parents, taxpayers, minority group leaders, politicians, businessmen all are pressing for greater participation in educational decision-making. Their demands for "a piece of the action" and for public accountability can no longer be ignored; urban school boards are beginning to realize, moreover, that political isolation merely exacerbates the demands for participation and impairs the mechanisms for coping with or mollifying them.

Much of the militancy behind the demands has been stimulated by the historic failure of urban schools to submit to public scrutiny and to set up channels of communication between school and community. And much of the current impotence of urban schools in the face of these demands is a direct result of their long-term political isolation. One observer has commented:

> If the schools are separated from the rest of the community's political system, they may be more easily exposed to the protests or demands of groups which are disaffected from that system, unable to work their will within its often labyrinthine structures, but able to organize direct populace support. And if they attempt direct protest action, they can make life most difficult for schoolmen who are unable to retreat into positions of mutual support among city officials with many other programs and agencies and client groups. Unable to trade off one group against another, the schools may be and often are the targets of protest which may well have its roots in other facets of the city's life, but

are directed against the schools precisely because they are autonomous and vulnerable.[8]

Consequently, educators who were once fervently committed to
insulating public schools from municipal politics now find it not
only prudent but mandatory to participate in urban social action
programs with other governmental units and with private organizations. Moreover, because these programs deal with racial discrimination, poverty, unemployment, inadequate housing, a burdened
system of public welfare, and other maladies of urban life, urban
educators have been either stimulated or forced to develop new
strategies for achieving racial and socioeconomic integration, decen-
tralized decision-making, and metropolitan governing units.

Urban school systems have thus been literally backed into political collaboration by the force of events. One may hope that their
new political awareness will encourage them to relinquish their traditional stand against lay influence. They may yet be able to realize
the long-denied dreams of progressives like George Counts and
Harold Rugg, who envisioned schools as major instruments of social change. Political involvement in public education, however uncertain its outcome, can hardly be more costly than continued
efforts to maintain the artifice of political isolation and professional
autonomy.

The Character of Bureaucracy in Urban Schools

In his study of the organizational society, Robert Presthus describes a bureaucratic model that seems particularly relevant to urban school systems.[9] According to that model, a bureaucracy is characteristically so *large* that none of its members can interact face to
face with more than a relative few of all the others. Although big
organizations need not be bureaucratic, bureaucracies are large by
definition. Closely related to their size is their dependence on *specialization of labor*; that is, as the size of an organization increases,
so too do the complexity of its operations and the need for a greater
number and variety of specially qualified personnel. As any organi-

zation becomes more bureaucratic, the number of generalists in it decreases while the number of specialists increases. Theoretically, the increased specialization of the work to be done by any one member of the organization leads to greater organizational effectiveness and efficiency; but it also leads to tension between the specialists and generalists in the organization. Administrators in a bureaucracy not only are required to prove their legitimacy as generalists in an organization of specialists, but must also mediate between competing specialized units of the organization.

A third characteristic of a bureaucracy is its hierarchical structure. Typically, this structure is depicted as a triangle, with the highest positions in the organization at the apex and the lowest positions at the base. This hierarchy of positions determines the *status* accorded each member of the organization—that is, the allocation of prestige, authority, income, deference, rights, and privileges. As one moves down the hierarchy, the number of positions increases, the relative degree of status decreases.

The hierarchy of positions also governs the channeling of communication in a bureaucracy—that is, who talks to whom and about what. Because information is a prerequisite to participation in decision-making, and because the design of the hierarchy is triangular, the few individuals at the top have considerable power to manipulate and control both the issues that are raised for consideration and the information available to those who resolve them. Ultimate authority and control in a bureaucracy are thus held by a small number of its members. Presthus suggests that this tendency toward *oligarchy*—rule by the few—is almost inevitable to bureaucracy:

> When organizations become large, communication is difficult and the power of decision tends to be restricted to a few leaders. Some elites enhance their power by concealing information; but in any event the problems of disseminating information and providing for widespread participation present almost insuperable obstacles. The pressure of demands for quick decisions often makes consultation impracticable. The highly technical character

of many decisions tends furthermore to limit participation to those who have the requisite skills and knowledge—this despite the fact that the ramifications of the decision may extend throughout the organization. Thus the intensity of oligarchy probably increases in some sort of geometric ratio to organizational size.[10]

Related closely to the oligarchic tendency of bureaucratic organization is the function of *cooptation*, the process by which those in power designate their successors. By placing high value on seniority, loyalty, and cooperation, cooptation leads inevitably to a "sameness" in the behavior of organization members and thus to a kind of inbreeding.

Finally, a bureaucracy is characterized by *rationality* and *efficiency* and, at least in principle, by *freedom from conflict*. Rationality may be defined as the capacity for objective, intelligent action; it is sought in a bureaucracy by the imposition of rules and procedures that limit diffusion of the decision-making process, and provide for recruitment and assignment of personnel on an objective and systematic basis. In principle, rationality leads to increased efficiency in the allocation and use of available resources; and because each component of the bureaucracy has clearly defined functions to perform and its own unique role to play in the total organization, there is, in theory, minimal room for conflict among components.

In summary, the structural characteristics of Presthus' bureaucratic model include size, specialization, hierarchy, status, authority, oligarchy, cooptation, rationality, efficiency, and freedom from conflict. These characteristics produce a distinctive work environment. Expected behavior is clearly prescribed. Interpersonal relations and the flow of information are governed by refined distinctions of authority, status, and rank, thus reducing ambiguity or uncertainty about what is expected of each member. And the organization's posture toward its environment is deliberately designed to protect personnel from rather than involve them with hostile and competing forces.

Bureaucracies in Urban Education

The nation's big-city school systems exhibit to a considerable degree the organizational characteristics described in Presthus' bureaucratic model. The number of students they enroll, personnel they employ, and dollars they expend each year indicate clearly that as organizations urban school systems are undeniably large and complex. Their size and complexity preclude face-to-face interaction among more than limited segments of their total membership, and likewise inhibit the development of meaningful school–community relationships. Urban school personnel, particularly those at the school and neighborhood level, thus face constituents who frequently feel, and usually are, unable to influence decisions regarding the education of their children; and frustration leads many of these constituents to develop negative, or even openly hostile, attitudes toward the "system" and those who control it.

Specialization of labor is a second major organizational characteristic of urban school systems. In any school district, some employees teach young children, others teach adolescents; some teach reading, others teach science; still others serve as counselors, librarians, supervisors, or principals; some drive buses or care for buildings; some function within a single building, others have authority throughout a district; some make policy, others implement it; and so on. Because of its magnitude and complexity, an urban school system requires not only a high degree of specialization, but also a large number of individuals to fulfill each role.

Perhaps ironically, it should also be noted that despite the creation of specialized roles in urban schools in recent decades, those of teacher and building principal have changed little and are still rather roughly defined. As their responsibilities have grown and their tasks have become more and more complex, teachers and principals have increasingly experienced "role overload," the burdening of an individual with so many tasks that none can be performed well. Even in the most modern urban school facilities, the time and energy of most teachers and principals are taken up by an astounding variety of instructional and noninstructional tasks.

> While some distinctive roles have been created—guidance counselor, librarian, nurse, custodian, remedial reading teacher, supervisor—most schools boast a principal, two or three specialists, and twenty or thirty classroom teachers. The teachers prepare their classrooms, operate duplicating machines, telephone parents, conduct classes, write examinations, grade papers, select library books, supervise students, diagnose learning problems, counsel students, conduct assemblies, keep records, monitor cafeterias, and otherwise perform as if they had no help. The principal and his assistant (if he has one) schedule classes, oversee the budget, interview candidates, telephone parents, attend school and community meetings, supervise custodians and cafeteria workers, solve bus problems, and, if they find time, work with teachers to improve curricula and classroom instruction.[11]

Hierarchy is a third organizational characteristic of big-city school systems—with a school board at the apex of the triangle and students constituting its base. Between the two, in descending order of authority and status, are the district's administrative staff, its building principals, and its teachers. As in any bureaucracy, the hierarchy determines the status of each individual in the school district, and with it the degree of authority, earnings, and information received, privileges enjoyed, and deference and prestige accorded. The triangular structure of the hierarchy sets up an oligarchy among administrative school personnel: nearly all critical decisions are made at its highest levels, and by a relatively few individuals—the school board, the superintendent, and a half dozen administrative personnel in the central office. One important result is that local school personnel typically believe it is impossible to influence school policy except through the central office. The centralized control that typifies urban systems is a major source of complaint from those both within and outside those systems.

In urban school systems, cooptation is also evident. Standardization, attention to detail, maintenance of the status quo, and dedication to the system are rewarded; those who raise questions about the system, who evaluate its performance and work to bring about change are not. Promotion "through the ranks" to higher and higher positions in the organizational hierarchy—from teacher to counselor to vice-principal to building principal to central office administrator—thus usually favors school personnel who have not deviated along the way, and who have not questioned either the philosophy of the system or the adequacy of its current operations.

> Studies have shown that administrators favor teachers who maintain orderly classrooms, keep accurate records, and maintain stable relations with parents and the community. Other studies reveal that middle managers in the educational system, such as principals and supervisors, tend to be recruited from among teachers who demonstrate these orderly qualities. Because they are rewarded for maintaining the system, administrators are not likely either to challenge it or to reward subordinates who do.[12]

That urban school systems became bureaucratic as they developed is understandable and was, to a degree, even desirable. In part, as Callahan trenchantly notes, the new vocation of school administration that developed in the early 1900's over-identified itself with the new science of industrial management and its worship of efficiency and economy. But bureaucratic practices also grew out of the need, around the turn of the century, to protect public schools —particularly those in large cities—from the inroads of political patronage and pressure by special interest groups. To assure their separation from political influence, school systems created their own administrative structures, notably including impersonal rules on hiring, promotion, and tenure for professional personnel. These bureaucratic practices have benefited both the educational process and the operation of urban schools, since they have given teachers protection against formal reprisals for innovation or for challenging existing conditions. They also have protected administrators from the pressure to make decisions for solely political reasons; and they have given all school personnel an equal opportunity for advancing their careers.

In another sense, however, many of the bureaucratic reforms instituted in the first half of the century—even including some advocated by progressive reformers—now prevent urban school systems from responding effectively to changing needs and conditions both within their organizational boundaries and in the larger community. Most bureaucratic practices help to protect the system; they encourage organizational inbreeding, they tend to reduce differences among personnel in values and styles of action, they encourage buck-passing and thereby centralize authority. They reward passivity, conformity, caution, smoothness, and superficial affability rather than boldness, creativity, and innovation. They breed a stronger loyalty to the organization than to professional principles or to human needs, encouraging personnel to place extrinsic rewards above the intrinsic satisfactions of teaching.

Ultimately, as one critic has suggested, the bureaucratic model is inconsistent with the kind of organizational structure required for maximum learning and creative teaching:

> . . . in virtually every important respect, the behaviors and attitudes appropriate for bureaucracies are quite the opposite of those appropriate for education. Educational relationships are diffuse, the student is treated as a "whole" person, but the hallmark of bureaucratic interaction is its specificity; education best proceeds in personal settings, through "primary" contacts, but bureaucracies are formal and impersonal; educational behaviors are consummatory, motivation is "intrinsic," but bureaucratic activities are entirely instrumental; education is responsive to the needs of the student, instruction is "individualized," but bureaucracies are first and always agencies of control; and so on. For schools which seek to educate through personal and responsive methods, then, a bureaucratic organizational structure is highly inappropriate and, theoretically speaking, perhaps the worst imaginable.[13]

Resistance of Urban School Systems to Change

Chapter One contained excerpts from a report on the effort to introduce extensive resources from New York University into a ghetto school—an effort that a year later ended in failure. The National Teacher Corps, created ostensibly to prepare teachers for inner-city schools, has not produced a substantial effect on the operation of those schools. Even an apparently successful pilot project in New York, Higher Horizons, failed when it was expanded into the More Effective Schools Program. The list of projects that have produced "no significant results" is discouragingly long. As one observer has noted, "Most attempts to reform large urban school systems have seemed to end in failure. Whether reform is initiated inside the system, as are most programs of compensatory education, or outside, like the thousands of short-term institutes and workshops set up by universities, little or no large-scale system-wide change seems to occur. . . . Most school children in the inner-city are affected not at all; the large systems stand unmoved."[14] Another observer, after interviewing personnel from over one hundred schools in a number of major metropolitan areas of the country, also concluded: "It is dangerous to generalize about something as large, complex, and presumably diverse as schooling in the United States. . . . As far as our sample of schools is concerned, however, we are forced to conclude that much of the so-called educational reform movement has been blunted on the classroom door."[15]

A voluminous literature on organizational change has been produced in the past decade. In school systems throughout the country, funds for innovation have been provided by Title III of the Elementary and Secondary Education Act. It would be infeasible to examine here all the hundreds of projects that have been conducted in urban school programs. Among the noteworthy projects are model schools such as the John Dewey School in New York, the Parkway School in Philadelphia, and the John Adams School in Portland, Oregon. The history of these and similar innovative projects is still too recent to permit a judgment of their long-term worth. If past experience is any indicator, however, they will all gradually wither with the departure of their original leadership, and as other interests in the school district compete for funds. Even more to the point is the question of how much in these innovative programs can be successfully incorporated into the regular programs of school systems. The fate of such experiments has in general been quite discouraging.

The multiple factors in this resistance to change, which tend to reinforce the basic conservatism of most urban school systems, include the following: (1) the organizational structure of most urban school systems, (2) the nature of their personnel, (3) the lack of incentives, and (4) the lack of educational planning.

Ultimately, the most serious obstacle to change is the complexity of the problems to be solved. Often, the effort toward an innovative solution aggravates them and puts new stresses on the organization. Edward C. Banfield claims this dynamic in the War on Poverty; that many training, employment, and housing programs associated with it left their clients worse off than before.[16] The military efforts by the United States in South Vietnam during the past decade may be seen as a colossal instance of this dynamic.

Decadent Organizational Structures

It is estimated that over one hundred additional functions have been assumed by the nation's public education system within the past several decades. Yet most of its urban school systems were designed to meet the educational needs of an earlier era: that is to supply "uniform instruction in basic skills at a minimum level of quality and at a low per pupil cost to the mass of the population at a time when farming and simple factory work occupied most of the people." Even today, ". . . the graded school of the past, with its ten-month year, five-hour day, thirty-pupil classes, technologically primitive classrooms, undifferentiated staffing, and continuously talking teachers is still the American standard."[17]

In most urban schools, despite their size, the definition of who does what, when, and to whom is little different today from what it was sixty years ago. The predominant reason for this maintenance of the status quo is, of course, the bureaucratic design of urban

schools. Their hierarchies so inhibit lateral and vertical communication among personnel that decisions made at the top, except on
purely administrative matters, rarely affect operating practices to
any notable degree. In addition, centralized administrative controls
discourage independence, experimentation, and idiosyncrasies of
style and attitude; and building principals, who might most logically put innovation into effect, are frequently inhibited by a central office staff at the district level, which "gives the orders on
teacher assignment, controls the flow of substitutes, shapes the
curriculum, dispenses the budget, promulgates 'circulars' by the
hundreds, and demands reports in equal volume."[18] Rewards are
given not for performance but for seniority or for pursuing university courses that may be only remotely related to work in an urban
school. Finally, promotions within the hierarchy encourage uni-
formity. As a result, most urban schools, along with most other
public schools, are still geared to processing students through the
standardized format of an industrial assembly line.

Resistance Among Professional Educators

Educators have worked for decades to establish their professional
status and to achieve appropriate social recognition and pay; in the
process, they have blocked interference in their domain by nonpro-
fessionals. Thus, schools of education operate to indoctrinate potential members; accreditation agencies, professional organizations,
and teachers' unions monitor curriculum development, hiring practices, and working conditions; certification laws control entry into
the profession. Education, as Michael Katz notes, "acquired a core
of career professionals—high school principals and administrators—
that would expand in size until it controlled all aspects of local
school affairs. . . . Soon teachers would have a machine so large
that they would be able to talk only to each other."[19] And "professional organizations" of educators have now developed a political
arm strong enough to thwart any move to diminish their newly acquired status and power.

The organizational behavior of most urban school personnel,

particularly administrators and supervisors, is typically self-protec-
tive. The culture of urban schools seems to forbid the admission of
error or failure. An urban school administrator rarely questions his
own competence, and regards those who criticize either him or the
system as misguided enemies of public schools. The previously
mentioned study of building principals reported "an angry defense
of the virtues of the school system, of the difficulties of dealing
with ghetto children, and the absurdity of letting 'unqualified,'
politically motivated insurgents take over the schools from those
who have had a lifetime of service, experience, and commitment in
public education."[20]

Martin Mayer, who served for five years as chairman of a subdistrict school board in New York City, has described the self-
protective behavior of most urban school administrators as a kind
of deafness:

> When a working mother suggests that it might be a good idea
> to open a school at 8 rather than 8:30 so women like herself
> could leave their children in a supervised place before going to
> work, the answer is that there's no budget for that. When moth-
> ers whose children ride a disorderly bus to and from school volun-
> teer to take turns keeping peace on the vehicle, the answer is
> that the system's insurance policy covers only children supervised
> by licensed personnel. These are supposed to be real answers, but
> what they mean, obviously, is that nobody's listening.
>
> Parents don't realize that teachers get the same sort of answers.
> At one of our meetings, a junior high teacher came forward to
> complain that she had spent the summer working at a university
> on the problems of teaching illiterate 13-year-olds to read. Now
> she had a class of illiterate 13-year-olds, and her principal
> wouldn't let her give her children the books she had learned to
> use; he said they weren't on the Board of Education's "approved
> list" of materials that could be bought for the classrooms. The
> teacher, who had been conditioned to obeying silly rules, was pre-
> pared to accept this answer, but she was puzzled about why the
> books hadn't been approved. When she checked up, she found
> that they really were on the approved list, but they were new

and her principal had an old list. Then the principal told her all the money was spent, so she still couldn't have the books that she was sure would help her desperate class.[21]

Lack of Incentives for Change

A third obstacle to innovation in urban schools is simply the lack of effective incentives for change. One reason for this is that the power of the bureaucracy to use its reward system to control behavior and maintain the status quo is considerable, as this observation suggests:

> So long as members of the school staff know that the principal source of approval and promotion is at the central headquarters, it is to that "community" that they will look for appraisal and recognition. As the typical city system now operates, there is little incentive for a principal or a teacher to be deeply concerned about what his local community expects of him. So far as his professional progress is concerned, that community possesses neither carrot nor stick. The lines of authority, stimulation, and reward now center at a single point. Until that situation is altered and the local community is given a larger voice in setting expectations for the professional staff and rewarding their attainment, most other schemes for placing the control of schools in the hands of local citizens will remain exercises in futility and largely an illusion.[22]

A second condition that reduces the incentives to change is that salaries paid to school personnel are often unrelated to the quality of their work. It is not student performance but seniority in the district and/or course work at a university, that governs increases. And those with tenure are virtually assured of their jobs for as long as they want them, regardless of the harm or good they do in the classroom.

Third, urban school personnel are without meaningful models or systematic training that would encourage innovation. Proposals for change are typically co-opted out of existence; in-service training is sporadic, usually consisting of one- and two-day workshops; and efforts at organizational reform are generally superficial.

Finally, any change at all is somewhat threatening to everyone concerned because of the uncertainty it brings. Human beings have a strong inclination to avoid uncertainty. Only when continuation of things as they are becomes more painful than rewarding are human beings likely to change their ways. For most urban schoolmen, this shift in the balance does not yet seem to have occurred.

Poverty of Educational Planning

Most urban school systems have failed to develop processes for managing information or planning for change. It is typical of school districts generally to carry out their activities in relative isolation. Rarely, for example, does a district testing program address itself to specific classroom objectives as teachers themselves define them; rarely does the budgeting process take account of the data collected by the testing program; and rarely is there close coordination of district-wide goals, curriculum guides, and individual lesson plans. Neither the separate activities within a typical public school district nor those affecting the district as a whole are systematically carried out. In urban school districts, this lack of systematic planning is especially unfortunate.

Underlying the poverty of educational planning in urban schools is, first of all, the lack of any real system for managing the information that is generated in such massive quantities. Computers are typically used as nothing more than sophisticated accounting machines—for scoring tests, recording attendance, preparing payrolls, and printing report cards—rather than as aids for data-analysis, planning, and decision-making. Second, planning itself is still primitive in most urban school systems. Usually it

> . . . is limited to simple linear extrapolation and the use of formulas to compute needs: 100 more students equals three new teachers; next year's budget equals this year's budget plus 8 per cent for salary raises and other rising costs; five school buses become seven years old and thus need to be replaced; the maintenance schedule calls for the auditorium to be painted every ten

years, and so on. Alternative arrangements are rarely generated, priced, and rated in terms of their probable effect.

Few schools have planning processes for coping with serious shifts in the social setting: erosion of the tax base, the arrival of bilingual students, rising teacher militancy, or the sale of drugs on campus. Plans for handling emergencies—violence, for example—are outdated or nonexistent.[23]

Third, the complexity and rigidity of budget-making discourage the financing of innovation, given the diversity of special interest groups to which an urban school district must listen and respond, and the pressure to minimize costs that is integral to the process of preparing annual budgets in any public school district. In addition, a number of the simplifications that have been developed over the years to facilitate the preparation of urban school budgets have had the undesirable effect of rigidifying the entire process of allocating resources. As budgetary decision-making has been increasingly centralized, the opportunities for building principals to make instructional and administrative changes at their own level have been reduced. Formulas for allocating various items in the budget among schools have standardized the process still further. For example, teachers are usually allotted on the basis of expected student enrollment, custodians on the basis of square footage, and supplies on the basis of expected average daily attendance. Because it is generally difficult to adjust these formulas from one year to the next, it is likewise difficult to develop alternative expenditure allotments to support desirable instructional and administrative changes.

An enormous amount of energy is expended in urban school systems simply to maintain the status quo. This resistance to change is exacerbated by decadent organizational structures, self-protectiveness among professional employees, a lack of incentives for innovation, and inadequate procedures for planning and decision-making. One other factor inhibiting change in urban schools, the severe financial squeeze that increasingly plagues all large central city school systems, will be treated in Chapter 7.

7 The Financial Condition of Urban Schools

In 1968 the public schools of Youngstown, Ohio, closed their doors for six weeks because the district had simply run out of money. Throughout the spring and summer of 1969, the threat either to close or to impose cutbacks in current programs hung over such large central city school districts as Philadelphia, Milwaukee, and Los Angeles.

A year later, the financial condition of many other large urban systems had become even more desperate. In Chicago, a strike-averting settlement was finally reached in January, 1970, between the Chicago Teachers Union and the city's Board of Education; but that single settlement added $26 million to operating costs in the district, and Superintendent of Schools James F. Redmond predicted deep cuts in school programs if the Illinois state legislature did not provide more financial aid. Prospects for obtaining that aid, however, were not very good: in the past, representatives of rural areas who dominated the Illinois state legislature had shown little sympathy with big-city problems: for example, in the previous year neither the governor of the state nor the mayor of

Chicago had been able to produce the $10 million necessary to balance the district's operating budget.

America's public schools are unlikely ever to obtain sufficient financial support to do all that is expected of them, particularly in central city school systems. In fact, the limits of municipal resources for financing city school systems may soon be reached. As their workload and areas of responsibility have expanded, they have increasingly been forced to defer expenditures, to limit development of the curriculum, and to reduce staff, transportation services, athletic programs, and summer activities. According to one group of school finance experts, "The city school system is thus caught in the double bind of facing dramatically increasing demands for services, indeed of having thrust upon it tasks that strain the capabilities of its present structures, at a time when its resources are steadily dwindling, with no turning point yet in sight."[1]

Three variables commonly used to assess the financial state of public school districts are (1) *expenditure per pupil*; (2) *community wealth*, as measured by family income and assessed valuation of property; and (3) *tax rates* for educational and other services. The expenditure per pupil is generally considered the best single indicator of the quality of education within a school district. The wealth within the district is an index of its ability to provide for educational needs, and the tax rate provides an estimate of local effort or community willingness to support existing school programs. These three variables are interdependent; taken together, they are useful in assessing the financial condition of a public school system and thus the quality of education it provides.

Two important qualifications should be kept in mind regarding the financial data presented here. First, comparisons between school districts in large central cities and those in suburban areas are based on a loose assumption that both areas are sufficiently homogeneous to permit valid generalization. In fact, differences *within* groups are often as great as those *between* groups, if not greater. This is particularly true of suburban school districts, where wealth, state aid, noneducation expenditures, and so forth are typically as great within a group of suburban districts as between that group and one or more central city districts. Given our broad focus on urban education, we have chosen to ignore within-group differences and to emphasize instead the fiscal inequities between urban school systems and suburban districts taken as a whole.[2]

Second, most of the financial data given in this chapter are approximate rather than exact. Comparable fiscal data for public school districts are never easy to obtain; for an entire metropolitan area the task is even more difficult, since budgetary categories and procedures for computing school taxes vary from state to state, from city to city, and from district to district. Boundaries for municipal districts are rarely contiguous with those for school districts. And the older the data, whether from the same or different sources, the more difficult it is to achieve comparability among them, for practices vary considerably *across* districts at any particular time and *within* districts over a period of years. Consequently, inferences from the comparisons presented in this chapter should be drawn with caution.

Urban Expenditures: Mammoth and Becoming More So

In 1970 nearly twelve billion dollars, over one-quarter of the total cost of operating public elementary and secondary schools in the United States, were spent to operate schools in 250 central cities of the nation's Standard Metropolitan Statistical Areas. Nearly half this total was spent in the nation's fifteen largest urban school systems; over a sixth went to operate the New York City public schools alone.

Public education in the nation's largest cities is clearly big business, and each year the business is becoming bigger. Table 7–1 indicates the degree to which *total* expenditures for public education increased in fifteen cities between 1960 and 1970. The largest increase during the decade was in Detroit, where total expenditures rose by 281 per cent. (It may be remembered from Chapter Five that teachers in the Detroit public schools are now among the best paid in the country.) In thirteen of the fifteen districts, total expenditures at least doubled during the decade; in the fifteen as a whole, total expenditures were nearly one and a half times greater.

A comparison of increases during the first and second halves of the decade shows that total expenditures in central city schools have been increasing at an accelerated rate. During the first half of the decade, total expenditures for all fifteen cities listed in Table 7-1 increased by 28 per cent; during the second half of the decade, the increase was over 50 per cent. A similar pattern characterizes each of the fifteen individual districts: total expenditures increased

TABLE 7-1   Increase Between 1960 and 1970 in Estimated Total Expenditures by Fifteen Selected Large Central City School Districts

SCHOOL DISTRICT	ESTIMATED TOTAL EXPENDITURES (IN MILLIONS)				PERCENTAGE INCREASE BETWEEN 1960 AND 1970
	1960–61	1965–66	1967–68	1969–70	
Washington, D.C.	$51.5	$87.3	$119.6	$195.9	281
Philadelphia	113.7	136.3	295.0	383.1	237
Cleveland	54.1	72.6	97.3	151.9	181
Houston	54.7	75.2	157.0	151.0	176
Dallas	40.7	54.5	89.8	110.7	172
Baltimore	69.2	87.1	144.0	187.4	171
New Orleans	29.9	38.8	77.5	81.0	171
Boston	31.5	49.3	60.2	84.0	167
Milwaukee	45.8	54.0	89.6	122.0	166
New York	611.6	820.0	1,212.0	1,595.0	161
Los Angeles	274.3	327.1	481.0	626.3	128
St. Louis	39.7	51.9	68.0	89.2	125
San Francisco	56.6	57.8	79.7	123.0	117
Chicago	272.5	259.3	371.0	538.5	98
Detroit	144.9	147.0	167.3	205.5	42
Total	$1,890.7	$2,318.2	$3,509.0	$4,644.5	145
U.S. Total	$16,800.0	$26,200.0	$31,900.0	$39,500.0	135

SOURCE: National Education Association, *Selected Statistics of Local School Systems, 1960–61* and *1965–66; Financial Status of the Public Schools: 1970;* U.S. Department of Health, Education, and Welfare, Office of Education, *Fall 1967* and *Fall 1969 Statistics of Public Schools.*

TABLE 7-2 Increase Between 1960 and 1970 in Estimated Current Expenditures per Pupil in Fifteen Selected Large Central City School Districts

SCHOOL DISTRICT	ESTIMATED CURRENT EXPENDITURE PER PUPIL[1]				PERCENTAGE INCREASE IN EXPENDITURES PER PUPIL BETWEEN 1960 AND 1970
	1960–61	1965–66	1967–68	1969–70	
Philadelphia	$447	$576	$789	$1144	156
San Francisco	451	634	726	1106	145
New York	535	898	1042	1300	143
Milwaukee	400	470	613	940	135
Cleveland	377	510	558	880	133
Washington, D.C.	435	674	693	1013	133
St. Louis	421	555	623	936	122
Chicago	453	523	618	972	115
Baltimore	409	518	669	862	111
New Orleans	333	424	684	676	103
Dallas	282	410	502	570	102
Boston	400	596	719	768	92
Houston	287	359	450	535	86
Los Angeles	453	546	631	775	71
Detroit	451	556	571	722	60
Average	$409	$550	$593	$888	117
U.S. Average	$393	$537	$634	$766	95

SOURCE: National Education Association, *Selected Statistics of Local School Systems,* 1960–61 and 1965–66; U.S. Department of Health, Education, and Welfare, Office of Education, *Digest of Educational Statistics: 1968* and *Fall 1969 Statistics of Public Schools.*

[1] Current expenditures per pupil presented in this table are based on "average daily attendance."

nearly twice as fast during the second half of the decade as during the previous five years.

These increases reflect the growth in student enrollment experienced by nearly all big-city school systems during the decade of the 1960's as a result of the postwar "baby boom" and as the influx of rural Americans to the nation's major metropolitan areas began to peak. They also reflect the substantial increases in salaries which most urban systems have been forced to grant to increasingly militant employees, the inflationary trend of the economy, and the increased costs of those instructional innovations that have been attempted, such as television, individualized instruction, team teaching, computer-assisted instruction, differentiated staffing, and compensatory education programs.

Expenditures *per pupil*, as the data in Table 7–2 indicate, also rose significantly between 1960 and 1970, though not quite so rapidly as *total* expenditures. In the nation's fifteen largest urban school systems, total expenditures increased by 145 per cent between 1960 and 1970, whereas the average expenditure per pupil rose by only 117 per cent. Nonetheless, the *rate* of increase in expenditure per pupil in central city school systems once again was nearly twice as great during the second half of the decade as during the first half.

Urban Expenditures Compared with National, State, and Suburban Levels

When *expenditures per pupil* in major central city school systems are compared with those in the nation as a whole, in their respective states, and in their respective suburbs it becomes clear that the nation's urban school systems in the early 1970's expended more dollars per student than most other public school systems in the United States, and considerably more than they had a decade before. Despite glaring inadequacies in such cities as Chicago and Los Angeles, expenditures for public education actually appear to be increasing more rapidly in the nation's largest central city school systems than anywhere else.

City Schools Within the Nation

Table 7–3 presents comparative data on expenditures per pupil between 1960 and 1970 in the nation as a whole and in the nation's fifteen largest urban school systems. Estimated current expenditures per pupil are shown as a percentage of the national average, thus permitting relatively easy comparisons. The degree to which the expenditure per pupil exceeded the national average in Phil-

TABLE 7-3 Estimated Current Expenditures Per Pupil Between 1960 and 1970 in Fifteen Selected Large Central City School Districts Expressed as a Percentage of the National Average

SCHOOL DISTRICT	ESTIMATED CURRENT EXPENDITURE PER PUPIL[1] EXPRESSED AS A PERCENTAGE OF THE NATIONAL AVERAGE				CHANGE IN PERCENTAGE BETWEEN 1960 AND 1970
	1960–61	1965–66	1967–68	1969–70	
Philadelphia	114	107	124	150	+36
New York	136	167	164	170	+34
San Francisco	115	118	115	144	+29
Milwaukee	102	88	97	123	+21
Washington, D.C.	111	125	109	132	+21
Cleveland	96	95	88	115	+19
St. Louis	107	103	98	122	+15
Chicago	115	97	97	127	+12
Baltimore	104	96	106	113	+8
New Orleans	85	79	108	88	+3
Dallas	72	76	79	74	+2
Boston	102	111	113	101	−1
Houston	73	67	71	70	−3
Los Angeles	115	102	99	101	−14
Detroit	115	103	90	94	−21
Average for these fifteen systems	104	102	94	116	+12

SOURCE: National Education Association, *Selected Statistics of Local School Systems*, 1960–61 and 1965–66; U.S. Department of Health, Education, and Welfare, Office of Education, *Digest of Educational Statistics: 1968* and *Fall 1969 Statistics of Public Schools*.

[1] Current expenditures per pupil presented in this table are based upon "average daily attendance."

adelphia, for example, rose from 14 per cent in 1960 to over 50 per cent by 1970. Eleven of the fifteen districts similarly registered an increase in the percentage of the national average; and the ratio of the average expenditure per pupil for all fifteen districts to the national average increased by 12 per cent during the decade.

Table 7-4 places these data in a larger historical context. When expenditures per pupil by local school districts are shown as a per-

TABLE 7-4   Historical Review Between 1921 and 1970 of Estimated Current Expenditures Per Pupil in the United States and in Four Selected Large Central City School Districts, Expressed as a Percentage of the National Average

YEAR	AVERAGE ESTIMATED CURRENT EXPENDITURE PER PUPIL[1] IN THE UNITED STATES	EXPRESSED AS A PERCENTAGE OF THE NATIONAL AVERAGE, THE ESTIMATED CURRENT EXPENDITURE PER PUPIL IN			
		Boston	Chicago	San Francisco	New York
1921–22	$ 67	155	133	141	154
1929–30	87	155	139	149	163
1941–42	98	153	145	180	185
1949–50	209	135	130	144	145
1951–52	244	141	123	145	144
1953–54	265	125	115	172[2]	141
1957–58	341	114	113	123	137
1959–60	371	108	111	121	138
1961–62	419	105	109	114	145
1965–66	537	111	97	118	167
1967–68	634	113	97	115	164
1969–70	766	101	127	144	170
Change in Percentage Between 1921 and 1970		−54	−6	+3	+16

SOURCE: Based on data compiled by Seymour Sacks and on data presented in U.S. Department of Health, Education, and Welfare, Office of Education, *Digest of Educational Statistics: 1968* and *Fall 1969 Statistics of Public Schools.*

[1] Current expenditures per pupil presented in this table are based upon "average daily attendance."

[2] Includes junior colleges.

centage of the average for all school districts in the country, several clear trends during the past fifty years become evident. It will be noted that in 1921–22, for instance, expenditures per pupil in Boston, Chicago, San Francisco, and New York ranged from 33 to 55 per cent higher than the national average. During the next fifty years, as the nation's average expenditure per pupil increased steadily, the relative fiscal position of these four large urban districts just as steadily declined. Only in the last few years has there been a reversal of the downward trend. By 1970, school systems in three of the four cities listed in Table 7–4—Chicago, San Francisco, and New York—were again receiving substantially higher fiscal support than those in the nation as a whole.

City Schools Within Their Respective States

As Table 7–5 indicates, the nation's urban school systems have also begun to regain fiscal preeminence within their respective

TABLE 7-5   Historical Review Between 1929 and 1970 of Estimated Current Expenditures Per Pupil in Fourteen Central City School Districts, Expressed as a Percentage of Their Respective State Averages

SCHOOL DISTRICT	ESTIMATED CURRENT EXPENDITURES PER PUPIL[1] EXPRESSED AS A PERCENTAGE OF THEIR RESPECTIVE STATE AVERAGES				CHANGE IN PERCENTAGE BETWEEN 1960 AND 1970
	1929–30	1960–61	1965–66	1969–70	
Cleveland	133	90	98	129	+39
Chicago	122	93	85	121	+28
Philadelphia	133	106	99	131	+25
New Orleans	NA	86	72	109	+23
San Francisco	NA	98	108	120	+22
New York	109	91	103	105	+14
Dallas	NA	85	86	98	+13
Milwaukee	134	94	90	107	+13
St. Louis	183	119	108	131	+12
Boston	127	92	103	102	+10
Houston	157	87	78	92	+5
Baltimore	116	97	94	98	+1
Los Angeles	111	99	93	84	−15
Detroit	95	106	100	86	−20

SOURCE: U.S. Department of Interior, *Statistics of City School Systems: 1929–30* and *Statistics of State School Systems: 1931–32*; National Education Association, *Estimates of School Statistics: 1961–62* and *Selected Statistics of Local School Districts: 1960–61*; U.S. Department of Health, Education and Welfare, Office of Education, *Fall 1966* and *Fall 1969 Statistics of Public Schools.*

[1] Current expenditures per pupil presented in this table are based on "average daily attendance."

states. In 1929–30, all but one of the districts for which data were available spent more per pupil than the average school district within their respective states. By 1960–61, however, this fiscal superiority had all but disappeared; expenditures per pupil were lower than state averages in eleven of the fourteen cities listed. The thirty-year downward trend finally began to shift during the 1960's, and by the end of the decade, expenditures per pupil surpassed state averages in nine of the fourteen cities listed. In Philadelphia, St. Louis, and Cleveland, central city expenditures per pupil exceeded their respective state expenditures by more than $200. Only in Los Angeles and Detroit did expenditures per pupil still appear to be falling significantly behind their respective state averages.

City Schools Within Their Respective Metropolitan Areas

Although the financial position of urban schools within the nation as a whole and within their respective states has improved since 1960, a comparison of expenditures in urban school systems with those in their respective suburban districts gives a somewhat less encouraging picture. In a sample of thirty-six major metropolitan areas in 1957, *total* expenditures per pupil in the central city school districts of those metropolitan areas averaged $366, as compared with $419 for all districts in the suburbs surrounding those central cities.[3] In fact, however, the higher expenditures outside central cities during the 1950's were due almost entirely to massive school building programs in new and growing suburbs. Factoring out such capital expenditures and examining only *current* expenditures per pupil in the two geographic groupings of districts actually reverses the discrepancy: in central city school systems in 1957, *current* expenditures per pupil were $312, as compared with only $303 in the surrounding suburban systems.

By 1962, however, *current* expenditures per pupil in suburban districts had forged ahead. Although enrollments were growing twice as fast in the suburbs as in the central cities, thus imposing severe financial burdens, this development also provided the incentive for increased public support for suburban schools, and tended perhaps to deflect attention from the needs of urban education. In those thirty-six central city school districts previously mentioned, *current* expenditures per pupil between 1957 and 1962 increased by only 21 per cent, from $312 to $376. During the same five years, however, comparable current expenditures in the suburbs surrounding those cities increased by over 44 per cent, from $303 per child to $438 per child. Three years later, the gap had widened even further: by 1964–65, central city districts were spending $449 per child, only slightly more than the expenditure by suburban districts three years earlier, whereas suburban districts were now spending over $573.

As might be expected, the disparities between urban and suburban districts in *per capita* support for education were generally comparable to those in expenditure *per pupil*. By 1957, for example, in a sample of thirty-six SMSA's, approximately $69 per capita was being spent in central cities for public education, as compared with more than $126 for the suburbs. Only in the middle of the 1960's did the gap between the two begin to close: by 1965, central cities were spending $82 per resident for public education, whereas suburban expenditures had declined to $113 per resident. During the second half of the 1960's, the massive injection of both federal and state money for compensatory education programs, particularly that allocated under Title I of the Elementary and Secondary Education Act, tended to favor urban over suburban school districts. As a result, by the late 1960's the yearly expenditures per pupil in the slums and in the rich suburbs of any one of twenty large central cities in the United States were nearly equal; sometimes, in fact, they were even favorable to the poor.[4]

A decision handed down in mid-1971 by the California Supreme Court may lead eventually to parity in per pupil expenditures, not only between urban and suburban school districts, but perhaps among all school districts in the country. During the latter half of the 1960's, plaintiffs in class action suits filed in several states—including Illinois, Texas, Michigan, and Virginia—argued that the heavy dependence of public school districts on the property tax (the source of approximately 50 per cent of revenue for the average school district) and the great variations in property wealth among districts inevitably lead to severe disparities in the total revenue available to districts, and thus to unequal educational expenditures per pupil. In all these cases, the courts had acknowledged the inequalities of wealth among local school districts, but had ruled that neither these inequalities nor their supposed educational results were unconstitutional, since the U.S. Constitution does not require that school expenditures be based on pupil needs or that they be equal.

In the California case, the parents of a group of Los Angeles County school children filed a class action against state and county officials. In 1971, the state's Supreme Court declared that the entire public school financing system of the state of California was unconstitutional because its dependence on the local property tax resulted in discrimination against the poor. The court ruled that the financing system then in effect denied equal protection of the law to residents of poorer and of less industrialized areas. Although taxed at a higher rate to cover school costs than persons in wealthier and more highly industrialized areas, these residents of poorer areas were unable to provide the same degree of dollar support for each child in their public schools. Justice Raymond L. Sullivan, who wrote the opinion, argued that basing school financing on each individual district's taxable resources

> . . . invidiously discriminates against the poor because it makes the quality of a child's education a function of the wealth of his parents and neighbors. Recognizing as we must that the right to an education in our public schools is a fundamental interest which cannot be conditioned on wealth, we can discern no compelling state purpose necessitating the present method of financing. We have concluded, therefore, that such a system cannot withstand constitutional challenge and must fall before the equal protection clause.
>
> . . . the richer district is favored when it can provide the same educational quality for its children with less tax effort. Furthermore, as a statistical matter, the poor districts are financially unable to raise their taxes high enough to match the educational of-

ferings of wealthier districts. Thus, affluent districts can have their cake and eat it too: they can provide a high quality education for their children while paying lower taxes. Poor districts, by contrast, have no cake at all.

By our holding today, we further the cherished idea of American education that in a democratic society free public schools shall make available to all children equally the abundant gifts of learning.[5]

Whether other state courts will concur, and whether the U.S. Supreme Court will uphold the decision, when and if it is appealed, remains to be seen. But should the California opinion prevail, the consequences would be monumental. Local property taxes might no longer be the primary source of revenue for public school districts. Expenditures per pupil, at least within states, might have to be equalized, leaving each state with the task of finding alternative means both of financing public education and of equalizing per pupil revenues. For instance, state income taxes might have to be increased or statewide property taxes imposed; and, as one school finance expert asserts, states might have either "to assume the full cost of public schooling from local districts" or "to make up the entire difference between what a district itself can raise, from a property tax based on equal rates and equal assessment throughout the state, and the total district costs, based on an identical cost-per-child amount throughout the state."[6]

Ultimately, if the California decision is carried to its logical outcome, equal protection of the law will not be fully achieved until the educational dollars available for each child are equal, not only within each state, but throughout the nation. If this should occur, current disparities in expenditures between central city and suburban school districts would of course be greatly minimized, if not completely removed.

Factors Behind the Financial Crunch in Urban Education

Given the comparative data already presented, the financial future of urban school districts might seem not nearly so bleak as many have suggested. Such data, however, can be distracting. Simply to achieve financial equity among public school districts is not a sufficient goal for public education, if the massive problems that now beset the nation's urban schools—curricular, instructional, organizational, and administrative—are to be dealt with effectively. The problems plaguing urban education are so much more complex than those typically faced by rural and suburban school districts that it would be a delusion to suppose that urban school problems could be met without a massive infusion of new money over an extended period of time. The burdens imposed by socioeconomic conditions in the cities will never be reduced if city schools in which a majority of those enrolled are found to be educationally disadvantaged receive no more financial support than the rest.

Of the reasons behind the financial crunch faced by urban education, some can be traced to the convenient view of many citizens and their legislators that equality of educational opportunity means simply guaranteeing equality of input, regardless of special needs, varied socioeconomic backgrounds, or inequalities in the outcome. Most of these reasons, however, can be traced to a special set of urban conditions that make it costly to operate public schools and difficult to raise adequate funds for the purpose. The remainder of this chapter will survey some of those conditions.

Greater Costs of Education in Central Cities

The costs of operating public schools are considerably greater in central cities than in either rural or suburban areas for several reasons: the costs of constructing and maintaining buildings are higher; personnel costs are exceeded only in the wealthiest suburbs; there is a greater need for costly special educational programs; and the concentration of publicly financed housing in central cities substantially reduces the revenue available to public school districts.

The Costs of School Construction and Maintenance. At a meeting in the mid-1960's, urban schoolmen offered the following comments on existing school plants:

—Our story is the same as in many other cities: heavy growth in concentrated periods and only enough money to meet the demands of new population growth, but never enough money to replace or modernize obsolescent school buildings.

—Fifty-nine buildings, or 29 per cent of our total school plants, were constructed prior to the turn of the century, and 85 buildings or approximately 41 per cent were constructed prior to World War I.

—Since most of the buildings requiring modernization and/or improvements are within the so-called inner core or central city, a section which no longer has community ties and traditions because of population change and mobility, we are faced with a very real problem in human psychology.

—The school plant has suffered because of inadequate funds. Extraordinary repairs have had to be curtailed, and many major educational projects have been postponed year after year because of lack of funds.

—It is evident that until greater resources are available for capital expenditures and/or the need for providing for new construction to meet pupil enrollment demands diminishes, we must necessarily conduct a restricted program for systematically modernizing school facilities.[7]

Less than one-fifth of the nation's urban school teachers work in buildings less than ten years old, and nearly two-fifths of them work in buildings more than forty years old.[8] A survey conducted in the nation's fifteen largest city school systems indicates that nearly 13 per cent of all school buildings in those systems were constructed prior to 1900, and more than 36 per cent prior to 1920. Thus, "more than 1,500 separate buildings still in use . . . were constructed before the advent of commercial air travel, television, and sound motion pictures—many of them before the invention of the electric light bulb or the automobile."[9]

Urban school construction reached a peak in the early 1920's, lagged during the Great Depression, and was virtually paralyzed during World War II. During the postwar period, as the nation's suburban population mushroomed, central cities were allowed to deteriorate. A dreary example is provided by the Boston City Schools. In 1962, over 40 per cent of all public school youngsters in Boston were housed in buildings over fifty years old, and nearly a third of this number were housed in buildings more than seventy years old. The city's last large-scale building program had ended in 1931; during the next three decades, Boston was able to construct only thirteen new schools, all after 1952. Of the sixty-three deteriorating buildings recommended for abandonment by 1960, only half had actually been closed by that date; the rest were still being used in the mid-1960's, including the historic Quincy Street School, originally constructed in 1847.[10]

For an urban school district, this lack of modern and adequate facilities seriously inhibits the design of educational programs suited to the needs of the 1970's. Egg-crate buildings inevitably isolate a teacher and his classes, obstruct the movement of students, and call for extensive regulations for maintaining order in the building. They practically forbid arrangements of space, time, and instructional facilities that will give students freedom to pursue individualized programs of study. Lacking such facilities as libraries, cafeterias, multipurpose rooms with folding partitions, gymnasiums and locker rooms, playing fields, and auditoriums, most urban schools are physically limited in their capacity to innovate instructional programs or to accommodate community groups during non-school hours.

The lack of modern and adequate facilities also increases markedly the costs of operating and maintaining a public school building. In buildings constructed half a century ago, heating units are obsolete and costly; plumbing is old and in need of replacement; decades of dust and grime and the coming and going of thousands through their corridors have left the woodwork marred and the floors buckled. Each year, vast sums of money must be spent literally to hold such buildings together for another cycle of forty school weeks.

If the costs of operating and maintaining urban school buildings are high, the costs of replacing them are enormous. Because the size of central city sites is necessarily limited, urban schools must be multistoried; this increases drastically the costs of construction, especially as compared with those in suburbs, where the availability of land allows for rambling, single-story structures. But construction costs are only part of the problem. The costs of urban sites themselves are astounding. During a five-year period in the 1960's, for instance, the average cost of a school site in the nation's twenty-one largest urban school systems was $68,156 per acre, as compared with only $3,074 per acre in a sampling of noncity school districts in the respective states of those urban systems. In New York City, the average cost per acre was $197,841; in Chicago it was $136,927; in Buffalo, $125,741; and in St. Louis, $112,081.[11] As one observer has commented, "In some instances, it costs as much to purchase a site in the central core of a large city as it does in most other districts to construct the entire school building."[12] As a result, more than half of all school sites in the nation's largest cities consist of less than two acres, severely limiting the range of indoor and outdoor facilities to innovate programs or simply to allow youngsters to move about.

The Costs of Personnel. A second major cost of education in central cities is for salaries. Militant teachers, especially members of the American Federation of Teachers, have been most successful in the central cities. Given the skyrocketing costs of living in the nation's major metropolitan areas and especially in central cities during the past decade, the continuous demand for higher teacher salaries is not surprising. In eighteen metropolitan areas, the cost of maintaining a "moderate" standard of living for a family of four, including a husband aged 35–54, a wife not employed outside the home, and two young children, averaged about $4,200 in 1951; by 1959 it had increased to $6,100, and by 1966 to over $9,000; today it exceeds $10,000 in nearly every major metropolitan area in the

United States. Yet in only one of the nation's twenty-five largest urban school systems did the average teacher's salary in 1968–69 equal the current "moderate" cost of living for a family of four in that city; moreover, the ratio of average salary to that cost of living was less than 90 per cent in a vast majority of the nation's largest central cities. It is hardly any wonder that teachers have become so militant.

Whatever benefits have been achieved by their militance have markedly tightened the crunch on urban school budgets. In an average school district, teacher salaries represent between 70 and 80 per cent of operating costs and nearly 90 per cent of "instructional" costs. Consequently, as salaries have increased, so too, proportionately, have total school budgets. During the 1960's, negotiated settlements rapidly pushed minimum and maximum salaries upward and reduced substantially the time required for teachers to move from the bottom to the top of a salary schedule. Because any urban school system is an integral part of a larger complex of metropolitan area school districts, moreover, the achievement of higher salaries and better working conditions in any one district almost inevitably stimulates increased teacher militance in surrounding districts. The resulting competition to obtain the best settlement in a metropolitan area simply provokes continuing cycles of teacher militance, negotiation, and budget increases.

The Costs of Special Programs. Large central city school districts must maintain a wide variety of special programs—for the physically, mentally, and emotionally handicapped; for the unemployed and underemployed; for those unfamiliar with the English language; for the socially and economically deprived; and, to an increasing degree, for preschool children; as well as for adults who wish to continue their education.

Each of these special programs places extra financial burdens on a school system, because it must be operated in addition to the district's regular instructional programs and often requires more expensive personnel and equipment. For instance, in a sample of twenty-six high schools located throughout the country, investigators discovered that expenditures per pupil were typically 27 per cent higher in vocational high schools than in regular, academic high schools.[13] Nearly every other special program mounted in the nation's public schools is similarly expensive. To a considerable extent, federal and state aid to support these special programs is available; but these additional monies, usually regarded as "start-up" funds, rarely cover either the indirect or continuing costs of the special programs, costs that inevitably must be borne locally.

It is in central cities that the density and variety of population intensify the demands for special services. Students in most suburban schools come from middle-class homes, are upwardly mobile, and tend to follow the less expensive college preparatory programs of study, whereas those in urban schools are more likely to enroll in vocational and technical programs. During one school year, for example, the public school system in Buffalo, New York, ". . . enrolled 22 per cent of the state's vocational, trade, or technical students, while it enrolled only 2 per cent of New York State's total public school student body. The comparable percentages for Chicago were 59 per cent and 26 per cent, for Cleveland 62 per cent and 7 per cent, for Detroit 96 per cent and 16 per cent, for St. Louis 68 per cent and 12 per cent. . . ."[14] When these percentages are translated into dollars for programs, the financial burden on urban public schools becomes obvious.

The Costs of Public Housing. Over 45 per cent of the nation's public housing units are located in its thirty-five largest urban school districts. In testimony as an expert witness before a Congressional subcommittee investigating the effects on public education of the federal government's Impacted Areas Law, Carl Thornblad explained how these public housing units create an additional financial burden for cities and their schools:

According to a recent study conducted by USOE in seven school districts (cities), it was learned that there were 114,994 public school pupils residing in the 70,321 low-rent housing units located in these cities and attending the public schools in these cities. These data produce a low-rent housing unit per pupil factor of 1.64. Assuming that this factor would be reasonably applicable throughout the Nation, we may estimate that there are 1,103,961 pupils living in the 673,147 low-rent housing units which were under management as of December 31, 1967.

The local contribution rate from public housing, as based on that portion of the payment in lieu of taxes which is made available for current operating purposes divided by the number of children residing in low-rent housing units and attending public schools in the local education agencies in the study, has been found to range from $0.00 per public school pupil in Atlanta, Seattle, and Memphis to $28.38 in Baltimore, with the average local contribution rate being $11.61 for the seven selected districts.

On the other hand, the local contribution rate as determined by the amount of current operating revenue per public school pupil, excluding low-rent housing pupils, which is derived from local sources was found to range from $153.69 in Memphis to $656.13 in San Francisco, with the mean rate being $415.79 for the seven selected cities.[15]

Thus, the usual payments in lieu of taxes made by the federal government to school districts serving low-income families in federally supported public housing projects fall far short of the cost of educating the youngsters who live in those housing projects; an average of only $11.61 is contributed to support an average cost of $415.79 per pupil. Ultimately, the already overburdened property tax base of an urban school system must absorb this disparity and make up the substantial difference between federal contributions and costs per pupil.

Greater Difficulties in Obtaining Adequate Resources

As Table 7-6 indicates, the nation's central cities typically tax themselves far more heavily than do the surrounding suburbs. For instance, in 1962 the percentage of income per capita required by residents of a central city for local taxes exceeded the comparable percentage for suburbanites in all but one of twenty-two major metropolitan areas. The maximum percentage difference between

TABLE 7-6   Measures of Tax Effort in 1962 in Central Cities and Suburbs of the Nation's Twenty-two Largest Metropolitan Areas

METROPOLITAN AREA	TAX EFFORT[1]		PERCENTAGE DIFFERENCE: CENTRAL CITY TAX EFFORT MINUS SUBURBAN TAX EFFORT
	In the Central City	In Surrounding Suburbs	
Newark	12.3	7.0	5.3
Boston	11.2	7.4	3.8
Cincinnati	8.2	4.5	3.7
Atlanta	6.3	3.7	2.6
Baltimore	6.9	4.4	2.5
Philadelphia	7.4	4.9	2.5
St. Louis	7.6	5.1	2.5
Pittsburgh	7.2	4.9	2.3
Cleveland	7.4	5.2	2.2
Dallas	5.7	3.7	2.0
New York	9.5	7.5	2.0
Milwaukee	8.4	6.5	1.9
Detroit	7.5	5.7	1.8
Los Angeles	8.4	7.0	1.4
Seattle	5.0	3.6	1.4
Chicago	7.4	6.1	1.3
Kansas City	6.0	5.4	.6
Buffalo	7.5	7.0	.5
Minneapolis	7.0	6.5	.5
Houston	5.9	5.6	.3
San Francisco	7.4	7.2	.2
San Diego	6.3	6.7	—.4
Mean	7.6	5.7	1.9

SOURCE: These data were originally computed by Woo Sik Kee and presented in Regional Research Institute, West Virginia University, *City-Suburban Differentials in Local Government Fiscal Effort*, 1967.

[1] "Tax effort" is defined here as the percentage of income used to pay taxes; more specifically, it is the per capita tax revenue in 1962 in each geographic area taken as a percentage of the per capita income in 1960 in that same geographic area.

the tax effort of the central city and of the suburbs was as much as 5.3 per cent in Newark; the mean difference for all twenty-two metropolitan areas was 1.9 per cent.

Data for many of the nation's major metropolitan areas suggest that local taxes typically require 8 per cent of an individual's personal income if he lives in a central city, but only 6 per cent if he lives in the suburbs; that is, by deciding to live outside a central city, the individual typically gains a 25 per cent break on his local taxes.[16] The variety of taxes city dwellers pay must be considered in order to understand why these geographical differences in tax effort exist: not only are property taxes significantly higher, but often a sales tax, an occupation tax, a wage or income tax, a use tax, a franchise tax, and even an amusement tax may be imposed as well.

Despite this greater tax effort, the nation's largest cities continue to find it difficult to finance their public schools. "Municipal overburden," an inadequate urban tax base, the loss of human capital, and the domination of state legislatures by rural interests all combine to tighten the financial squeeze on big-city school districts.

Municipal Overburden. As the density of population in an urban setting increases, the cost per capita of governing and providing public services rises at an accelerated rate. Police protection, transportation facilities, traffic control, fire protection, waste removal and disposal, hospital services, sanitation facilities, snow removal, pollution control, street maintenance, welfare programs, cultural activities, and the maintenance of public libraries, museums, and auditoriums are but a few of the public services a big-city government must provide to *both* urban and suburban residents. Moreover, all these services necessarily compete with the city's public school district for a share of the municipal revenue.

Given these disparate demands in central cities for a piece of the revenue pie, it is useful to examine some figures on educational and noneducational expenditures inside and outside central cities. By the late 1960's, for example, in the nation's thirty-seven largest metropolitan areas, noneducational expenditures constituted 68 per cent of all local expenditures in the central cities, but only 47 per cent in the surrounding suburbs.[17] For particular cities, the contrast was even more striking: Philadelphia devoted 58 per cent of its local tax revenues to noneducational activities, whereas the average for the state of Pennsylvania was only 22 per cent; San Francisco devoted 71 per cent of its local tax revenues to noneducational activities, but the average for the state of California was only 49 per cent; and Buffalo devoted 76 per cent of its local tax revenues to noneducational activities, while the average for the state of New York was less than 50 per cent.[18] As Seymour Sacks has observed, the nation's central cities typically spend $50 more per citizen than do the surrounding suburbs to provide necessary municipal services; at the same time, though, they spend $50 less per citizen to support their public schools.[19]

TABLE 7-7 Municipal Overburden as Indicated by the Comparative Percentages of Property Taxes Used for Noneducational Purposes in Ten Central Cities and in Other Local Governments Within Respective States

CENTRAL CITY	PERCENTAGE OF PROPERTY TAXES USED FOR NONEDUCTIONAL PURPOSES		DEGREE OF MUNICIPAL OVERBURDEN: DIFFERENCE BETWEEN THE PERCENTAGE FOR THE "CENTRAL CITY" AND THE PERCENTAGE FOR "OTHER LOCAL GOVERNMENTS"
	In the Central City Itself	In Other Local Governments in Its Respective State[1]	
Pittsburgh	61	22	39
Philadelphia	58	22	36
New York	77	49	28
Buffalo	76	49	27
San Francisco	71	49	22
Milwaukee	66	47	19
Chicago	60	40	16
Detroit	57	48	9
Los Angeles	54	49	5
Boston	73	73	0

SOURCE: Research Council of the Great Cities Program for School Improvement, *The Challenge of Financing Public Schools in Great Cities*, 1964.

[1] This statistic is an average percentage for all other local governments in each state.

When we look at revenues obtained solely from property taxes—the chief local source of revenue for public education—the contrast between central city and suburban expenditures for schools is even sharper. As Table 7-7 indicates, noneducational services typically absorb a greater proportion of available property tax revenues in central cities than they do in nearly all other local governmental units within the respective states. Furthermore, comparative data derived from 1966–67 reports of the Census Bureau indicate that the public schools in 83 out of 96 cities in the United States typically receive less than half the property taxes collected within each city. And a third study conducted in the late 1960's shows "that although central cities raised more than $90 per capita in property

TABLE 7-8   An Inadequately Growing Tax Base: Changes During a Recent Five-Year Period in Per Pupil Taxable Assessed Valuation in Fourteen Selected Large Central Cities

| | PER CENT OF CHANGE DURING A FIVE-YEAR PERIOD[1] | |
CENTRAL CITY	In the Central City	In the Remainder of its Respective State
Baltimore	−19.3	+10.0
St. Louis	−10.6	+3.1
Cleveland	−9.9	+4.2
Milwaukee	−9.6	−1.1
Buffalo	−8.6	+26.1
Chicago	−6.0	−0.2
Detroit	−5.7	+3.4
Boston	−5.3	NA
Houston	−2.8	+18.9
Philadelphia	−0.6	+13.6
Pittsburgh	+2.2	+13.6
Los Angeles	+5.1	+5.6
San Francisco	+5.9	+5.6
New York	+32.4	+26.1

SOURCE: Research Council of the Great Cities Program for School Improvement, *The Challenge of Financing Public Schools in Great Cities*, 1964.

[1] Change was for the most recent five-year period prior to 1964 for which data were available.

taxes to their suburbs' average of more than $70, the suburbs spent
an average of $60 per capita on schools, excluding capital outlay,
while the cities spent about $50."[20] The proportion of property
taxes used to support public schools is clearly much smaller in central cities than in the surrounding suburbs.

Thus, municipal overburden—the need for cities to provide extensive municipal services, not only for city residents but for all
who live in a metropolitan area—increases drastically the competition for central city tax dollars and simultaneously reduces the resources available to support any one of those city services, schools
in particular.

An Inadequate Tax Base. Municipal overburden is not the sole
drain on the resources available for urban education. Equally important is the lack of increase in the tax base—that is, the total assessed valuation—which has barely remained stable in most of the
nation's largest urban centers, and has actually declined in others.
During a recent five-year period, while the total taxable assessed
valuation was increasing in Philadelphia by 3 per cent and in St.
Louis by slightly more than 1 per cent, it was simultaneously decreasing in Detroit by 2 per cent, in Cleveland by 3 per cent, and
in Baltimore by nearly 11 per cent.[21] As Table 7-8 indicates,
changes during the first half of the past decade in the amount *per
pupil* of taxable assessed valuation in fourteen of the nation's largest
central city school districts were even more dramatic, particularly
in view of corresponding changes in the states in which each city
is located. During that five-year period, the tax base behind each
student declined in ten of the fourteen central cities, even as it
was increasing in all but two of the states. Only in New York City
did the tax base per pupil increase significantly more than in the
state.

Moreover, as Table 7-9 shows, while the tax base expressed on a
per capita basis has increased to some extent during the last four
decades within each of the nation's major central city school districts, in none of these districts has the increase in tax base equaled
the dramatic increase in expenditures per pupil during the same

TABLE 7-9 An Inadequately Growing Tax Base: Estimates of Per Capita Value of Taxable Property in Fifteen Selected Large Central Cities in 1930 and 1960

CENTRAL CITY	ESTIMATE OF PER CAPITA, FULL-MARKET VALUE OF TAXABLE PROPERTY[1]		PER CENT OF INCREASE BETWEEN 1930 AND 1960
	1930	1960	
Houston	$2,281	$6,869	201
St. Louis	2,477	6,611	167
Washington, D.C.	3,009	7,883	162
Los Angeles	2,852	7,264	159
Detroit	2,379	5,990	152
Cleveland	2,782	6,986	151
San Francisco	4,992	10,826	117
Baltimore	3,071	5,907	92
Milwaukee	2,407	4,388	82
Chicago	2,958	5,018	70
Buffalo	2,443	3,350	37
Pittsburgh	2,734	3,418	25
Boston	2,786	3,207	15
New York	3,072	3,518	15
Philadelphia	2,714	2,862	6

	AVERAGE EXPENDITURE PER PUPIL		PER CENT OF INCREASE BETWEEN 1930 AND 1960
	1930	1960	
All public schools in U.S.	$87	$393	352

SOURCE: H. Thomas James, James A. Kelly, and Walter I. Garms, *Determinants of Educational Expenditures in Large Cities of the United States,* 1966.

[1] Derived from assessed valuations by applying ratios of assessed value to full-market value and then dividing by populations reported by the U.S. Bureau of Census. Because of variations in assessment practices within assessment districts, rigorous comparisons on the basis of these data should be avoided.

forty-year period. In fact, between 1930 and 1960 the per capita, full-market value of taxable property doubled in less than half the fifteen systems listed; in one city, the increase during those thirty years was only 6 per cent. Meanwhile, during the same period the average expenditure per pupil in the nation as a whole (and in each of the cities as well) more than tripled. Clearly, the tax base for urban schools has not kept pace with the increased demand for educational expenditures.

Several conditions account for stagnation or decline in an urban tax base. First, most of the growth in large central cities, and so most of the construction of new single-family residential structures in cities occurred between 1890 and 1930. Later, as rural families migrated to the cities during the period following World War II, new areas for residential construction were either nonexistent or available only at a high premium. Consequently, existing structures were simply subdivided, so that instead of housing a single family, they now crowded three or four families into the same living space. Over the years, as a consequence, residential housing in the nation's central cities became outmoded and, unless offset by unusual efforts at maintenance, dilapidated.

As more and more city homeowners who could afford to maintain two pieces of property moved to the suburbs to live and rented their city property to the nation's new urban migrants, tenants replaced homeowners in urban housing, and real property was allowed to deteriorate. It is usually more profitable for an absentee landlord "to let his aging tenement sit and decay, while he pays low taxes on the building and the site, than for him to develop the site or sell it to a private builder who will."[22] This tactic severely hurts a city, for as urban residential property is allowed to age and to deteriorate, its contribution to an urban property tax base declines proportionately.

Second, most American cities can no longer attract new taxpaying industries. Since land is scarce and thus expensive, and construction costs are considerably higher than in most other locations, many industries and businesses have had to locate in the surrounding suburbs instead of the central city. As suggested in Chapter 3, this dispersal of economic activity in the nation's major metropolitan areas reflects not only the need to reduce construction costs, but also the introduction of new, single-floor production processes, the development of extensive interstate highway systems which skirt central cities, and the ascendance of the truck and automobile in the nation's suburbs. All have contributed to the shift of business and industry from city to country.

Evidence of the shift is plentiful. In twelve major metropolitan areas, the proportion of manufacturing employment in the central cities declined from two-thirds in 1929 to less than two-fifths in 1970.[23] In all but one of the nation's twenty-two largest metropolitan areas, retail sales between 1948 and 1958 increased more in the entire metropolitan area than in either the central city as a whole or its primary business districts.[24] The spread of suburban shopping centers has nearly destroyed the fiscal solvency of downtown shopping zones. Lastly, to illustrate developments in just one major city, "Of the billion-and-a-half-dollar industrial expansion enjoyed by the Cleveland metropolitan area in the postwar years [prior to 1960], one billion dollars' worth [was] located in the suburban municipalities."[25] With each increase in this pattern of economic dispersal, the tax base on which urban schools must depend simply shrinks a bit more.

Third, during the last two decades many central cities have witnessed the removal of considerable amounts of taxable property from their public tax rolls. The impact of this loss on urban school finances was predicted nearly a decade ago:

One of the crucial problems is the diminishing amount of tax property, particularly in large cities, which results in part from the activities of the Federal Government in the cities—the increasing demand for acreage for freeways, public housing, etc. In the case of property removed from tax rolls and condemned for construction of freeways and traffic arteries, the lost revenues cannot be recovered. In the case of housing projects, an annual payment is agreed upon in lieu of taxes, but a considerable time may elapse before the payment is available to schools, and the payment often amounts to a lower figure than (1) school taxes paid by a private apartment development or (2) taxes from the original properties which housed a much smaller pupil population. In urban renewal areas, it may be years before the full amount of taxes for redeveloped land is available. Yet successful renewal requires great capital investments for new schools. Thus, the need for educational services may increase while public payments for such services decrease.[26]

Fourth, two assessment practices sometimes employed in large urban settings have tended still further to reduce the tax base in central cities. One of these is "the tendency in most [central cities] to allow the ratio of assessed values to full-market values to de-

TABLE 7-10 Ratios of Assessed Valuation to Full-Market Valuation in Fifteen Selected Large Central Cities in 1930 and 1960; Assessment Ratios in 1962 on Residential Housing Only

CENTRAL CITY	ASSESSMENT RATIOS IN 1930	1960	DEGREE OF CHANGE IN RATIOS BETWEEN 1930 AND 1960	1962 ASSESSMENT RATIO ON RESIDENTIAL PROPERTY ONLY[1]
Detroit	90	50	−40	42.9
Cleveland	80	45	−35	35.4
St. Louis	65	30	−35	35.6
Washington, D.C.	90	55	−35	47.2
Los Angeles	50	23	−27	20.4
Baltimore	90	64	−26	55.5
Boston	90	66	−24	34.6
Philadelphia	90	68	−22	57.7
Buffalo	80	60	−20	NA
Milwaukee	73	53	−20	48.4
Houston	50	33	−17	NA
San Francisco	38	25	−13	11.8
Pittsburgh	66	55	−11	35.8
New York	90	82	−8	47.6
Chicago	37	55	+18	35.5

SOURCE: H. Thomas James, James A. Kelly, and Walter I. Garms, *Determinants of Educational Expenditures in Large Cities of the United States,* 1966.

[1] These ratios are derived from reports prepared by the U.S. Bureau of the Census.

cline, thus reducing the exposure of property to taxation."[27] As Table 7-10 indicates, assessment ratios declined between 1930 and 1960 in every one of the fifteen cities listed; unfortunately, corresponding tax rates did not increase sufficiently during the same period to produce adequate revenues for the many municipal services these cities were required to provide.

A second practice that has contributed to decline in a city's property tax base is the tendency of many urban tax assessors to underassess residential housing and to overassess commercial property.

This is an extraordinarily difficult phenomenon to study because of the secrecy surrounding assessment practices in a great many jurisdictions. Yet persons who are informed generally concede that the tendency is to underassess residential properties, particularly those which are owner-occupied, and most especially those which have been under one ownership for a long time. This phenomenon is most conspicuous in jurisdictions where assessors are elected, but can often be seen where they are appointed. This is in recognition of the fact that residents control many more votes (and the older residents wield much greater influence) than the corporate bodies who own the commercial and industrial properties. Where the discrepancy between the assessment ratio for all property and for residential property is very large, it almost certainly implies a tax overload on corporate properties. In the long run, one would expect such arrangements to be a factor favoring the decision of industries and commercial ventures to move to other jurisdictions, and a factor weighing against decisions for new industries and commercial units to settle in cities where this is the practice.[28]

The data in Table 7-10 suggest the degree to which this second assessment practice has been used in the nation's largest central cities. In at least twelve of the fifteen cities, the assessment ratios for residential property alone were substantially less in 1962 than their respective overall assessment ratios had been just two years earlier.

Taken together, these four conditions at work in the nation's major central cities—deterioration of real property, inability to attract and hold business and industrial activities, removal of significant amounts of property from the tax rolls, and the practice of discriminatory assessment procedures—have all contributed to a steady erosion of the tax base on which city governments and thus urban schools, must depend.

Loss of Human Capital. Neither municipal overburden nor an inadequate tax base in cities is fully responsible for the decline of financial support for urban schools. A third contributor to these difficulties is the continuing loss of what is popularly referred to as a city's "human capital."

As outlined in detail in Chapter 3, the flight of white, middle-class Americans to the nation's suburbs and the concomitant influx of poor, nonwhite Americans to its central cities have significantly changed the socioeconomic characteristics of most major metropolitan areas. The educational level of city residents, measured in terms of median years of schooling, has been steadily declining, whereas that of suburban residents has been just as steadily increasing. Similarly, and closely related to these educational differences, economic disparities between central city and suburban residents exist on nearly every indicator—family income, rate of unemployment, number on welfare, number in low-income public housing projects, occupational levels, and so forth. These inequities are greatly exacerbated by the heavy concentration of poor and nonwhite residents in central city slums and ghettos, where the pathologies resulting from socioeconomic disadvantage are most severe.

For a big-city school system, the loss of its human capital has ominous implications. Expatriate landlords living in suburbs and intent on profiting from their city property can hardly be expected either to appreciate or to support a city school system's need for additional financial resources. Similarly, residents of city neighborhoods characterized by low socioeconomic levels are unlikely either to recognize the issues concerning quality education or to mount and maintain viable pressure groups for support of it.

It is much easier, therefore, for suburban rather than urban school systems to press their demands for additional money. Residents of middle-class suburbs are typically more interested in and supportive of public education. Suburbs and small towns are more likely than large cities to be inhabited by people who bring similar income levels, tastes, values, and backgrounds to bear upon educational questions, thus facilitating efforts to achieve community consensus and support for particular tax and expenditure levels. The diverging effects of urbanization and secularization—mobility, anonymity, pluralism, and so forth—are obviously felt most in a central city.

One group of observers has described the impact upon a city of this loss of human capital as follows:

> In our society, the educated are capital assets to a community and the uneducated are liabilities. As long as a city either has empty spaces within its boundaries or can extend its boundaries, it matters little that educated citizens who are able to win social and economic privileges move out to the edges of the city and [that] those who cannot [move] remain at its core. It is when the educated cross the boundary and leave the city, subtracting their productive skills and their capital wealth from the pool in the city, and adding both to another civil division, that the city is weakened. If for each educated person it loses, the city must accept in exchange an uneducated person, then, as long as that pattern of exchange persists, the decline of the city is inevitable.[29]

Lack of State Support. No city government in the United States collects enough money through local taxes to cope singlehandedly with all the problems that confront it. Yet, as already indicated, city governmental units typically collect more taxes per capita than any other municipal form of government. It would logically be expected, therefore, that state governmental agencies would design financial aid programs to reduce this inequitable tax burden on central cities—that state aid to cities would take into consideration the effects of municipal overburden, the declining urban tax base, and the continuing loss of human capital. In fact, however, state aid programs typically aggravate rather than relieve the financial problems faced by city governments and their public school systems.

The central city–suburban disparities that today exist in state aid programs for public schools have their roots in history. In many states, aid formulae for schools were developed decades ago in an effort to help finance nonurban school districts which were then terribly disadvantaged. Cubberley, at the turn of the century, asserted that schools outside the nation's cities would require vast sums of money if they were ever to be as good as the urban schools: "In two -thirds of the States of the Union, no adequate provision is made for the maintenance of the smaller schools of the state, and usually these are maintained in a most unsatisfactory manner and at a sacrifice entirely out of proportion to the local benefits received. On the other hand, the cities with their aggregations of people and wealth are able to maintain excellent school systems on a relatively small expenditure. . . . There is little excuse for a system of state taxation for education if the income from such taxation is to be distributed in a larger proportion to the communities best able to care for themselves."[30] Sparked by Cubberley and others like him, state aid programs in the first half of the century focused primarily on the nation's nonurban school districts and stimulated a remarkable upgrading of these districts at a time when assistance was badly needed.

The times, however, have changed drastically since 1900. Many of what were once rural areas in need of state support are now affluent and thriving suburbs. Conversely, most of the nation's larger cities have either lost their fiscal preeminence or barely retained it; and, even more important, most have been severely affected by decay, poverty, and social dysfunction. Meanwhile, formulae for state aid have remained relatively unchanged; they continue to favor suburban districts, increasing still further the inequity between city and suburb. This inequity has traditionally been considerable. From their 1962 study of thirty-five large urban school systems, however, Seymour Sacks and David Ranney concluded that "suburban school systems benefit much more from the present system of state aid to education than do central cities."[31] Clearly, at least in those thirty-five large districts, on either a per student basis (a difference of $40.62) or a per capita basis (a difference of $16.93), state governments tended to invest significantly less money in the education of children attending big-city schools than in the education of those attending schools outside the central cities.

Two additional state-related conditions intensify the financial squeeze on urban school systems. First, there is a tendency in many states to place more stringent limitations on property tax practices in central cities than in the suburbs of those cities. In his study of fourteen large urban districts, H. Thomas James discovered that "in seven of the fourteen cities, the state constitution or statutes restrict the access of city school districts to property tax revenues more severely than they do smaller districts in the same states," even though the percentage of property tax revenues used to support noneducational activities was higher in large central cities than it was in smaller municipalities.[32] These restrictions presumably reflect the historic suspicion and fear with which legislatures dominated by rural areas have long viewed large cities.

The second condition intensifying this financial squeeze is the unintended result that higher state aid for schools in suburbs has on the costs of public education in cities. Expenditures for education outside central cities are a very important determinant of expenditures inside them. Not only must central city school systems compete financially for personnel with the suburban districts that surround them, but they must also struggle to maintain a standard of education (defined in terms of dollar inputs) comparable to that which suburban districts, with their growing tax bases and their disproportionate share of state aid, are better able to support. As the gap in state aid between central cities and their suburbs widens, the financial pressure on urban districts rapidly intensifies.

Efforts to date at remedying the inequities in state aid programs have been only mildly successful. Because it is usually easier to raise money for education in suburbs than in central cities, and because it is politically astute not to pressure rurally dominated state legislatures for additional funds for urban institutions, state departments of education have generally been reluctant to press vigorously for complete equalization of the tax burden between rich and poor districts, and are not at all inclined to press for a disproportionate share of state aid for big-city school districts.

The political reality is that state departments are answerable most directly to state legislatures, and legislators are in turn answerable directly to their constituents. Perhaps as the U.S. Supreme Court decision on reapportionment, with mandate of "one man, one vote," begins to influence the makeup of state legislatures, their attention to urban needs, and especially to those of urban schools, will become more favorable, so that state aid programs more accurately reflect the peculiar needs of each school district. Then, too, if the 1971 California Supreme Court decision on public school financing is upheld, state legislatures will be under considerable pressure to develop school financing programs that will guarantee an equal expenditure per pupil, at least throughout each state, and perhaps even throughout the nation.

In Conclusion

Expenditure levels in urban school systems are large, and growing at an accelerated rate. Since the mid-1960's, urban districts appear to be on their way to obtaining greater financial support than most other districts—at least in terms of expenditure levels per pupil. In most of the largest central city school districts, expenditures per pupil today exceed both the national average and the particular averages within their respective states; whether city expenditures will eventually equal those in suburban districts remains to be seen.

Although it is certain that the nation's largest urban districts are relatively well supported financially in the 1970's as compared with a decade ago, and despite evidence that the competitive position of city school districts vis-à-vis other districts is steadily improving, the financial squeeze which has beleaguered urban education throughout the last three decades continues to tighten. Most central city school systems find it increasingly difficult to raise sufficient financial resources to meet the dramatically increased social and educational demands placed upon them. The cost of operating public schools in an urban setting increases each year as building and maintenance costs accelerate, staff salaries and wages increase, and expensive special programs are mounted. At the same time, the difficulties faced by all public school districts in their efforts to obtain adequate financial support are aggravated substantially for central city school systems by their need to compete for dollars with a multitude of other social and governmental agencies; by the steady decline in their property tax bases; by their loss of valuable human capital to the suburbs; and by their lack of financial support from state legislatures. In sum, despite some encouraging signs, the financial squeeze in urban education is probably greater than ever.

As Sacks concludes in his comprehensive recent study of urban school finances, "The current inferior financial position of large city school systems is a reflection of their past superiority." When fiscal policies designed originally to help smaller rural systems were applied to suburban systems as well, they merely aggravated the fiscal plight of large city systems. To break what he describes as "the historically determined degenerative cycle of public school finance," Sacks argues for "a pinpointed federal program that will deal with financial needs of the large cities. . . . The financial requirements of suburban and rural school systems can be most adequately dealt with by the system of state and local finance which has been able to provide such large sums of money since the end of World War II. Large cities, on the other hand, present problems which are very different and probably can be dealt with only on a national scale with a national resource base."[33]

In recent years, many other observers have urged that the federal government assume greater financial responsibility for the future of cities and their social institutions. None has been more forceful than Mark Shedd, former Superintendent of Schools in Philadelphia, who recently called for the complete "nationalization" of big-city school systems.

I see a national school system in the big cities, federally funded and operated, as the only solution. When a hurricane devastates the Gulf Coast, the government immediately declares a national disaster and steps in with great sums of money to rebuild what the storm tore down . . . I contend that urban education today is a national disaster and nothing short of massive federal intervention will save it. And if education isn't saved, I don't think even massive federal help will be able to rebuild the great cities of this nation if they ever get torn down.[34]

III Prospects for Urban Education

8 Trends and Probable Outcomes

In this chapter we shall discuss the probable size and character of public school enrollments in large central cities; changing industrial and employment patterns in the United States; the prospects for education and employment of urban nonwhites and for their residential integration in cities and suburbs; some probable future strategies to reconstruct ghettos and their urban setting; and, finally, the prospects for metropolitanism, both as a form of political organization and as a way of thinking about and acting upon urban problems.

Trends in Public School Enrollments in Large Central Cities

In the 1970's each of the nation's fifteen largest city school systems enrolled between 100,000 and 1,000,000 youngsters, employed between 4,000 and 60,000 teachers, and spent between $100 million and $1.5 billion a year.

The rate of growth in most of the nation's largest and oldest central cities has, however, gradually begun to level off. The effects of the post–World War II baby boom already have reached their peak. Those goods-producing industries which require large numbers of workers have little incentive today to locate in central cities. Child-rearing families find cities even less attractive. For nearly a decade, the balance of population in the nation's metropolitan areas has tipped in favor of suburbs; that this balance will ever again be reversed seems remote. Some cities—particularly their central cores—may not even maintain their current level of population.

Evidence of this leveling off in urban school enrollments can be seen in the following statistics. In 1960, 12.3 million students between the ages of five and seventeen were enrolled in central city schools, both private and public, throughout the United States. By 1965, this number had increased by approximately 8 per cent, to 13.2 million. During the next five years, however, public school enrollments in those same central cities actually declined by nearly 100,000. Urban school enrollment is likely to rise again, but at a relatively slow rate. Given the natural increase in the total population and the prospect of rebuilding America's central cities, the increase of 900,000 students in the nation's fifteen largest city school systems between 1960 and 1970 is probably a more valid indicator of the future than the slight decline that occurred during the last five years of the decade.

If entire metropolitan areas are eventually consolidated into single governmental units, their impact upon urban education will be tremendous. Many of these consolidated metropolitan school districts will quickly be comparable in size to the city school districts currently found in New York, Chicago, and Los Angeles. This prospect, remote as it may now seem, heightens the need for reform in large city school systems.

In most large cities, racial and socioeconomic segregation is already a fact of life. It is thus not a question of *what* will happen, but of *how long* it will be until city school enrollments come overwhelmingly from racially segregated and/or socioeconomically disadvantaged neighborhoods. The distribution by age of nonwhite children in fifteen of the nation's largest central cities, for example, foreshadows the increase that can be expected. The data in Table 8-1 show that in 1960, in every one of the fifteen cities listed, the percentage of nonwhite children in the youngest age group was largest, and that in the oldest age group was smallest. In Chicago in 1960, for example, Negroes comprised less than 23 per cent of all youth fifteen to nineteen years of age, but more than 34 per cent of those under five. In Detroit, the comparable figures were less than 28 per cent and more than 39 per cent; in San Francisco, less than 18 per cent and more than 30 per cent. Between 1960 and 1970 the comparative proportions across age levels in each of these major cities remained relatively constant; thus it appears that, as younger

TABLE 8-1 Nonwhite Percentage of School-Age Population in Fifteen Selected Large Central Cities of the United States in 1960

	NONWHITE PERCENTAGE OF POPULATION				DEGREE TO WHICH "UNDER 5" PERCENTAGE EXCEEDS "15–19" PERCENTAGE
CENTRAL CITY	15–19 Years of Age	10–14 Years of Age	5–9 Years of Age	Under 5 Years of Age	
Washington, D.C.	53.4	69.3	74.7	72.6	19.2
San Francisco	17.7	26.3	31.2	30.4	12.7
Detroit	27.7	32.5	39.2	39.8	12.1
Chicago	22.7	26.8	32.8	34.2	11.5
St. Louis	29.2	35.6	40.4	40.1	10.9
Baltimore	35.8	40.2	45.3	46.5	10.7
Philadelphia	26.4	30.6	34.6	35.5	9.1
Cleveland	27.5	32.2	37.5	36.5	9.0
Buffalo	12.6	15.9	20.1	20.9	8.3
Boston	8.1	11.8	14.4	14.7	6.6
Milwaukee	8.2	10.6	13.6	14.5	6.3
New York	14.2	16.2	19.6	20.4	6.2
Los Angeles	16.8	17.6	20.0	22.5	5.7
Houston	23.6	21.6	25.5	28.0	4.4
Pittsburgh	17.1	19.5	21.1	21.5	4.4
United States Average	12.2	12.7	13.9	14.6	2.4

SOURCE: U.S. Department of Commerce, Bureau of Census, *Census of Population and Housing: 1960.*

children fill the spaces vacated by older children, the percentage of nonwhite students in public schools, at least in these fifteen cities, will inevitably increase.

In its 1968 report, the National Advisory Commission on Civil Disorders predicted that by 1985 the proportion of Negroes in central cities throughout the country will have risen from 12.1 million in 1966 to 20.8 million, for a nineteen-year increase of 72 per cent. Natural growth is expected to account for 6.0 million of this increase and in-migration for the remainder. If realized, according to the Commission, "this growth would increase the proportion of Negroes to whites in central cities by 1985 from the present 20.6 per cent to between an estimated 31.0 and 35.6 per cent."[1] By 1985, Negroes would comprise at least a majority of students in the public school districts of New Orleans, Richmond, Baltimore, Jacksonville, Gary, Cleveland, St. Louis, Detroit, Philadelphia, Oakland, Chicago, Dallas, Pittsburgh, Buffalo, Cincinnati, Harrisburg, Atlanta, Louisville, Indianapolis, Kansas City, Hartford, and New Haven.[2]

If the high correlation between being nonwhite and being socioeconomically disadvantaged continues, it seems inevitable that as the Negro portion of the populations in central cities increases in the decades ahead, so will the number of socioeconomically disadvantaged. As this occurs, racial and socioeconomic imbalance in public school enrollments will increase, thus intensifying the socioeconomic disadvantage in those larger populations. Only a significant growth in the urban Negro middle class might begin to operate against this trend—and, as data to be presented in this chapter indicate, there is some evidence that such growth may be under way.

Another ray of hope in an otherwise bleak prognosis has been discerned by Daniel Levine and Robert Havighurst. In their study of enrollment in the Kansas City public schools, these investigators discovered some signs that the *rate* of increased segregation in urban school enrollments is beginning to be arrested. These signs include the following:

1. The wellsprings of Negro migration to the cities have all but dried up in many parts of the South.

2. As technological change has reduced opportunities for unskilled and semi-skilled employment, the cities no longer are so strong a magnet for untrained migrants from the rural areas.

3. As a result of these two developments, it appears that the volume and rate of Negro in-migration to the cities are much less than in the period between 1945 and 1960. . . . In general, it appears that Negroes are still migrating in appreciable numbers to the west coast and to some cities on the east coast, but the national trend is toward a slackening in the rate of migration from the rural areas and the south to the large urban areas of the north and west.

4. Because the relatively young Negro in-migrants who came to the cities in the past two decades have now passed through the primary childbearing age, it appears that at least in some cities the number of Negro babies being born is no longer undergoing a rapid annual increase as it did in the postwar period.

5. Each year, thousands of urban Negroes with working-class backgrounds are moving up to middle-class status. Recognizing social class differentials in fertility, it can be predicted that birth rates among urban Negroes will undergo a decline.

6. Urban renewal of the kind which required extensive demolition of dwelling units occupied by low income Negroes not only has been undertaken much less frequently than heretofore, but also is encountering increasingly effective opposition wherever such renewal projects are being proposed.

7. Although mortgages are more readily available than in the past three or four years, financing is nevertheless more difficult to obtain than was the case during the rapid suburban expansion of the postwar period.

8. In many cities, whites who are most inclined to make prejudgments detrimental to nonwhites were the first to panic and leave desegregated neighborhoods. Whites who remain in desegregated parts of the city, conversely, tend to be more tolerant of other people with backgrounds different from their own.[3]

When these factors were taken into consideration, projections of student enrollment in Kansas City contrasted sharply with projections based simply on an extension of past trends. Levine and Havighurst predicted, for instance, that Negro students would constitute 46 rather than 50.7 per cent of the enrollment in 1970; 51 rather than 60 per cent of the enrollment in 1975; and 54 rather than 69.5 per cent of the enrollment in 1980. Thus, it would be in 1975—rather than 1970, as previously predicted—that Negroes would constitute a majority of the public school enrollment in Kansas City, and the percentage increase between 1970 and 1980 would be 8 per cent rather than 20 per cent. Whatever the accuracy of these projections, they suggest that there has been at least a modest alleviation of the socioeconomic and demographic pressures that have intensified racial segregation in large cities throughout the past decade.

In summary, racial and socioeconomic imbalance in the nation's central city schools will probably continue to increase, at least in the immediate future. The *rate* of this increase, however, will gradually decline as the Negro portion of the nation's urban population begins to level off and as an urban Negro middle class begins to develop in significant numbers and to spread throughout a metropolitan area. Nevertheless, a gradual decline in the rate at which urban school enrollments become segregated is not the same as achievement of racial and socioeconomic balance. In the foreseeable future, all urban institutions and agencies, particularly urban schools, will continue to be encumbered by the major burden of racial and socioeconomic segregation.

The Prospects for Industry and Employment in Urban Centers

Changes in the economy since World War II, especially in patterns of industrial activity, have profoundly affected the distribution of jobs and the requirements for entry and progress in most occupations. New production processes, market demands, and industries have generated new occupations and made many others obsolescent.

One example of these changes is the increase in expenditures for research and development in the United States over the past two decades from less than $5 billion in 1953 to well over $27 billion by 1970. In giving rise to new industries and to a diversity of re-lated industries—those in aerospace, for example—research and de-velopment has created a host of new specialized occupations and manpower requirements. At the same time, changes in national priorities during the early 1970's led to substantial cutbacks in areo-space production and thus to unemployment of highly skilled per-sonnel—an illustration of how the employment problems of Ameri-can workers have been compounded. Such trends impose special demands on public educational systems, since workers must now not only qualify for entry into the labor force but also be adaptable to rapidly changing occupational requirements. Schools and col-leges are also being enlisted to provide retraining programs for workers affected by cutbacks and adjustments in the economy.

A further development has been the dramatic shift in America's labor market from a preponderance of blue-collar, production-oriented occupations to those that are white-collar and service-oriented. In 1950, there were a million more blue-collar than white-collar workers in the United States. By the early 1970's, white-collar workers outnumbered blue-collar workers by nearly eleven million. This growth in white-collar, service-oriented occupations stems from the proliferation of banks, loan companies, brokerage houses, department stores, insurance companies, business schools, car rental agencies, airlines, restaurants, franchise businesses, motels, and credit card companies.

This shift is relevant to schools because such service occupations typically require of their workers a higher level of basic education and of technical competence than do goods-producing occupations. They tend to demand greater facility in language, in mathematics, and in interpersonal communication, whose cultivation depends importantly on the quality of education and life experience available to an individual. This requirement has serious implications for public schools, especially for those with large proportions of youngsters who are educationally disadvantaged. Traditional blue-collar jobs as well increasingly require individuals equipped to learn new skills rapidly as job specifications undergo continuous revision. Prior training, even for these jobs, is rapidly becoming mandatory as the number of trained persons increases and the number and range of jobs available to any one worker continue to shift unreliably.

Even more serious in its repercussions is the change in geographic distribution of the nation's work force, as cities have lost even those goods-producing industries traditionally located within their boundaries. In the past, heavy industries were located in large cities specifically because a massive supply of manpower was available. Early in the twentieth century, some manufacturers even sent representatives to Europe to recruit potential immigrants. These newcomers from Europe joined migrants from the rural areas of America in company towns and in the mushrooming industrial neighborhoods of large cities. In their daily lives, city and factory, work and home, became intertwined.

World War II and its aftermath brought massive changes. With the adoption of single-level, assembly-line methods of production, the traditional multistory factories of the inner city became obsolete. Increasingly congested traffic and rising tax rates made operation of large industrial plants in cities less and less profitable. At the same time, vast acreages of inexpensive open land, accessible to highways and to new housing construction, gradually opened up the communities surrounding central cities to industrial development. It is ironic that as vast numbers of Mexican-Americans, Negroes, and rural poor whites during the 1950's and 1960's were being supplanted by mechanized agriculture and forced to move to major central cities, the nation's large goods-producing industries, which historically had assimilated immigrants into the work force, were rapidly deserting those central cities and relocating in the suburbs.

A few statistics suggest the extent of this relocation. In 1929, central cities accounted for 66.1 per cent of all manufacturing employment in the nation's twelve largest metropolitan areas. By 1947 the figure had declined to 60.8 per cent, and by 1970 to less than 40 per cent.[4] On a national scale, by 1970 considerably less than one-half of all new mercantile and industrial construction was taking place in central cities; the remainder was in their suburban fringes.[5] And as goods-producing industries have moved out of the nation's largest central cities, service industries have moved in, for it has been in cities that their clientele are most numerous, potential employees are best trained, and communications are most highly developed.

For post-World War II immigrants to cities, therefore, the development of service-oriented occupations and the geographic redistribution of jobs have led to critical employment problems. An immigrant from Europe in the early 1900's could, with minimal formal education, find an adequate job within walking distance or an easy ride from his home. But today's immigrants from Appalachia, from the deep South, or from Midwestern farms are not nearly so fortunate. Although they may know the language, and although they may feel themselves to be part of American culture, their difficulty in finding adequate employment continues to be acute. To find unskilled or semiskilled jobs, they must increasingly go into the suburbs. To find any of the few blue-collar jobs that remain in a city, they must surmount the hurdles to job entry set up by trade unions. And to qualify for jobs in a service industry usually means obtaining further education and training. In the 1970's, the new immigrant to urban America is clearly in the wrong place at the wrong time with the wrong talents.

Unfortunately for present and future central city residents, there is no sign that these trends in the occupational and geographic distribution of the nation's work force will be reversed. Tables 8-2 and 8-3 give data on actual and projected employment both by occupational group and by type of industry. Table 8-2, showing employment by occupational group, points to a continuing steady in-

TABLE 8-2 Actual and Projected Employment in the United States Between 1960 and 1975, by Major Occupational Group

OCCUPATIONAL GROUP	ACTUAL EMPLOYMENT				ESTIMATED EMPLOYMENT		
	In 1960		In 1970		In 1975		ESTIMATED PER CENT OF CHANGE BETWEEN 1960 AND 1975 IN THE NUMBER OF EMPLOYED
	Number (In Millions)	Percentage of Total in All Occupational Groups	Number (In Millions)	Percentage of Total in All Occupational Groups	Number (In Millions)	Percentage of Total in All Occupational Groups	
White-Collar Workers:							
Professional and technical workers	7.5	11.2	11.3	14.4	12.9	14.8	+72
Clerical workers	9.8	14.7	13.8	17.6	14.8	16.9	+51
Service workers (e.g., private household, waitresses, policemen)	8.3	12.4	9.7	12.4	12.0	13.8	+45
Sales Workers	4.4	6.6	4.7	6.0	5.6	6.4	+27
Managers, officials, and proprietors	7.1	10.6	8.2	10.5	9.0	10.3	+27
Total	37.1	55.5	47.7	60.9	54.3	62.2	+46
Blue-Collar Workers:							
Craftsmen and foremen	8.6	12.9	10.0	12.8	11.4	13.1	+33
Operatives (e.g., truck drivers, assemblers)	12.0	18.0	13.8	17.6	14.7	16.9	+23
Nonfarm laborers	3.7	5.5	3.6	4.6	3.6	4.1	−27
Total	24.3	36.4	27.4	35.0	29.7	34.1	+22
Farm Workers:	5.4	8.1	3.2	4.1	3.2	3.7	−41
Total Employed in All Occupational Groups	66.8	100.0	78.3	100.0	87.2	100.0	+31

SOURCE: U.S. Department of Labor, Statistics on Manpower: A Supplement to the Manpower Report to the President, 1969; U.S. Department of Commerce, Bureau of the Census, Statistical Abstract of the United States, 1970.

TABLE 8-3 Actual and Projected Employment in the United States Between 1960 and 1975, by Type of Industry

| | ACTUAL EMPLOYMENT[1] | | | | ESTIMATED EMPLOYMENT | | |
| | IN 1960 | | IN 1970 | | IN 1975 | | |
	Number (in Millions)	Percentage of All Industrial Employees	Number (in Millions)	Percentage of All Industrial Employees	Number (in Millions)	Percentage of All Industrial Employees	ESTIMATED PER CENT OF CHANGE BETWEEN 1960 AND 1975 IN THE NUMBER OF EMPLOYED
Service Industries:							
Government: federal, state, and local	8.4	15.4	12.3	17.7	14.1	18.6	+68
Services: personal, business, and professional	7.4	13.6	11.0	15.9	12.9	17.0	+74
Finance, insurance, and real estate	2.7	5.0	3.5	5.0	3.7	4.9	+37
Wholesale and retail trade	11.4	21.0	14.4	20.7	16.1	21.2	+41
Transportation, communication, and public utilities	4.0	7.4	4.4	6.3	4.6	6.1	+15
Total	33.9	62.4	45.6	65.6	51.4	67.8	+52
Goods-Producing Industries:							
Construction	2.9	5.3	3.3	4.7	4.2	5.5	+45
Manufacturing	16.8	31.0	20.0	28.8	19.7	25.9	+17
Mining	.7	1.3	.6	.9	.6	.8	−14
Total	20.4	37.6	23.9	34.4	24.5	32.2	+20
Total Employed in Service or Goods-Producing Industries	54.3	100.0	69.5	100.0	75.9	100.0	+40
Agriculture	5.7		4.2		3.7		−35

SOURCE: U.S. Department of Labor, *Statistics on Manpower: A Supplement to the Manpower Report to the President*, 1969; U.S. Department of Commerce, Bureau of the Census, *Statistical Abstract of the United States*, 1970.
[1] These data include all full- and part-time employees who worked during, or received pay for, any part of the pay period reported. Excludes proprietors, self-employed persons, unpaid family workers, domestic servants, and Armed Forces.

crease, at least until 1975, in the percentage of professional and technical, clerical, and service workers employed in the nation's work force. Simultaneously, the table projects a steady decline in the percentage of operatives, nonfarm laborers, and farm workers, who usually require only minimal training. The data indicate that the percentage of blue-collar workers will continue to decline as the percentage of white-collar workers increases.

Table 8-3, showing projected employment requirements within industries, indicates that the number of employees in agriculture, mining, and manufacturing will grow only slightly or may even decline by 1975, and that the number of employees in service industries will increase nearly two and one-half times as fast as those in goods-producing industries. During the fifteen years between 1960 and 1975, the number of personnel in goods-producing industries is expected to increase by slightly more than 20 per cent, from 20.4 million to 24.5 million workers, and the number of personnel in service industries by more than 52 per cent, from 33.9 million to 51.4 million workers. By 1975, the number of personnel employed to provide services is expected to be more than twice the number employed to produce goods. Within specific service industries, some of the largest increases in employment are expected to be in state and local government; in personal, professional, and business services; and in wholesale and retail trade. The one goods-producing industry in which a significant need for workers is expected is contract construction.

Similarly, established trends in the geographic distribution of American business and industry are likely to continue. The widely publicized handful of goods-producing plants built in urban ghetto locations by a few pioneering companies are primarily experiments or simply "public image" gestures, and are not likely to be duplicated on any significant scale. The high cost of construction, the problems of assembly, and the limited amount of available land in central cities make it infeasible to accommodate a large number of single-level factories. Moreover, in any part of a central city, the high crime rate, the threat of vandalism, high taxes and exorbitant insurance rates, transportation delays and parking problems make it unattractive to business firms.

The growth of industry and business requiring large numbers of semiskilled and unskilled workers will thus occur principally in suburbs. Central cities will be transformed into office and professional complexes, headquarters or communication nerve centers for major service industries. Although there will be a continuing need for skilled technical, managerial, and professional personnel in these cities, future employment needs will continue to be greatest in their suburban fringes. In many metropolitan areas, it is predicted that four out of every five new jobs will be located in suburbs; that twenty-five of the nation's largest central cities will lose three million jobs by 1975; that there will be a 20 per cent shift in employment from cities to suburbs by 1975; and that eventually, over half of all jobs in any metropolitan area will be located in its suburbs.[6]

As a result of these trends, the nation's public schools, particularly those located in large central cities, will be called on more than ever to help students develop technical and professional skills, including the ability to shift from one occupation to another.

The Prospects for Education, Employment, and Residential Integration of Nonwhites

In the early 1970's, the prospects for nonwhites in the nation's major urban centers were still uncertain. Indicators and statistics could be cited, for instance, to show that the position of nonwhites, particularly of Negroes, in American society improved markedly during the 1960's: the black population in suburbia doubled between 1960 and 1970, presumably as a result of more liberal housing practices and stricter enforcement of open-housing legislation; nonwhites were better educated, moved into higher-paying occupations, and improved their socioeconomic status; and the federal government encouraged nonwhites to believe that future urban development would benefit them.

In a now famous memorandum to President Nixon early in 1970,

Daniel Moynihan, then a special adviser to the President, offered the following as evidence of progress made during the prior decade:

The nineteen-sixties saw the great breakthrough for blacks. A third (32 per cent) of all families of Negro and other races earned $8,000 or more in 1968 compared, in constant dollars, with 15 per cent in 1960.

Young Negro families are achieving income parity with young white families. Outside the South, young husband-wife Negro families have 99 per cent of the income of whites! For families headed by a male aged 25 to 34, the proportion was 87 per cent. Thus, it may be this ancient gap is closing.

Income reflects employment, and this changed dramatically in the 1960's. Blacks continued to have twice the unemployment rates of whites, but these were down for both groups. In 1969, the rate for married men of Negro and other races was only 2.5 per cent.

Black occupations improved dramatically. The number of professional and technical employees doubled in the period 1960–1968. This was two and a half times the increase for whites.

In 1968, 19 per cent of Negro children three and four years old were enrolled in school, compared to 15 per cent of white children. Forty-five per cent of Negroes 18 and 19 years old were in school, almost the equal of the white proportion of 51 per cent. Negro college enrollment rose 85 per cent between 1964 and 1968, by which time there were 434,000 Negro college students.[7]

The data in Table 8-4 corroborate Moynihan's optimistic contention that Negroes are steadily moving into the more skilled and higher-paying occupations. The data in the table indicate that for metropolitan area Negroes, there were encouraging increases between 1960 and 1970 in employment as professionals, managers, clerks, and craftsmen, along with a comparable decline in the percentage employed as laborers, farmers, and menial servants. In 1960 the percentage of metropolitan Negroes employed in low-paying, unskilled jobs was three times as great as in higher-paying, skilled

TABLE 8-4   A Growing Urban Negro Middle Class: Changes Between 1960 and 1970 in Occupational Distribution of Male Negroes Residing in All Metropolitan Areas of the United States

	NUMBER EMPLOYED		PERCENTAGE EMPLOYED		CHANGE IN PERCENTAGE BETWEEN 1960 AND 1970	PERCENTAGE OF ALL MALES EMPLOYED (ALL RACES)	
OCCUPATION	1960	1970	1960	1970	1970	1960	1970
Professional and technical workers	82,000	211,000	3.8	6.7	+2.9	2.4	4.2
Managerial workers	37,000	139,000	1.7	4.4	+2.7	1.2	2.9
Clerical workers	183,000	339,000	8.4	10.8	+2.4	7.6	12.1
Sales workers	47,000	54,000	2.2	1.7	−.5	2.2	2.7
Craftsmen	239,000	480,000	10.9	15.2	+4.3	4.2	7.4
Operatives	649,000	958,000	29.7	30.4	+.7	11.8	15.9
Nonfarm laborers	511,000	558,000	23.4	17.7	−5.7	28.8	27.3
Service workers	396,000	388,000	18.1	12.3	−5.8	21.2	17.0
Farm workers	40,000	21,000	1.8	0.7	−1.1	7.7	6.5
Total	2,184,000	3,148,000	100.0	100.0			

SOURCE: U.S. Department of Commerce, Bureau of the Census, *Social and Economic Characteristics of the Population in Metropolitan and Nonmetropolitan Areas: 1960–1970.*

occupations; by 1970, the two percentages were nearly equal. Finally, Table 8-4 notes the improving status of metropolitan Negroes vis-à-vis metropolitan whites. In 1960, only 4.2 per cent of all craftsmen in metropolitan America were Negro; in 1970, that percentage had increased to 7.4 per cent. Similarly, during the decade, the proportion of Negro professional and technical workers, managerial workers, clerical workers, sales workers, and operatives increased, whereas the proportion of Negro nonfarm laborers, service workers, and farm workers declined.

These U.S. Department of Commerce statistics confirm Moynihan's assessment of educational achievement and income parity for Negroes, and provide some evidence that an urban Negro middle class is, in fact, expanding significantly. This is further substan-

TABLE 8-5 A Growing Urban Negro Middle Class: Increases Between 1960 and 1970 in Level of Education of Negroes Residing in All Metropolitan Areas of the United States

LEVEL OF EDUCATIONAL ACHIEVEMENT	PERCENTAGE OF NEGROES IN ALL METROPOLITAN AREAS		INCREASE IN PERCENTAGE BETWEEN 1960 AND 1970
	in 1960	in 1970	
Completion of at least four years of high school	42.1	61.0	+18.9
Completion of at least four years of college	4.7	6.9	+2.2

SOURCE: U.S. Department of Commerce, Bureau of the Census, *Social and Economic Characteristics of the Population in Metropolitan and Nonmetropolitan Areas: 1960–1970.*

tiated by the data in Tables 8-5 and 8-6, showing sizable increase between 1960 and 1970 in the percentage of metropolitan area Negroes who completed four years of high school, and an increase from 4.7 to 6.9 per cent in the percentage of Negro college graduates in metropolitan areas—slight but definite increases that con-

TABLE 8-6 A Growing Urban Negro Middle Class: Increases Between 1959 and 1969 in Annual Income Levels of Negroes Residing in All Metropolitan Areas of the United States

LEVEL OF ANNUAL INCOME FOR A YEAR-ROUND WORKER	PERCENTAGE OF NEGROES IN ALL METROPOLITAN AREAS		INCREASE IN PERCENTAGE BETWEEN 1959 AND 1969
	in 1959[1]	in 1969	
Over $7,000	10.1	40.9	+30.8
Over $10,000	2.1	10.0	+7.9
Over $15,000	.4	1.7	+1.3

SOURCE: U.S. Department of Commerce, Bureau of the Census, *Social and Economic Characteristics of the Population in Metropolitan and Nonmetropolitan Areas: 1960–1970.*

[1] Income figures for 1959 are adjusted to 1969 dollars to offset the effects of inflation.

trast sharply with the negligible shifts in prior decades. The considerable pressures on colleges and universities during the latter half of the 1960's and the early years of the 1970's to admit and graduate more nonwhites assures an even greater increase during the current decade.

Closely related to these educational achievements in the 1960's is the increase in annual income. In 1960, only 10 per cent of all metropolitan-area Negroes earned more than $7,000 a year; by 1970, the percentage had increased to nearly 41 per cent. Given that the median income for all Americans in 1968 was approximately $8,600, it would be reasonable to conclude that by 1970 nearly a third of all metropolitan Negroes had achieved a middle-class standard of living; in addition, five times as many metropolitan Negroes earned more than $10,000 a year in 1970 as in 1960.

These noteworthy achievements should not be allowed, however, to obscure a whole range of discouraging indicators about the future of urban Negroes. The data in Table 8-6 also indicate that 60 per cent of all metropolitan-area Negroes, although residing where costs of living are extremely high, earned less than $7,000 in 1970. Negro unemployment continues to be twice as high as white unemployment, and is worst in cities. The percentage of whites who are college graduates is still nearly three times as great as for Negroes. Most important, residential housing patterns in the late 1960's belie the frequent claims that suburbia is open to Negroes and that integration of the races is proceeding well. In fact, racial integration of housing has made relatively little progress in America. To move individual nonwhite families into suburbs is one thing; to integrate all-white neighborhoods is quite another!

In the late 1960's, Seymour Sudman, Norman Bradburn, and Galen Gockel made an extensive survey of racially integrated housing in the United States.[8] Focusing on a geographically representative sample of "neighborhoods" as they were identified in U.S. Census tracts, the researchers defined a neighborhood as *integrated* if both whites and Negroes could move and/or were moving into it, or as *segregated* if it was essentially closed to such in-migration.

TABLE 8-7   Estimated Percentage of White and Negro Households Located in 1967 in Integrated and Segregated Neighborhoods in the United States

RACIAL CHARACTERISTICS OF HOUSEHOLD AND NEIGHBORHOOD	GEOGRAPHIC AREA			
	In total U.S.	In all metropolitan areas	In central cities of those metropolitan areas	In suburbs of those metropolitan areas
Percentages of White Households				
In integrated neighborhoods	19.6	22.8	33.0	16.6
Characterized as "open"[1]	6.1	9.1	11.5	8.0
Characterized as "integrating"[2]	4.5	6.6	9.5	4.8
Characterized as "substantially integrated"[3]	2.4	3.3	5.2	2.1
Other[4]	6.6	3.8	6.8	1.7
In segregated neighborhoods	80.4	77.2	67.0	83.4
Percentage of Negro Households				
In integrated neighborhoods	13.6	15.0	10.9	12.7
Characterized as "open"	0.1	0.1	0.1	0.2
Characterized as "integrating"	0.9	1.2	0.5	2.5
Characterized as "substantially integrated"	8.9	12.7	9.5	9.6
Other	3.7	1.0	0.9	0.4
In segregated neighborhoods	86.4	85.0	89.1	87.3
Percentage of All Households				
In integrated neighborhoods	19.0	22.0	28.2	16.4

Characterized as "open"	5.5	8.3	9.0	7.6
Characterized as "integrating"	4.2	6.1	7.5	4.7
Characterized as "substantially integrated"	3.0	4.1	6.2	2.4
Other	6.3	3.5	5.5	1.7
In segregated neighborhoods	81.0	78.0	71.8	83.6

SOURCE: Sudman, Bradburn, and Gockel, "The Extent and Characteristics of Racially Integrated Housing in the United States," *The Journal of Business of the University of Chicago*, January, 1969.

[1] Integrated "open" neighborhoods were defined as those having less than 1 per cent Negro population.

[2] "Integrating" neighborhoods were defined as those having between 1 and 10 per cent Negro population.

[3] "Substantially integrated" neighborhoods were defined as those having more than 10 per cent Negro population.

[4] "Other" includes all neighborhoods in localities with very few Negroes and/ or in integrated rural areas.

Table 8-7 presents definitions and data in support of the following conclusions:

1. Only 19 per cent of all households in the United States in 1967 were located in *integrated* neighborhoods. Only a fifth of these—4.2 per cent of all households—were located in neighborhoods that could be considered both *integrated* (open to in-migration of both races) and *significantly* (more than 10 per cent) *Negro*.

2. The highest incidence of racial integration in 1967 could be found in central city neighborhoods, particularly those in the nation's ten largest metropolitan areas; the lowest incidence could be found in suburban neighborhoods.

3. This does not suggest, however, that racial integration in central cities had reached a desirable level; even in those cities where

racial integration was most prevalent in 1967, many *integrated* city neighborhoods were less than 1 per cent Negro.

4. Whether the unit of analysis is central cities, suburbs, or entire metropolitan areas, the proportion of Negroes living in *integrated* neighborhoods in 1967 was consistently smaller than the comparable proportion of whites.

5. For most whites living in *integrated* neighborhoods in 1967, the integration was only *slight*; by contrast, for most Negroes living in *integrated* neighborhoods, the integration was *substantial*.

None of these statistics indicates that substantial residential integration has been occurring or is likely to occur in the near future. Since most *integrated* neighborhoods in central cities are already substantially integrated (considerably more than 10 per cent Negro), these are the neighborhoods most likely to be affected by any future exodus of the white middle class to suburbia, and thus most likely to become rapidly segregated if that exodus continues. At the same time, although suburbs have the greatest statistical potential for racial integration, the independence and the intense desire of many suburbanites to maintain the status quo, to "avoid trouble" and "protect property values," inevitably will make future residential integration in most American suburbs a conflict-ridden and agonizingly slow process.

Given the probable future character of populations in metropolitan areas, and the changing nature and distribution of the job market, central cities will in all likelihood continue to be inhabited by disproportionate numbers of citizens who are nonwhite, poor, undereducated, and unlikely to find employment. Job and residential discrimination will continue to make it difficult for nonwhites to join labor unions, move into executive positions, obtain the necessary capital to finance their own businesses, or find moderately priced housing in the middle- and upper-income neighborhoods of the nation's major metropolitan areas. The life prospects for nonwhites in urban centers, particularly those who are also poor, are far from cheerful.

The Prospects for Reconstructing Ghettos
and Their Urban Settings

During the first half of the 1960's, unprecedented attention was given to the "urban crisis" and particularly the conditions prevalent in the ghettos of most large American cities. The stimulus came from the civil rights movement, the coverage of demonstrations by the mass media, the obviously increasing gap between the nation's haves and have-nots, and the support by two successive Presidents of programs for coping with urban poverty, inadequate education, poor housing, unemployment, and insufficient health care. By 1965 the nation appeared to have made a considerable commitment to urban problems, especially in the ghettos.

Since the mid-1960's, however, that commitment has been greatly eroded. Other concerns have absorbed the nation's resources and political energies: an undeclared war in Vietnam and the polarization of attitudes toward it; black militance and the hardening of attitudes among whites toward the problems of black people; inflation and the decline of confidence in the economy; campus unrest and the political repression that followed; and concern for the physical environment. Consequently, government action to reform the ghettos and their larger urban settings—especially at the federal level, the source of most funds—has been slow and halting. Even a strategy of reform, aside from the highly publicized community development programs associated with the War on Poverty, remains to be designed and validated. The sections that follow deal with strategies that are under consideration or are actually being tried out, although only in very limited ways.

Basic Strategies for Dealing with Urban Ghettos

If and when public attention focuses once again on urban America, it is likely that each of three strategies employed since World War II will be given more extensive trial. The first of these strategies is one of "enrichment." Supported by a limited number of corporation executives and principally by Black Power leaders, its aim is black capitalism: that is, to develop sufficient economic power within the ghetto itself so that residents can obtain substantial employment, own their own businesses and homes, and participate in the free enterprise system. It calls for a wide diversity of ghetto-based programs: vocational education, both privately and publicly financed; development of new businesses and industries within the ghetto; massive loan and grant programs to black-managed or black-owned businesses that locate in a ghetto; black ownership of banks and of other sources of capital; and the strengthening of local development corporations to encourage, support, and monitor the expansion of black economic power. The intent of this strategy is thus to build sound economic structures within the ghetto itself, to provide the capital and the enterprises that will enable black businessmen to offer jobs for ghetto residents and to compete in the market place with established firms.

A second strategy is "relocation–reconstruction." On the premise that both the ghetto and the city as now constituted are beyond repair, it argues against simply demolishing old ghettos and setting up new ones—an unintended consequence of much urban renewal activity in the years following World War II—and in favor of starting all over again in virgin territory. Advocated vigorously by real estate developers and home builders, it calls for the total destruction of existing ghettos and the gradual redistribution of current ghetto dwellers among "freshly minted, privately built new towns." As one writer describes the strategy, it proposes "systematically encouraging much of [the ghetto's] population to move to new, carefully integrated communities—complete with industry, variously priced housing, and white families—to be built mostly beyond existing metropolitan areas."[9]

A number of privately financed experimental communities are currently being developed; Columbia in Maryland, and Reston in Virginia are two that have been well publicized. According to the U.S. Department of Housing and Urban Development, which has begun to help developers through federal loan guarantees, some seventy privately developed "new towns" are now under way.

Whether these developments really will be worthy of being called "new towns"—whether, that is, they really will be any more "livable" than the typical middle-class suburban community—remains, of course, to be seen. Even more important, no one really knows whether "new towns" will attract sufficient residents from ghettos to ensure that they are integrated.

It is already possible to identify several features of this second strategy that discourage its wide adoption, at least in the immediate future. First, it assumes that we already know enough about the political, social, economic, and psychological dynamics that accompany urbanization to be able to avoid the errors of the past as we go about creating new cities, whereas current events would indicate that we are still wondrously ignorant. Second, building new cities takes time and, because conditions in twentieth-century America change so rapidly, the rationale that undergirds the design and development of a model city may well become antiquated before it is fully operational. Third, the strategy depends for success on the ability of developers to build cities so attractive and so functional that a diversity of individuals representing a wide range of races, value systems, and socioeconomic strata will both desire and be able to live there compatibly with each other; the events of the past decade offer little basis for the hope that this degree of consensus and brotherhood is likely.

Fourth, in order to replace existing urban ghettos, where anywhere from ten to twenty million nonwhite and poor persons are now estimated to live, a massive number of "new towns" will have to be built. Fifth, a dominant tendency in any new city will be for it gradually to take on and foster the characteristics of white, middle-class America; many current ghetto residents may not be willing or able to substitute such a culture for their own. Sixth, to build entirely new cities is a terribly expensive venture, one that cannot be financed fully by private capital; their extensive development, therefore, will depend on considerable assistance from federal, state, and local governments. To date, the American public has given little evidence at a state and local level that it is concerned with the problems of urban America, particularly those of big-city ghettos, and willing to approve and provide for such an expenditure of funds.

A third general strategy is "dispersal." Perhaps the most conservative of the three strategies, it assumes that population growth, economic activity, building construction, and residential integration are most likely to occur not in the nation's central cities but in the metropolitan regions surrounding them. Its ultimate objective, therefore, is to encourage a substantial movement of urban ghetto dwellers during the next few decades into metropolitan areas where economic opportunity and employment needs are likely to be greatest.

Studies to date indicate that employment programs requiring reverse commutation—travel from a home in the city to a job in the suburbs—are too time-consuming and expensive to be attractive to the ghetto poor. Thus, in the Philadelphia area, where the central city lost 50,000 jobs between 1951 and 1965, and the surrounding suburbs gained over 200,000 jobs, less than 2 per cent of the suburban work force in 1968 was composed of nonwhite commuters from the central city; furthermore, those who did commute to the suburbs represented less than 9 per cent of the employed nonwhites in the central city.[10]

Rather than depend on reverse commutation to improve the economic condition of ghetto dwellers, therefore, this third strategy attempts to use future employment opportunities in the suburbs as a stimulus to increased suburban residential integration. Its essential aim is to sever "the suburban 'white noose' around our core cities, making the metropolitan housing–real estate market work the same for the Negro as for the white, and forcing cities to accept nonwhite and lower-income families in significant volume and in a harmonious manner."[11]

Several tactics can be employed to achieve these ends. Open-housing statutes can be enforced, despite the unlikelihood that the force of law will produce significant changes in racial attitudes. Suburban land can be rezoned for small lots and multiple dwellings, thereby encouraging new construction of moderate- and low-cost housing in suburban growth areas. Nonprofit corporations can be formed to participate in low-interest government housing programs. Countrywide public agencies can be organized to take advantage of publicly supported rent-supplement programs. And the economic muscle of the nation's business and industrial leadership can be employed to make available industrial locations and capital for building, as well as to influence zoning laws and real estate practices. Projects in line with this strategy, however, such as the planting of low-income housing in suburbs and in middle-class areas of large cities have, perhaps predictably, met with militant resistance from those already living in those areas.

Strategies for Reconstruction of Cities

Although enrichment, relocation–reconstruction, and dispersal are the strategies most likely to be pursued in the years ahead, a variety of others are likely to be attempted as part of an overall effort to make the nation's central cities more livable. Some of these are conventional, others futuristic. Some are intended to make urban life more humane, others are designed to make it more efficient by applying technological principles and practices.

1. To reduce both congestion and air pollution, severe restrictions will be imposed on automobile, rail, and truck traffic within a central city. Although these restrictions may be initially on an hourly or daily basis, a total ban will eventually be placed upon all gasoline-powered vehicular traffic. Central cities will be fringed by parking lots and freeways, and extensive rapid transit systems—trams, subways, monorails, moving walkways, escalators, and elevators—will whisk those who use the city for business, pleasure, or residence to their destinations.

2. Intercity transportation systems will consist of electronically controlled superhighways, high-speed trains, and jet-powered airplanes capable of vertical landings and takeoffs from rooftop landing pads and floating barges moored in nearby waterways.

3. Electricity will be the primary, if not the only, source of power for operating the nation's cities—for heating buildings, preparing food, powering mass transit, lighting streets, and operating the thousands of gadgets available to urban residents; an extensive network of nuclear reactors will provide electricity sufficient to meet the maximum needs of an entire metropolitan area.

4. Desalination processes will be sufficiently developed that most American cities, including all within five hundred miles of either coast, will obtain their water supplies directly from the ocean rather than from fresh-water sources that are miles away and diminishing annually.

5. Techniques will be developed for reclaiming most refuse for useful purposes, and will not only spawn new industries and new jobs but also eliminate the current need to burn refuse, bury it, or dump it in the ocean.

6. Central cities will become massive communications switchboards, crisscrossed by intricate systems, both audio and visual closed-circuit television, picture-telephones, one-way and two-way portable radios and telephones, and a massive computerized information system capable of storing and retrieving information at a moment's notice.

7. Public outcry will force government and private industry to commit sizable resources to pollution control. Effective technology will be brought to bear upon the problem, and stringent pollution laws will be passed and then rigidly enforced. Cities will finally be capable of maintaining air, water, and noise pollution at tolerable levels.

8. Public health services in the nation's central cities will be vastly expanded. Overcrowding in medical facilities will be eliminated by massive, publicly financed hospital construction programs. The shortage of adequately trained medical personnel—doctors, nurses, specialists, attendants, and supporting staff—will be reduced significantly by the continuing shift from goods-producing to service occupations and industries, by extensive development of medical technology, and by the expansion of schools and programs for

training prospective medical personnel. The escalating costs of medical treatment—for professional services, medication, and hospital care—will finally be brought under control through extensive, publicly supported health insurance programs and modified forms of socialized medicine.

9. Cities will become public recreational and cultural centers of the nation. No longer will the costs of attending an opera, a symphonic concert, or even a professional football game exclude the majority of urban residents from enjoying live performances. Through a metropolitan-based program of public subsidies, central cities will be able to offer metropolitan area residents a wide array of cultural, athletic, and recreational opportunities.

10. By the 1980's, most American cities, particularly those in the East and Midwest, will have undergone a complete physical transformation. Buildings constructed prior to World War II will largely have disappeared and have been replaced by giant new architectural forms, multistoried, sparkling, and distinctively designed. Glass, concrete, and plastics will be the dominant building materials. Height will be no limitation. Architectural design will strive for both a form compatible with the urban environment and a functionalism to protect the amenities of privacy and quietude. Each building will serve a wide array of purposes. Some floors will provide space for business offices, conference rooms, and large auditoriums; others will accommodate shopping centers, restaurants, hotels, and even public schools; still other floors will be designed for private residence. Connecting these many floors will be an extensive network of elevators and escalators and an elaborate telephone and closed-circuit television system; and while ample parking facilities will be constructed beneath each building, attractive walkways, gardens, and tunnels will connect the various buildings, and rooftop landing facilities will provide easy access to an intercontinental system of airports.

11. Finally, the distinction between cities and suburbs will no longer be meaningful. Rather, entire metropolitan areas will have become the major unit of urban life—and the level at which such

aspects as employment, residential development, education, governmental services, culture, pollution control, are dealt with.

12. We shall then be well into what Melvin Webber has described as the "post-city age," one in which

> . . . the large metropolitan centers that used to be primarily
> goods-producing loci have become interchange junctions within
> the international communications network. Only in the limited
> geographical, physical sense is any modern metropolis a discrete,
> unitary, identifiable phenomenon. At most, it is a localized node
> within the integrating international networks, finding its signifi-
> cant identity as contributor to the workings of that larger system.
> As a result, the new cosmopolites belong to none of the world's
> metropolitan areas, although they use them. They belong, rather,
> to the national and international communities that merely main-
> tain information exchanges at these metropolitan junctions.[12]

The Prospects for Metropolitanism in Urban Settings

In the late nineteenth century, the United States committed itself irreversibly to a shift from an agricultural to an industrial economy and from a rural to an urban society. Between the late 1800's
and the pre-Depression years, great numbers of Americans moved
from the open country and from small towns and villages to large
central cities where jobs were plentiful in an expanding industrial
economy. Throughout that half century there was still a sharp de-
marcation between the city, with its houses, shops, and factories
laid out in predictable patterns of streets, and the irregular spaces
of the surrounding countryside. Rural areas could still be distinguished from urban areas and country-dwellers from city-dwellers.

After World War II, however, as the nation's industrial and
business interests began to decentralize, and Americans began
streaming from central cities to their outlying areas to live and, increasingly, to work, city and country became less distinguishable
from one another. Mushrooming between the two, a host of new
suburban communities promised to meld into one style of life the

best of both country and city living. With the development of these suburbs came recognition of the concept of a metropolitan area and of *metropolitanism* as a way of thinking and acting in an urban setting.

As a demographic concept, the term "metropolitan district" was first used by the U.S. Bureau of the Census in 1910; but it was not until 1949 that the first standard definition of a metropolitan statistical area was issued by the Bureau of the Budget. Today a Standard Metropolitan Statistical Area (SMSA) is defined as an integrated economic and social unit containing either a central city with a population of at least 50,000 inhabitants, or twin cities with a combined population of at least 50,000, in which 75 per cent of the labor force are employed in nonagricultural occupations, and there is social and economic interdependence among the communities comprising it, as evidenced by newspaper circulation figures, traffic data, geographical distribution of bank accounts and charge accounts, and the like.[13]

The complex causes of metropolitan growth have been set forth in earlier chapters: industrial expansion, population pressure, and improved transportation and communication systems:

> The motor car and the truck have radically extended the radius of feasible commuting trips and made the distribution of goods and services vastly more flexible. The telephone and the radio have enlarged the individual's range of communication, widening the geographic reach of his business, leisure, and consumer activities. Meanwhile, the lure of open space and detached dwellings has pulled families to the suburbs, a pull facilitated by affluence and by public policy that has encouraged home ownership.[14]

Statistically, the growth of metropolitan areas has been awesome. Over 75 per cent of the nation's total population increase between 1950 and 1970 occurred in metropolitan areas; two of every three Americans now live in one of the approximately 250 areas designated by the Bureau of Census as an SMSA. By the turn of the century, it is expected that more than 85 per cent of the nation's

total population will be concentrated in either the central cities or
the suburbs of major metropolitan areas. The need for new governmental entities to serve a massively redistributed population is
becoming increasingly acute.

As defined for demographic purposes, an SMSA is a group of
demonstrably interdependent cities and suburbs; yet as David
Minar points out, "the metropolitan area is essentially a product of
the uncoordinated growth of the social and political aspects of urban life."[15] For while metropolitan areas have become enormously
complex social and economic entities, the development of viable
political structures within them has been sluggish and uneven.
Initially, the nation's central cities simply extended their municipal
boundaries in order to incorporate or annex newly developed areas.
In the 1920's, however, state legislatures, dominated by rural interests and seeing large urban and suburban municipalities as a threat
to their power, eliminated annexation as a legitimate response to
metropolitan development. Thereafter, communities that developed
outside central city limits had either to expand their own existing
political jurisdictions or to create entirely new ones. As Minar observes,

> The uneven distribution of existing governments and the uneven-
> ness of suburban growth have meant that patterns of political de-
> velopment have seldom been rational. Jurisdictions once estab-
> lished have proved to possess much staying power and little
> flexibility. Needs for services have developed in uncoordinated
> parts and have been made the province of special service districts.
> Small and specialized units of government have been cherished
> and have multiplied in pursuit of the Jeffersonian ideology of the
> simple political system kept close to the people. Thus, the gov-
> ernmental structure of the metropolitan area has come to be as
> we know it today, the jerry-built product of half-measures and
> accidents.[16]

Without exception, every one of the nation's approximately 250
SMSA's is characterized today by extreme political fragmentation,
some of whose causes are peculiar to metropolitan areas, whereas

others are common to all governmental units in the United States. Their combined effects, however, have all but stifled the possibility of effective political action and interaction at the metropolitan level. In one respect, political fragmentation is inevitable to the American federal system of government, in which national, state, and local government agencies often become rivals. Although urban problems now transcend local governmental units and produce repercussions in both state and nation, the traditions of home rule safeguard the autonomy of local municipalities and serve to block state and national governments from developing comprehensive solutions to what are, in reality, areawide problems.

In a second respect, political fragmentation results naturally from the multiplication of local units of government. This has occurred extensively during the last half century. Some political units have been set up to govern new, incorporated geographical areas—townships, villages, and cities; others have been set up to provide some special service—education, water, sewerage, fire and police protection, parks and recreational activities.

> Governments have been piled on top of other governments and have been allowed to overlap, many of them attending to different but closely related aspects of social needs. It is not uncommon for the metropolitan resident, for this reason, to be served by six, eight, or even ten local units: a county, a municipality, perhaps a township or town, special-function districts for such services as transit, recreation, conservation, or sanitation, and one, two, or even three school systems. The nation's 212 standard metropolitan statistical areas in 1962 contained 18,442 local governmental units. Of these, 6,004 were school districts, 4,142 were municipalities, and 5,411 were special-purpose districts; townships, towns, and counties accounted for the remainder.[17]

The combination of these governmental units, whether defined spatially or functionally, naturally differs widely across metropolitan areas, but overlapping and fragmentation are characteristic of all metropolitan regions of the country.

In a third respect, political fragmentation characterizes the internal workings of nearly all governmental units, whether they be school districts, municipalities, or special service districts. Internal fragmentation is inevitably produced by systems of checks and balances imposed on governmental units at all levels; by the use of bargaining and negotiation as the dominant means of political decision-making; and by the degree to which political energy is expended in the American system of government to inhibit rather than facilitate the exercise of power—e.g., in the creation of municipal boards and commissions, the separation of civil service from political activity, the sanctity of public hearings, and the sensitivity to public pressure. As a result of political fragmentation, action programs run a gauntlet of political tests before they can finally be implemented by a governmental unit.

These aspects of political fragmentation have meant that development of the nation's metropolitan areas has typically been irrational, unsystematic, and uncoordinated. Several portraits of metropolitan America, though drawn from varied sources, all point to this characteristic lack of design:

The political and bureaucratic structure of government in urban areas . . . is not a monolithic giant that encompasses all public personnel within its administrative tentacles. . . . Each unit, whether a school district, municipality, or county-wide sewerage district, has its own entrenched officials and employees and its own fenced-in areas of jurisdiction. . . . Water departments in the city and county vie with each other to become the metropolitan supplier. A county health department seeks to expand its authority at the expense of the municipal agencies. Autonomous sewerage districts resist efforts of a metropolitan agency to bring them under its jurisdiction. County and municipal police departments argue over their respective jurisdictional spheres. . . . In this interplay of forces, each segment or sub-unit of the structure cultivates clientele relationships and affords points of access to the private influence of the community. The king has many ears.[18]

Here a special district disposes of sewage wastes for half of one city, all of another, and none of a third, while serving sections of an unincorporated area. There a fire protection district exists as a county island completely surrounded by a city, stoutly resisting absorption by the larger more efficient city department.[19]

[The 100,000 residents of Highline School District, south of Seattle] are governed, taxed, or served by King County, the school district, Port of Seattle, four small cities, eight sewer districts, eleven water districts, six fire districts, a library district, a road district, a drainage district, and the County Housing Authority—thirty-six local governments, with over one hundred elected officials.[20]

[Many metropolitan communities are, unfortunately, characterized by] streets that do not meet, land uses that are incompatible, sewage from one area polluting the water of another, smoke from one area polluting the air of another, unvaccinated dogs from one section menacing another, and the duplicate purchasing of expensive equipment and facilities. . . . the education of the child [isolated] from the health of the child. . . . the most badly blighted areas [burdened with] the lowest tax resources. . . . the most able leaders [located] in separate political entities—frequently suburbs—and [isolated] from the core city's problems.[21]

The character and quality of such urban sprawl is readily recognized: neon bright strip cities along main-traveled roads; housing tracts in profusion; clogged roads and billboard alleys; a chaotic mixture of supermarkets, used car lots, and pizza parlors; the asphalt plain of parking spaces; instead of parks, gray-looking fields waiting to be subdivided. These are the qualities of most of our new urban areas—of our slurbs—our sloppy, sleazy, slovenly semicities.[22]

Political organization and action have simply not kept pace with economic and social developments in metropolitan America. The resulting problems are legion: slums, polluted air and water, electrical power shortages, inadequate transportation, racial discrimination in housing, inequities in financial support for schools, deficiency of cultural and recreational facilities. No one of these problems can be dealt with successfully by a single governmental unit, but this is precisely the affliction of metropolitan America. By their very existence, the relatively autonomous cities, towns, villages, and special districts in a metropolitan area safeguard stasis and prevent action. Developmental work is typically limited by tradition to the legal boundaries of existing municipalities, even though the problems toward which the actions are directed often transcend municipal boundaries.

Given the inexorability of urbanization, it seems inevitable that *metropolitanism* will become a necessary way of thinking and acting. Metropolitanism as a way of thinking requires that an entire region, not just a central city or its suburbs, be recognized as the "most useful geographical unit for thinking about the coordination and the organization of educational, governmental, and other social systems."[23] It requires that the metropolitan area be viewed as a new kind of community, one in which the boundaries between towns, cities, villages, and districts are open to change—to contraction and expansion in response to regional needs. In effect, metropolitanism requires that metropolitan areas be viewed as open systems, continually in flux and always sensitive to interdependencies both within and outside their geographic boundaries. As a process for acting, metropolitanism requires that an entire metropolitan area become the arena for planning and doing—that actions be coordinated across traditional geographic and functional boundaries and that human, natural, and financial resources throughout the metropolitan area be coordinated rather than expended to protect isolated enclaves of political power.

Metropolitanism thus calls for the dissolution of existing political structures, the development of a single areawide governmental unit, and participation by the entire metropolitan community in developing and executing policy. The prospects for such sweeping and comprehensive political reforms, despite their inherent rationality, are unfortunately slim.

One of the many inhibiting political conditions is, of course, home rule. To dissolve old political structures in favor of entirely new ones requires political support from a substantial number of those who will be affected by the changes. Political scientists have often noted that, ". . . however 'intrinsically right' our plans may be, they are only plans until someone harnesses the wild horses of diverse politics to them."[24] To achieve the necessary consensus of opinion within an urban setting is all but impossible. The principle of home rule not only permits, but actually encourages local municipalities to oppose unification. To protect their autonomy, local communities have historically tried to isolate themselves from the larger metropolitan region through restrictive zoning, racial and religious discrimination in housing, and the passage of local ordinances designed to maintain the status quo. In communities where such protective responses are almost habitual, it is unrealistic to expect local leaders either to initiate proposals for metropolitan unification or to support others who do so. This has been demonstrated amply in the recent history of efforts to consolidate small school districts—efforts which succeeded primarily because of political pressure from county and state agencies.

In his discussion of the merits and prospects of the metropolitan approach, Daniel Grant suggests three further factors that tend to discourage the adoption of metropolitanism in its ideal form:

1. The strong mutual distrust of the suburbs and core cities of each other militates against political union. In the suburbs, the core city image is one of corrupt city machines, graft, high taxes, heavy debt, the "great unwashed masses," and the "wrong side of the tracks." In the core city, the suburban image is one of wealthy, overprivileged, lily-white, anti-Negro people who enjoy a free ride on all the city services without paying city taxes.
2. Political party cleavage between Democratic core cities and many Republican suburbs almost guarantees the opposition of at least one group of party leaders to metropolitan merger proposals.
3. The popular fear of "big government" and the tendency to equate the metropolitan government concept with big govern-

ment places two strikes against any proposal for areawide government, regardless of how careful the proponents are to guarantee
the continuation of all existing local governments. The argument
that the creation of some kind of metropolitan community decision-making structure is the only way to avoid centralization of
decision-making at the state or national level is a rather sophisticated argument which is not easy to translate into votes from the
masses in a referendum. The "metro-monster" charges are much
easier to relate to popular fears of big government.[25]

Despite all this, urban developers and administrators have increasingly subscribed to modified forms of metropolitanism. Major
social organizations operating in America's major metropolitan
areas have come to define their functions as areawide rather than
as limited to central cities or to particular suburbs or groups of
suburbs. Chambers of commerce, for example, often cover entire
metropolitan areas, as do labor unions, church federations, and social organizations. Prominent department stores, specialty shops,
and banks establish branches in suburbs. Telephone, gas, water,
and electrical power companies organize their services throughout
entire metropolitan regions, as do symphonic and theater groups,
universities and community colleges, newspapers, and radio and
television stations.

In its ideal form, metropolitanism may well be infeasible, but a
number of factors encourage its continued development in these
modified forms. Between 1900 and 1950, suburbs were typically inhabited by persons with high income and considerable formal education, whereas those living in central cities were just as typically
persons with low income and poor educational backgrounds. During the past two decades, however, the shifting patterns in metropolitan population growth—the simultaneous influx to central
cities, exodus to suburbs, and movement between the two—have
tended to blur these differences. Whereas the working class and
the poor used to settle almost exclusively in central cities, they are
now beginning to spread themselves—the poor and nonwhites
more thinly than the rest—over entire metropolitan areas. As a re-

sult, the historic social and economic differences between cities and suburbs are being rapidly reduced; their problems today are more similar than not. The central city and suburban worlds are rapidly becoming "all of one piece," to recall once again Robert Penn Warren's analogy of the spiderweb.

It is to be hoped that the various geographic areas in a metropolitan region will come to recognize their common interests. As the problems of maintaining adequate water and power supplies, providing mass transit, disposing of sewage, constructing adequate highways, and controlling pollution become critical, so too will the demand for increased cooperation among metropolitan communities. The development of new and modified forms of metropolitanism will also receive some stimulus through financial incentives provided by state and federal governments. The Federal Highway Act stipulates, for example, that after 1965 no local governmental agency in a metropolitan area can qualify for federal highway funds unless its application is reviewed by an official agency engaged in comprehensive transportation planning for an entire metropolitan area, and takes into consideration the future effects of proposed action. Similarly, the relatively new Department of Housing and Urban Affairs requires that federally supported activities related to mass transit, residential housing, and urban renewal be carried out on a metropolitan areawide basis.

Such factors are likely to bring about increasing subscription to metropolitanism as a way of thinking and acting. Residents of a metropolitan area will gradually come to identify themselves as citizens of an entire region, perhaps even to the point of ignoring the smaller geographic entities in which they reside. Social organizations and institutions in metropolitan areas, both suburban and central will cooperate more extensively across traditional geographic boundaries. This cooperation will develop most rapidly in those subsystems concerned with technological needs—water supply, electrical power, sewage disposal, street maintenance, police and fire protection, mass media, air and water pollution—and most slowly in areas of government and education where traditional law and custom are strongest. Even there, however, we can probably expect the establishment of a substantial number of governing units functioning across metropolitan areas. Air pollution control agencies, countywide special education districts, areawide audiovisual libraries, and metropolitan planning commissions are clearly harbingers of the future. As Grant suggests in his concluding remarks on the future of metropolitanism, "The vacuum caused by a metropolitan society without metropolitan government will undoubtedly be filled during the next two or three decades by a growing nationally directed functional federalism, in cooperation with a variety of limited-purpose special districts and limited-area cities, towns, townships, and counties. The metropolitan government approach would be far more rational, but the 'intergovernmental megalopity,' with its myriad vertical and horizontal relationships, is a far more realistic prediction."[26]

9 Toward a Strategy for Urban School Reform

If mobility and change are central themes in the history of the city and in the development of an urban society, then a central problem in urban school systems is their inordinate resistance to change. Their design continues to reflect the high value placed on social order and stability by educational leaders in the latter half of the nineteenth century. Until around 1950, big-city public schools remained relatively isolated from the spectacular social changes occurring elsewhere in urban America. Such pre-World War II organizational reforms as civil service examinations and job tenure for teachers, while protecting city schools from incursion by municipal politics, served also to insulate them from valid social criticism and to dull the incentive to engage in self-study and innovation.

In the first few decades of the century, city schools achieved a modest reputation for success, particularly with children whose middle-class or upward-aspiring working-class parents had prepared them for what they were to experience in the classroom. For many of these children, to succeed in school, or at least to avoid failure, had been made a moral imperative. As for other, less well moti-

vated youngsters, the city school was relatively free of responsibility; the masses of those who did not succeed or who were uninter-
ested in school could leave it and readily find a place in the vast
urban market for unskilled workers.

Since mid-century, however, as massive migrations of Americans
have transformed the character of city neighborhoods, central city
schools have enrolled an increasingly large number of youngsters
whose caretakers at home have been unable to prepare them adequately for formal education; and simultaneously, because of a
diminishing market for unskilled labor and an increased demand
by potential employers for diplomas and other credentials, all public schools have been forced to retain youngsters longer. The previous safety valve of student dropout is thus no longer available to
schools—hence the unrelieved pressure built up by numbers of students who are academic failures and/or who are alienated from the
values and objectives of the school.

The inadequacies of public schools, particularly those in cities,
are being revealed with increasing starkness, as they and their students are forced, often to their mutual dismay, to live out an extended confrontation with each other's failure.

Developing a Methodology for Urban School Reform

A methodology for reform calls not merely for a collection of
methods or procedures but for a more subtle set of considerations,
including open attitudes toward social change, concepts of social
organization, and theories on the nature of urbanization and the
function of education in an urban society. Without such a con-
ceptual basis, a methodology for reform is likely to be unequipped
to distinguish, at any given time, the problems that can feasibly be
worked on from those that can not.

Models of Institutional Reform

Debate over social issues is inevitably complicated by antinomies
—that is, by the possibility of contradiction between two appar-

ently true or reasonable judgments. A classic antinomy is that of the water glass that can be described either optimistically as half full or pessimistically as half empty. In urban education, the assertion is often made by urban school administrators that, by and large, the schools have done a good job under difficult conditions; on the other hand, it is asserted with equal justification by their most radical critics that urban schools have failed dismally. Similarly, the documented views of a Moynihan or a Banfield that a black middle class has in fact rapidly developed during the past decade can be set against the equally valid evidence that an underclass of poor black families continues to grow at the core of most large American cities.

Debate about success and failure in urban America and in urban schools is shot through with such antinomies. Indeed, they are unavoidable. Not only do people look to different facts and bring differences of bias to their interpretations, but what they perceive in any situation depends to an important degree on the breadth and the depth of historical perspective from which they view it. Educational reform will, of course, inevitably be more fruitful to the degree that reformers remain aware of antinomies and try to minimize one-sided assertions about right and wrong or good and bad. Current criticism and debate over urban education are seriously lacking in this kind of objectivity.

No less important than the attitudes one brings to the subject of institutional reform are the models used to conceptualize that reform. Here, the distinction drawn by Morris Janowitz between "specialization" and "aggregation" as models for change seems particularly useful.[1] Specialization, the model that most American institutions have followed during the past century, involves the introduction of innovations on a piecemeal basis. Often, if not usually, such innovations have been developed by "specialists" outside an organization, who then confer their expertise on the practitioners in that organization. Thus, innovations in schools typically have involved the adoption of textbooks or packages of materials and procedures, sometimes including the training of teachers and ad-

ministrators. To the extent that a specialization model for change
has involved the transfer of expert knowledge and skills directly
from innovator to practitioner, it has provided a logical approach
to innovation; moreover, it has been a relatively economical and
efficient way to carry out change, for it has enabled many schools
and their professional staffs to be furnished simultaneously with
programs that are pretested and prepackaged. Among its most no-
ticeable effects, the specialization model has brought about considerable refinement of the teaching process, more specialized curricula, and more systematic approaches to school organization and
management.

Despite its benefits, however, the specialization model has led
mainly to inadequate short-term reforms. If for no other reason
than the political pressures generated by their failures, central city
schools will no longer be permitted to respond to the need for
change with merely temporary palliatives. Short-range experiments
and specific improvements in curriculum, instruction, or special
services to youngsters—most of which are consistent with a specialization model for change—have still not reduced appreciably the
large number of failures in central city schools. Increasingly, strategies are needed to bring about reforms not simply in curricular and
instructional practices, but also in the way schools as social systems
are organized and administered.

An aggregational approach to institutional reform, as Janowitz
describes it, would create ". . . a set of educational practices that
would transform the normative and moral order of the slum
school."[2] It would seek to redefine the authority and the roles of
teachers, administrators, and students in relation to one another. It
would recognize that the media through which students learn are
many and diffuse, and would thus emphasize the coordination of
all of a student's experiences within a well-defined yet "open" educational organization. Implicit in an aggregation model for change
is the belief that innovations are more likely to be invented or
adopted in a school organization when all those involved—students,
teachers, parents, and administrators—have been encouraged to

share their evaluations of what the school is doing and to work together toward improving it. In effect, therefore, an aggregational approach to institutional reform would require the school to operate as an "urban community school" rather than as a "four-walls school," according to Havighurst's distinction as described in Chapter 6.

The requirements imposed on a public school and its personnel by an aggregation model for change are substantial. First, students and staff would have to be convinced that school authorities "really mean it," and that significant improvements in the school and in their own situations within it are both feasible and worth the effort. Second, there would have to be a shared perspective among all participants regarding the goals of public education, the historical and structural aspects of school systems, the major problems they face, and appropriate directions and strategies for dealing with those problems. Perhaps ideally, such a perspective would be developed and shared as a preliminary step to planning changes in organization or practice. But schools are ongoing organizations, in which change must be instituted even as operations continue; thus, the perspectives of school administrators and teachers, as well as those of students and parents, would have to be sharpened and shared in the process of working together. A third requirement of an aggregation model for change would be encouragement of communication among all interested parties whenever a proposal is to be formulated or assessed. Although particular policy decisions, such as those related to budget or personnel, might ultimately rest with school officials, the political principle implied by an aggregation model would require participation and commitment of the widest possible range of individuals both in developing plans and then in carrying them out.

Until recently, because of the complexity they entail and the demands they place on an educational organization, programs consistent with an aggregation model for change have not been widely attempted in America's central city school systems. But given the failure of most specialized efforts at change, public disaffection with current urban school programs, and the growing interdependence among urban school, community, and governmental organizations, it would appear that innovations based on an aggregation model for change are worth attempting.[3] Later in this chapter, several specific suggestions for beginning to "open up" and modify the structure of a school will be examined.

Assessing Performance of Students and Schools

Characteristically, educational systems, like all "people-changing" institutions, operate without precisely defined criteria for effective performance. Only within certain disciplines, such as mathematics and the sciences related to it, do standardized achievement tests enable educators to compare degrees of student learning systematically and with some confidence, to define units and sequences of content to be learned, and to specify the probable conditions for mastery of that content. To date, most academic skills, and probably all educational outcomes associated with personal beliefs and values continue to elude translation into precise performance or behavioral objectives. A good deal of what the schools attempt, therefore, is extremely difficult to evaluate, thus making the causes of failure very hard to analyze and a judgment of what reforms would succeed very difficult to reach.

Even when reasonably valid and reliable measures of student achievement can be obtained, other problems tend to hamper reform. Efforts directed simply at improving mastery of particular subject areas may ignore other conditions, both in and outside the school, which severely impede learning. Most programs designed to reduce student dropout or to improve employability through special instruction and counseling have turned out to be incomplete or inadequate because they did not—and perhaps could not—get at the noneducational conditions within and outside the school that significantly affect student competence and motivation. Educators have not yet developed a systematic procedure for sorting out the multiple causes of student failure and for identifying the kinds of educational programs that will help students succeed. Consequently, we cannot know precisely why short-term increments in student performance based on intensive tutoring or exemplary Head Start programs typically have not been sustained after the students moved into regular school classrooms; or why even successful innovative curricular or instructional programs lose their potency when their personnel change or when they are introduced into new school settings. Most of the evidence collected to date, in fact, seems primarily to support the contention that the main causes of failure lie not within the school itself, but in the community beyond and especially in the labor market.

The methodological implication of all this is that we shall probably have to continue to approach the reform of schools—particularly those in large central cities—with only loose indications of what is wrong, how it came to be, and what specifically can be done about it. This uncertainty is all the more disturbing in view of the outrage, the name-calling, and the personal indictments that are part of the dialogue of school reform. It would be comforting to have more precise and hopeful answers to give to critics or to parents concerned that their children are "losing out." But answers of the kinds desired are simply not yet available. Given the problems of criteria and measurement faced by schools, with the resulting gap in information, it seems inevitable that any methodologies designed for urban school reform must be tentative and groping, at least for some years to come.

A basic methodological condition in urban school reform is therefore that the problems addressed will never have, in any real sense, a "solution." Problems that involve complex relationships among men or between man and his environment are thus part of a continuing social process and can never be fully solved; rather, they must be accommodated to and must always be treated tentatively. Lewis Schaw, in a very useful definition, speaks clearly to this principle of incrementalism when he writes that "work [is] . . . the replacement of a primitive problem in history by another, less primitive problem."[4]

For example, the construction of a dam is a deliberate, man-made intervention in natural processes, one intended to answer the need to store or control the movement of water. The construction of the dam, however, though it may temporarily alleviate the need for water supply or control, produces a host of new, less primitive needs and problems: it affects the ecology of the watershed, introducing a new set of natural and artificial conditions that have consequences for life in and beyond the region. So too, when a community builds a school, when teachers organize for collective bargaining, or when remedial tutoring is attempted to meet the special needs of urban students, a whole new set of consequences is put into motion.

Such deliberate interventions may or may not realize the objectives intended; even if they do, however, the interventions can be thought of as "solutions" to problems in only a very restricted sense. Methodologically, therefore, any educational change or effort at reform can be viewed most usefully if, like work, it is viewed as part of a continuing process of replacing one set of problems with another less onerous, but perhaps in the end more complex. The process of change and of reform is endless.

Achieving Perspective on Urban School Reform

Anyone seriously interested in urban school reform continually faces two related challenges: that of "tracking" the conditions in the larger urban scene that underlie the problems he observes, and that of placing the daily conditions and problems he observes in a larger perspective. Lacking such perspective, efforts at reform are likely to be primarily crisis-stimulated, myopic, and in the long run ineffectual. While serving as a review of the major themes already presented, the remainder of this chapter will suggest some of the concerns to be addressed by anyone holding such a perspective.

Urbanization

There is a lack not only of suitable appreciation for the contribution city living has made to the growth of civilization, but also, as

Melvin Webber notes, of adequate concepts for understanding the emerging urban social order.[5] Urban living no longer means living in a city; in fact, for some members of the intellectual and business elite, and for those who are part of the "jet set," cities are mainly convenient centers of communication and take-off for commuting between locations throughout the world. The traditional distinction between urban and rural folk, Webber also notes, has been nearly reversed. Not only does one no longer have to live in the center of a teeming metropolis in order to carry on an urban style of life, but, ironically, those whose folkways are most genuinely rural now comprise the majority of newcomers to cities throughout the world.

Because urban America is no longer limited to a few particular geographic settings, many so-called urban problems are too widespread either to be attributed solely to conditions in the city itself or to be treated simply through municipal programs. Public school systems of themselves can do little to influence the conditions that spawn drug addiction, juvenile delinquency, or ghetto poverty, any more than they can alter the main growth trends within an urban society. But they can cooperate with other interests in an effort to reduce or ameliorate such problems. Despite their lack of direct influence, urban school planners and administrators can anticipate in a general way how new arrangements and patterns of urban living are likely to affect the life styles, educational chances, and job prospects of their students. Two particular concomitants of urbanization, high population density and racial and socioeconomic stratification, demand the continuing attention of all who are concerned with the fate of urban schools.

We sometimes take the high population density of cities so much for granted as a general condition that we ignore its special effects upon such city institutions as schools. Our discussion of city schools has called attention to the deleterious effects of their great size: the development of cumbersome administrative bureaucracies, organizational resistance to change, costly administrative overhead, and centralized authority and control. But high population density has an even more important effect on urban school youngsters since, paradoxically, high density tends to enforce increased homogeneity of social class, race, and ethnic background within particular neighborhoods, schools, and classrooms.

To the extent that this kind of socioeconomic fragmentation and segregation occurs, a traditional benefit of city living, namely the opportunity to interact with and learn from people with differing life styles, is severely reduced. In this sense, then, many urban residents are as confined psychologically as traditional villagers, but without the compensating security which authentic village life provides. Moreover, because a child's learning in school depends less on the "weak actions" of a school and its teacher than on his "intense interactions" with other children in a social environment, the socioeconomic segregation which increases with a city's population size and density curtails the child's opportunities to learn from his peers.[6] Although he may feel more comfortable—more "familiar"—in classrooms with other students from similar racial, ethnic, and social class groupings, a child living in a densely populated city may learn even less about the diversity of values and life styles in American society than his counterpart living in a suburban or rural setting. In this, urban schools are failing to provide city youngsters with socially integrative educational experiences.

High population density, however, is not the only major contributing factor in the socioeconomic fragmentation of central city neighborhoods, schools, and classrooms. Equally contributory are the large-scale movements of population into, out of, and within most large metropolitan areas. In any large city in the United States today, the following groups of residents can be identified: successful, middle-class blacks, who are increasing rapidly in number but have not yet moved to the suburbs, either because they have not been able to obtain adequate housing or because they do not wish to live there as isolates; the working-class members of non-white minority groups who cannot afford to relocate even though they may work steadily and aspire to move; the large number of persons of various ethnic backgrounds who are poor because of age,

illness, or other personal misfortune and who have no alternative
to living in a city's low-rent districts; the whites who have the resources to move out but have chosen to remain because of attachment to certain neighborhoods or preference for the life styles available in the city; the middle-class whites who probably will leave
eventually, but who have not yet made a final decision; and the
growing hard core of lower-class residents who are primarily nonwhite and who lack either the capability or the incentive to find
and hold a steady job.

It is mainly persons in this last grouping who live in the ghettos.
Trapped by race, poverty, and/or their lack of employable skills,
ghetto dwellers are preponderantly represented on welfare rolls and
other social service lists. A large proportion of the children born
into ghetto families are locked almost from the start into a pattern
of school failure, unemployability, and social alienation. The inability of schools to have a meaningful influence on these children
is the single most agonizing problem in urban education today. No
large-scale programs of compensatory education seem to have
proved effective; special programs of tutoring, counseling, and
other services have realized only unstable, short-term gains. As city
schools are currently designed and operated, they seem pathetically
incapable of motivating and helping ghetto youngsters to engage in
productive, sustained academic learning. Moreover—this is perhaps
most troubling of all to educators—it seems doubtful that any
urban school reform will be sufficient to reverse the academic failure of these youngsters unless substantial improvements can also
be made in their living conditions, their family morale and resources, and their prospects for employment when their formal
schooling is complete.

Racial Integration

Two decades of political debate and action on school reform
were initiated in 1954 by the U.S. Supreme Court decision on racial segregation in public schools. Ideally, that interpretation of the
U.S. Constitution should have signaled an immediate end to racial

segregation in schools; in fact, however, it became simply the opening move in launching a large and enthusiastic civil rights movement, and after that a continuing effort to achieve not only racial
integration but equality of economic and social opportunity for all
Americans in all institutions of society.

Although the Constitution itself provides sufficient warrant for
integrating the nation's public schools, the proponents of integration have presented a number of other arguments. As James Coleman discovered in his extensive study of educational opportunity
in the United States, there is an important relation between segregation and academic performance: when Negro youngsters attend
predominantly white schools, their achievement, on the average, is
higher than when they attend predominantly Negro schools.

Guided by the 1954 Supreme Court decision and by such sequels
as the Civil Rights Act of 1965, and pressed by civil rights activists,
public school boards and administrators have made considerable
efforts during the 1960's and early 1970's to bring about a better
racial mix within their student populations. A whole range of alternative strategies has been attempted, from redrawing attendance
lines and establishing open-school policies to pairing school buildings and busing students. When it became apparent that the residents in most communities were not really interested in integrating
their schools, and that many white parents would—quietly at first,
but later openly—resist sending their children to schools attended
by a significant proportion of black children, school boards and
administrators tried to create new programs and school designs that
would be more attractive to the recalcitrant whites.

In Pittsburgh, for example, Superintendent of Schools Sidney
Marland (who later became U.S. Commissioner of Education) initiated a massive new program of school construction, called the
Great High Schools, for which he obtained a commitment of $50
million. As envisioned by Marland and the Pittsburgh School
Board, these Great High Schools were eventually to make up five
giant educational parks, so situated within the city as to maximize
the racial integration of student enrollments. The plan won a good

deal of initial support and was skillfully promoted during its early years; but after five years of developmental work, during which Marland resigned as Superintendent and the plan was periodically criticized by various segments of the Pittsburgh community, it was allowed slowly to die. During the 1970–71 school year, the Board finally rescinded all prior decisions regarding the plan.

The reasons for the abandonment of Pittsburgh's Great High Schools and the accompanying educational parks are typical of the failure to date of most efforts to integrate schools in large central cities. The escalating costs of school construction—and thus of the major reform envisioned in Pittsburgh—eventually exceeded the level of cost that citizens were willing to support. The ratio of black to white students in the city shifted so rapidly during the 1960's that not even large educational parks would have achieved acceptable levels of racial integration; in addition, the pace of "re-segregation" indicated that redrawing attendance lines could be viewed realistically as only a temporary measure. Finally, racial unrest in several of the city's existing high schools, enrolling no more than from 1,000 to 2,500 students each, was viewed as an ominous portent of what might happen in a racially mixed educational park enrolling from 5,000 to 6,000.

The most heated educational issue of the past few years has been, of course, that of busing youngsters to achieve racial integration within all schools of a district. It is apparently a strategy that nobody really favors, to achieve a goal in which only a minority of white parents and an uncertain majority of black parents seem to believe. As David Cohen has observed, the resistance to busing as a means of achieving racial integration is attributable, to a considerable extent, to the failure of both white and black supporters of integration to develop a "politics of common interest."[7] Given the tumultuous political debate and the strong cross-currents of educational policy at all governmental levels, including the ambiguous and contradictory statements emanating from Administration sources, it is difficult to see how, at this time, busing can contribute positively to school integration. In fact, the acrimony raised by recent busing programs—particularly those attempted in 1971 in such cities as Boston, San Francisco, and Pontiac, Michigan—and by political debate over busing during the 1972 Presidential campaign may actually have obscured and confounded still further the many less inflammatory efforts being made to achieve racial integration in public schools.

Given the formidable political issues involved, those responsible for the operation of urban schools during the next decade will be forced to walk a precarious tightrope as they attempt to deal with the problems growing out of racial segregation. They are obliged to implement the mandate of the Constitution as interpreted by the courts. Yet the obstacles before them will continue to be formidable. A racial mix will be difficult enough to achieve when the concentration of blacks in central cities is increasing daily; but it will be impossible so long as a substantial public opinion opposes not only the procedures, such as busing, but also the goals of school and residential integration. The courageous black children and parents who defied hostile mobs at Little Rock and countless other places to break the tradition of segregation in the 1950's had a great moral purpose clearly before them as they acted. But today few parents, either white or black, who advocate racially integrated schools are likely to regard the moral issue as sufficiently compelling to place their children in situations where they perceive their safety to be threatened. Urban schoolmen, even as they try to integrate their schools, must therefore also be able to convince their constituents that they can maintain school buildings that are pleasant, safe, and educationally productive places for children.

Authority and Control

Legally, the authority of a local school board and its professional personnel comes directly from the state government, through the Constitutional provision that it is the responsibility of each state to provide, regulate, and operate public schools for the education of its young. To varying degrees throughout the United States, however, state governments have seen fit to delegate this responsibility to local school districts. Over the years, local schools have come to exercise this responsibility in relative insulation from their constituents and from other political interests in the community.

Events of the last decade, however, have rapidly cut through that insulation. For the first time in their history, the nation's urban schools face serious threats to their authority and control. An early breakthrough, as we have noted, was the court-imposed mandate in 1954 for the racial integration of schools; more recently, there has emerged a demand for the reduction of disparities in educational achievement among children of different neighborhoods, races, and socioeconomic classes.

To those demanding racial integration, the slow progress made during the last two decades has been at least partially understandable: the obstacles to progress are at least identifiable and susceptible to analysis. By contrast, the failure of urban schools to raise the educational achievement levels of their most disadvantaged students, most of whom are both poor and nonwhite, has no ready rationale and no easily identifiable guilty parties other than the schools themselves. For all the millions of dollars expended by special compensatory education programs, the indicators of success are frustratingly few. It is thus no surprise that many inner-city residents no longer regard the public schools as legitimate educational institutions. Despite whatever formal authority the states have conferred on them, an increasing number of urban schools have gradually lost the kind of authority that clients typically accord an institution on the basis of its competence. When institutions thus lose the support of client groups, they lose as well much of the base for their real authority and control.

The mounting crisis of confidence in relations between city schools and their constituents is unlikely to subside until the schools either meet the demands of their critics or alter their traditional prerogatives. Two interrelated strategies for the latter, decentralization and community control, will be discussed here. The first will be viewed as essentially a strategy for changing the internal hierarchy in a school or school district, the second as a strategy for radically reconstituting the interface between a school and its immediate geographic community.

Decentralization. As treated here, decentralization is the shift of decision-making within an organization in such a way as to bring the process as close as possible to the individuals who will implement the decisions made. Usually this means moving responsibility for decisions "downward"—that is, rather than keeping all decisions in the hands of some centralized authority, the process is delegated by stages to the various levels of the organization. For this reason, decentralization is often seen as a useful way to overcome some of the traditional dysfunctions of an urban school bureaucracy and to reduce administrative red tape, thus opening the way for more communication and participation by staff, students, and parents in the reform and operation of schools.

The concept of a "development" bureaucracy is a possible model for redefining the administrative and organizational structure of an urban school district;[8] it is one way by which schools might achieve order and system without becoming unnecessarily rigid, hierarchical, or isolated from their clientele. Even the largest school systems, with their several administrative layers between teachers and school board, might conceivably make real allocations of power and responsibility to teachers, students, and community groups, for specific purposes over specific periods of time. Authority would be allocated in accordance with "functional necessity"; relationships would be "lateral instead of vertical"; and staff relations would be organized in accordance with the principle of "non-dominance." In a "development" bureaucracy, administrative roles thus might well overlap, so that superior-subordinate relationships would be different from one functional area to another.

The main point is that, to be effective, decentralization efforts will probably have to be part of a larger and more conscious policy for coordinating the activities of a school system with those of its clients and its community. Unfortunately, most recent efforts to decentralize large city school districts have revealed little interest in redistributing power and responsibility. Decentralization plans typically have amounted simply to breaking a total district into several smaller units or subdistricts, each administered by a deputy superintendent. These efforts have rarely gone beyond the subdistricts to individual school buildings and classrooms; only minimal authority and independence seem to have been dispersed. For instance, decisions about curriculum, the recruitment and screening of teachers, the negotiation of contracts, and the allocation of dollars still tend to be made by the central administrative office. It is still too early to tell whether even the well-publicized Bundy Plan, which led to division of the New York City public schools into thirty-one subdistricts, has actually brought about a substantial reallocation of authority and resources, not only to those newly created subdistricts but also to building personnel within each subdistrict.

Community Control. Decentralization, as a strategy for modifying the internal hierarchy of authority and control in a school or school district, can occur without any involvement of a district's larger community. On the other hand, community control involves significant redefinition of the interface between a school and its community. It typically includes decentralizing authority and control; but it also implies other kinds of organizational changes as well.

Most communities, of course, can be said to exercise some measure of control over their local public schools through a representative board of lay citizens responsible for making policy. By electing the members of that board and voting on tax levies and bond issues, most citizens control, at least indirectly, the operation of their public schools. But current proponents of community control in large cities have in mind not this traditional kind of influence, but a far more direct and radical involvement of the community in school operations. Typically, the argument for community control is focused on a single school building or cluster of buildings rather than on an entire school district, and calls for participation of community residents in making policy through direct rather than representative means. Such responsibilities as the hiring of personnel, design of curriculum, and allocation of resources are usually claimed by proponents of change for community representatives rather than for professional personnel; perhaps most significantly, community control is based on the premise that each school building can best serve its students by remaining autonomous. Carried to its extreme, community control would allow each school building in a city to be independently "owned" and operated by residents of the community it serves, setting up their own curriculum, hiring and firing their own teachers, and, managing the building, facilities and human resources by themselves.

The pressure for community control of urban schools generally comes from minority groups that are socioeconomically most disadvantaged. But these groups often have two different objectives in mind when they argue for community control. Some proponents see it as the most promising way of improving the educational opportunities available to students, whereas for others, particularly in black ghettos, it is primarily a way to increase the power of certain political interests. Inevitably, these two motivations become intermixed. The pressure for community control in black ghettos is frequently based on the conclusion that urban schools are illegitimate and lacking in the competence to educate the city's black and poor children. But the achievement level of youngsters is not the whole issue; if it were, as some have observed, the political attack on legitimacy would probably not be made. What is at issue for most black leaders is their disillusionment with the entire American political system and their demand for a "new social contract" between minority groups and the social institutions that serve them, one that redefines institutional authority and guarantees considerably more power to the clients of an institution.

In this sense, then, urban schools are but one of several social institutions in a city over which leaders of minority groups would like to have control. This is somewhat ironic, for urban schools are less riddled by inequity and injustice than most other social institutions. Understandably, therefore, urban educators who have long regarded themselves as pioneers in the fight for equality of minority groups are chagrined when they and their schools are declared illegitimate by the leadership of those very groups. But so long as schools fail to stimulate achievement by nonwhite children equal to that of white children, those moderate leaders of minority groups who perceive the issue of community control mainly in terms of educational gain will remain allied with the perhaps smaller minority of leaders who are determined to create a new political authority. Simply because of their geographic location, urban schools will continue to be extremely vulnerable to confrontation. Furthermore, in view of the additional jobs and power over resources that community control would bring, it would be naive to expect most members of minority groups to be pious and loyal supporters of urban schools on the basis of the marginal sympathy and support they have historically received from educators. Thus, urban schools will continue to be faced with the dual challenge of adequately educating a city's children, particularly those of minority groups, and of sharing some measure of their authority with the immediate communities surrounding each school building.

How are urban schools to respond to this pressure? There are certainly good reasons to be skeptical about the prospects. The pressure could, for instance, give birth to new and pernicious forms of cultural and political segregation, with retrogressively parochial effects on the values of young Americans and thus on all social institutions. Yet so long as fundamental inequities and injustices in our national life continue to produce racial and socioeconomic ghettos, we shall have to cope with the political consequences.

Deliberate, exploratory grants of power and resources for such projects as community-controlled schools may be the most sensible response possible to political pressures from the ghetto. In part, this may represent a surrender in the interest of arriving at a truce with the most alienated political forces in the ghetto. However, although control can always be used inappropriately and illegitimately, even the most radical proponents of community control of urban schools are likely to remain concerned about improving educational opportunities for youngsters. Granting a community greater control of its school would represent a significant change in the politics of education, but it would not be an irreversible change. The activities of any community-operated school would still be subject to inspection and evaluation by governmental agencies, since its budget would still depend greatly on state and federal resources. Those in control of the school would still receive much unfriendly criticism from their political opponents. And parents and children themselves would inevitably compare their current educational experiences with those possible under other arrangements. In sum, experiments with community control in urban school districts would not only be a useful step in the direction of reform, but might also help reduce the alienation of those minority group leaders who are understandably impatient with the failures of the American political system.

In light of events during the past two decades, perhaps any discussion of decentralization and community control is merely academic. To the extent that professional educators and community groups become polarized over the issue of community control, it will be resolved in terms of political power rather than of educational theory. It may already be too late for the leadership of many big-city school districts to institute deliberate reforms and thereby avoid such a political showdown with community activists. It is futile to say of any institution that certain steps should have been taken a decade ago; if that institution had been of a different kind a decade before, it might have done so. It may be that the growth of urban political and intellectual elites and of middle-class minority groups will still permit the negotiation of a redistributed balance of authority on rational rather than purely emotional and political terms.

In any event, urban school boards and administrators have little choice but to make the best possible effort to share their traditional power and to establish more flexible definitions of the role of staff, clients, parents, and community groups in operating their schools. The political trends associated with population change and the other conditions of urbanization described in this book will no longer permit boards, administrators, and teachers simply to stand pat.

Employment and Schooling

Urban schools have been more closely tied to the industrial labor market than most educators seem to realize or are willing to admit. To a large degree, public education is a creature of industrialism, since, not withstanding the humane motives of educational reformers in the nineteenth century, the political forces that have shaped public school systems have been motivated largely by an economic consideration, that of creating pools of trained and employable manpower.

Since World War II, and especially since 1957 when the Russian sputnik galvanized federal support for the education of scientific and technical manpower, the nation's schools and universities have been intimately bound up with industrial development. Technological advances have generated new jobs and specialties, each requiring ever more sophisticated training in a range of scientific, professional, and technical fields. At the same time, technological changes, especially those connected with automation, have precipitated a large-scale elimination of jobs in particular plants, cities, and industries, thus evoking anxious predictions that all but the highly skilled will eventually be displaced from the labor market. Whether or not these predicitions are valid, they have had the effect throughout the past decade of stimulating extensive manpower training programs for unemployed adults and of placing heavy pressure on schools to improve employability and reduce the dropout rate. To meet such demands, the nation's public schools have been forced inevitably to define their priorities in terms of national manpower needs.

In addition, urban schools will continue to face the challenge of reducing ghetto unemployment—a challenge they have neither the power nor the resources to meet adequately. Unless there are reforms in the labor market itself, any efforts by urban schools to improve the employability of youngsters from inner-city ghettos will continue to be insufficient and perhaps largely wasted; and, the schools will be condemned for one more failure to improve the life chances of disadvantaged young people.

We have considered a few of the roadblocks that job applicants from an inner city encounter when they look for employment. If they neither desire nor qualify for technical or clerical jobs, they find only low-level service jobs available within convenient commuting distance of their homes. Most new industrial plants employing large numbers of workers and offering attractive entry wages have been built or relocated in the suburbs of major metropolitan areas. To reach one of these from a central city, simply to apply for a job, requires lengthy and expensive commuting. Nor are efforts to attract industry to the city or to finance minority group businesses within the city itself, as described in Chapter Eight, ever likely to produce an adequate number and variety of jobs.

Broad metropolitan strategies are needed to increase the free flow of people among jobs and neighborhoods. This means that a critical mass of families from similar minority groups must be encouraged to relocate; to be most beneficial, there must also be extensive construction of low-income housing projects in the suburbs and the relocation to them of significant numbers of ghetto residents. Tokenism will not suffice. That proposals to construct low income housing usually bring white suburbanites to the barricades simply bears out the methodological point that there are no real "solutions" to social problems, only temporary resolutions which bring with them another, more complex set of new problems.

A second obstacle to the employment of residents of the inner city is the continuing practice by employers of assessing job applicants primarily on the basis of years of schooling and scores on personnel tests. In his study of the relation between education and employment, Ivar Berg concludes that employers have raised educational requirements without evaluating their relevance to the actual performance of workers on the job. "Policies calculated to generate job opportunities for a growing population," he writes, "would seem to deserve higher priority than those designed to rationalize, by their stress on education, the considerable difficulties imposed on those without academic credentials."[9]

There is no convincing evidence that years of schooling, beyond what is needed to acquire a basic education, affect an individual's performance on a wide range of industrial and service jobs or even in white-collar occupations; nor is there evidence that extent of schooling is a reliable indicator of an individual's capacity to be trained or the likelihood of his being promoted. Similarly, although standardized personnel tests may have limited utility in predicting the success of some kinds of training, they are not useful for predicting job performance; they may serve to identify candidates who have outstanding potential or who are bad risks, but they usually fail to differentiate reliably among the mass of candidates who fall in the middle range.

That employers continue to screen candidates on the basis of schooling and standardized test scores is understandable. As Edward Banfield suggests, ". . . it is at least plausible for [the employer] to assume that a diploma is evidence of some sort of achievement, or—more likely perhaps—that there is probably 'something wrong' with a boy who does not finish high school now that most do."[10] Dispensing with such screening devices would, of course, increase the traditional influence of personal connections, nepotism, and subjective bias. On the other hand, it would force employers to dispense with smoke screens in their hiring practices, and to accommodate more readily to requests for open hiring and for action programs designed to increase the employability of inner-city residents. Perhaps the fairest strategy for selecting among a pool of candidates for entry jobs would be a lottery, similar to that used for selecting draftees for military service.

A third employment handicap for residents of the inner city lies in the way the job market actually functions. Except for those who move into the professions as a result of extended formal education or into upper-level management positions through extensive on-the-job experience, for most American workers the primary means of attaining job security and higher income is through attachment to some stable organization.[11] Traditionally, the emphasis in public school education and in vocational guidance has been on encouraging students to identify themselves with some particular occupation. Except for well-organized professions and crafts, however, this is unlikely to be sufficient, in view of the nation's present labor market. At some phase of their careers, most workers are forced to compromise between the desires for independence and for stability by joining "the company" or "the union" or some governmental organization. Once they have taken this step, their status and security on the job are determined by organizational policy or by contractual agreements between labor and management.

Lack of access to large, stable organizations has been one of the most serious obstacles encountered by job applicants from the inner city. Their entry has traditionally been blocked by racial discrimination; by rationalized but generally invalid personnel screening requirements; by apprenticeship regulations, nepotism and a variety of subtle barriers erected by workers in organizations to exclude new competitors. Although there are still subtle inequities in the civil service process, most of the more flagrant barriers to entry and promotion have gradually been removed in publicly supported organizations. But to gain access to employment in stable private corporations, or to break the monopolies on entry into many craft unions, will continue to require intense political effort. The recent cooperation between black community groups and the federal government in efforts to open apprenticeship and journeyman lists to black workers in the construction trades is exemplary here. The blacks exerted pressure by demonstrating; the federal government exerted pressure by withholding funds for construction projects until contractors and unions agreed to employ and train a significant number of workers from black and other minority groups.

Although real improvement in the service relationship between urban schools and the existing labor market calls for the removal of some of these roadblocks to employment, there are nonetheless a number of things that urban schools themselves can do to improve the chances of their students. Improving the basic education of elementary school students—the ability to read, write, speak, and compute—is probably the single most critical step. For a number of years, the influence of automation, the elimination of jobs in specific industries, and rigorous personnel selection procedures used by employers fostered the illusion that job opportunities for unskilled and semiskilled workers would become increasingly scarce. Recent studies by manpower specialists, however, have largely dispelled that illusion: most jobs in both service and industrial occupations can be performed competently by workers *so long as they have an adequate basic education and some minimal on-the-job training*.[12] The failure to provide substantial numbers of students, particularly those in inner-city schools, with a basic education adequate to qualify them for jobs has become *the* major failure of urban education; more than any other cause, it has precipitated the current loss of confidence—particularly among blacks—and the pressure for radical reform.

Urban secondary schools must also continue the effort to develop viable alternatives to the academic curriculum for those students who are unwilling or unable to go on to college. To a large extent, city schools have been pioneers in vocational education, vocational guidance, work-study programs, and curricula designed to stimulate career planning. Over the years, however, most of these programs have been carried out in a sterile and desultory fashion; moreover, they have typically failed to portray the "world of work" in a realistic way. Students have frequently found the programs dull and irrelevant, if not a total waste or an imposition.

There is some hope that the new emphasis by the U.S. Office of Education on "career education" will stimulate vocational development activities in urban schools. Proposals have recently been made, for example, that every student in high school be assigned to paid employment during part of the school day: for an hourly wage, set on a sliding scale according to age, the student would perform a variety of tasks in school and out. Acceptable progress in regular studies would have to be demonstrated in order to remain in paid employment. At first blush, the proposal appears extravagant; but given what we know of human motivation and of the conditions necessary for effective learning, it might provide students with an incentive well worth the cost.

Yet another action that urban schools—in fact, all schools—can take to improve the relation between employment and schooling is to reexamine and possibly modify some of their basic assumptions about how much formal education is really needed. In the United States, the extension of formal schooling has come to be equated with the expansion of opportunity. That a college education is at least theoretically accessible to all students when they enter high school has gradually led to the uncritical view that the more schooling the better, regardless of individual interests, abilities, and employment prospects. Naturally, all students—including those in inner-city ghetto schools—are entitled to an equal opportunity to attend college, and should be encouraged to do so if their past school achievement and personal disposition make this a realistic course; but, as students move into the higher school grades, they should also be encouraged continually to reassess all the alternatives.

These are simply the traditional aims of educational and vocational guidance programs. Less traditional is the proposal that leaving high school early be a real option for some, or even most, young people. Ideally, exercising this option should be related to a plan for work; but even if it is not, students and their parents ought to be given the choice. The expansion of work-study programs in which students spend part of their school day on the job is one of many possible strategies for those students who plan to leave school early. Regardless of the strategy chosen, it is a waste and an indignity to force adolescents to sit in a classroom as players in educational games which they see as largely irrelevant.

Ultimately, of course, the onus of failure is not on the student but on the school. By and large, public secondary schools have failed to provide students with a suitable range of alternative learning situations. Enabling students to leave school with a certificate of completion, perhaps as early as the ninth grade, could have several important payoffs: it could make a real connection between employment and schooling; it could foster a realization by students that decisions about work are ultimately theirs; and it might foster a more creative approach by school administrators and teachers to their own responsibilities.

Obviously, any such revision of policy or programs will be ineffectual unless conditions in the labor market become more hospitable to young people. Here, once again, the prospects for change and reform in the nation's urban schools depend precariously on needed reforms in society itself.

School Organization and Programs

Most discussions of educational reform focus on proposed changes in school organization, programs, and practices. The term "educational innovation," for example, is applied almost exclusively to the internal workings of a school district. Throughout our treatment of urban education, we have tried to emphasize the interdependence between urban school systems and the larger urban setting. Thus, current efforts to equalize dollar resources and educational opportunities for students will be only minimally effective unless they are part of a larger strategy for bringing about urban change.

Equalizing Resources and Opportunities. Many proposals for school reform assume that equality of educational opportunity in public schools is in itself a worthy goal—and that it can be achieved if only we equalize the expenditures for education. To date, this assumption has not been supported by empirical evidence. We have yet to prove, in fact, that even *unequal* expenditures necessarily benefit those for whom they are made. A vast array of compensatory education programs have been initiated during the past decade, and millions of dollars have been made available to local school districts, for tutorials, special after-school activities, instructional specialists, and smaller classes. Unfortunately, however, these programs generally have failed to produce significant educational gains for students.

Follow-up studies of the Head Start Program gave the first indications of failure: when disadvantaged youngsters left Head Start and entered first grade, the ground that had been gained through special services was quickly lost. In 1966, Coleman concluded from his study of educational opportunity in America that spending more money on buildings, equipment, and special services had had little differential effect upon student achievement. Of all the variables examined, he found that the social class of a student's parents, perennially the chief indicator in twentieth-century social science research, continued to be so for success in school.

Finally, evaluations of the many compensatory programs financed under Title I of the Elementary and Secondary Education Act confirm that although the programs have tended to improve school conditions, enliven attitudes, raise attendance, reduce vandalism, and make teachers happier, very few produced significant gains in student achievement. As David Cohen has observed, "The evidence from children in programs of compensatory education . . . was no better than that of comparable children who had no more money spent on them. And some programs (such as the More Effective Schools program in New York City) have invested much more—up to $500 per pupil per year; the evidence there is mixed, but even the most enthusiastic reading indicates that it reveals only a small achievement gain."[13]

In addition to the fact that children learn not only at different rates, but in different ways, one of the principal reasons for the general failure of compensatory education programs is believed to be that too little was spent too late to make any real difference in the educational experiences of disadvantaged children. In 1967–68, Title I of ESEA increased instructional expenditures for each participating child by about $65. This represented less than 15 per cent of the average expenditure per pupil throughout the United States. As Cohen suggests, "The simplest way to figure the amount of educational improvement that an increase like that can buy is in terms of the time a teacher devotes to her children. If a teacher has thirty students and works a five-hour day (and if we imagine that she divides the day into a series of tutorials), then each student receives a ten-minute daily tutorial. An increase of 10 per cent in the teaching staff would add one minute to the daily individual attention a student receives."[14] Cohen wryly concludes, "That does not exactly constitute an educational revolution." Perhaps, as Harold Howe observes, a "critical mass" of additional services is needed to make a real difference; for instance, in programs in California and Connecticut, there were significant achievement gains after adding three hundred dollars per child each year for compensatory education.[15] This last observation suggests that compensatory education has not really "failed," but rather that efforts to implement programs have been too sparse and too haphazard to permit careful assessment.

In mid-1971, a new breakthrough in efforts to equalize educational opportunities occurred when the California Supreme Court ruled in *Serrano* v. *Priest* that disparities among school districts in their expenditures per pupil, even though resulting from differences in the wealth of those districts, are unconstitutional in that they deny children equal protection under the Fourteenth Amendment. After that decision, similar challenges to current school finance practices were made in a number of other states. If the California decision is upheld, legislatures in all states—with the possible exception of Hawaii, which already has a single, statewide school system—will be pressed to devise new procedures for equalizing the funds available to support each child's education. In public education, the case could be a legal milestone equal to the 1954 decision by the U. S. Supreme Court on desegregation: if states are compelled to equalize their expenditures per pupil, it is almost inevitable that the local property tax will be de-emphasized or eliminated as a major source of school revenue. Instead of forcing school districts to depend on local dollars for the majority of their funds, thereby allowing for considerable disparities in expenditure across districts, the states most likely will be forced to assume the full costs of elementary and secondary education, and to equalize expenditures per pupil by limiting or stabilizing spending in wealthy districts and providing additional funds where needed in poorer districts. Traditional "equalization formulas"—which in fact have rarely equalized—will have to be significantly revised, and state school resources considerably increased.

The extent to which the effort to equalize the dollar resources available to school districts will benefit urban school systems remains to be seen. Given the continuing high costs of education in large central cities, and given the high cost of effective compensatory education programs, a formula to equalize educational expenditures across a state simply on a dollar-for-dollar basis will be unfair and detrimental to big-city school districts. On the other hand, the prospect of breaking the traditional rural stranglehold on state education funds is cause for some optimism on the part of urban schoolmen.

Opening Up the Schools. A basic lesson of compensatory education programs is that substantial school improvement requires significant changes in attitudes and behavior, not simply revisions in organization, procedure, and materials. Schools are best conceived as "labor intensive" rather than "capital intensive" organizations. Thus, it is encouraging that educational reformers have gradually rejected the strategies for change, popular in the 1950's, that were directed primarily toward consolidating small units, putting up large buildings, and making more economical use of expensive laboratories and technological devices. Today, educational reformers seem to be moving gradually toward accepting proposals consonant with the aggregation model described in this chapter. They are less concerned simply with adding special programs and facilities, and more with seeking changes that will liberalize the climate of the schools and the relations between teachers and students, while maintaining disciplined activity and a sound organizational structure. The concern of reformers with the quality of relations among students, teachers, parents, administrators, and paraprofessionals, as opposed to curricula and instructional methods, are reflected to some degree in such terms as "organizational development," "administrative team," "planning unit," and "self-renewal."

One of the most effective ways to open up a school, as has been suggested, is to decentralize authority. This means spreading responsibilities for decision-making throughout the building, giving sanction for all personnel to participate in the decisions relevant to them, and focusing the process at the precise point where the decision will be implemented. But this kind of decentralization will rarely be effective if it is attempted simply by mandate; it will need thorough discussion and collective participation by all personnel in a particular building.

Mario Fantini offers several operational suggestions for facilitating this process, with teachers in particular.[16] Initially, he suggests, teachers should be brought together in small groups as frequently as possible during the school day. This may well require reshaping the school's daily schedule, a step that should not be taken reluctantly; that is, the time for teachers to meet should not be grudged, as though they were wasting time that could be better spent in the classroom. Among the more short-sighted norms in education is the assumption that one is a teacher only when he is standing before a class, and its corollary, that planning is not nearly as important as teaching.

There is also a need for someone in the school to play the role of instructional leader and serve as a consultant to teachers about curricular planning and instructional practice. As a consultant, he should have little or no administrative authority and should not be placed in the position of having to evaluate for the school record the teachers with whom he consults. It would therefore be difficult for a building principal to play this role of instructional leader. To play it successfully, one must be able to free himself for part of the time from the "administrivia" which occupies the usual work day of a principal; he must be freed of the responsibility for official evaluation of the teachers' performance, and he must be able to minimize the authority of his status when working with teachers. Although such a role might be perceived by a principal as robbing him of some of his traditional status, the loss, if any, should be compensated by the prestige and personal satisfaction of creating a staff of teachers who have more autonomy, higher morale, and increased competence.

Team meetings at first are likely to accomplish only minimal tasks. For most teachers, accustomed to working with youngsters in "egg-crate" classrooms, responsible group planning during the regular work day will be entirely new. They will need experience with the group process itself, as well as perceptive support from the consultant, if they are to develop skill in evaluating what they do or to initiate promising changes. Those teachers who are not able to adapt successfully to a team approach must be permitted to find their own best way to function. Others will gradually emerge as natural leaders; as they do, it may be useful to incorporate them in a "school cabinet" where their efforts to stimulate and coordinate developmental activities throughout the school can be given formal sanction. This cabinet should not merely be an arm of the principal, but should have its own set of responsibilities for curricular and instructional decision-making.

Attitudes toward the teaching-learning process also are important in opening up schools and classrooms. Learning can occur whenever two human beings interact, and so need not be perceived as some mysterious operation peculiar to the interactions between student and teacher. In fact, a significant amount of a child's learning in school results from his interactions with classmates. The goal of successful reform is not simply "open classrooms" and "open schools" —although these may be a desirable objective—but a climate for learning in which each student recognizes that he is ultimately responsible for the process and that all other individuals in the school, including his peers, are potential resources. This is not to suggest that teachers either can or should be absolved from direct responsibility for their students' learning, or that students should simply be encouraged to be spontaneous and creative. Rather, a structured curriculum evolves, but it is oriented to individuals and carried out in an open and flexible learning environment.[17]

Some educators argue that, a structured curriculum is inconsistent with an open classroom. In practice, however, there is no reason why a classroom environment cannot be one in which students sometimes work individually under the guidance of a teacher and at other times with structured curricular materials. In their comprehensive plan for an urban school, Robert Meeker and Daniel Wyler have proposed just such a synthesis.[18] Their model school would have an open-ended curriculum, including presentations, small group meetings, and self-directed individual study; at the same time, it would have a structured curriculum for helping students acquire certain basic skills and information that are prescribed by the state or district in a standardized course of study. As proposed, the two curricula would be separately maintained so that neither takes staff time, commitment, or resources from the other; each would have its own "faculty," selected on the basis of professional competencies and interests. How strict a division between the two curricula would actually need to be drawn for both to survive in an open school or open classroom remains to be tested; Meeker and Wyler's proposal, however, suggests an operational strategy for enabling students to make the most productive use of each.

Local Power and Central Coordination. Efforts to open up schools and classrooms may actually be enhanced by refining and strengthening certain functions in the central administration of a school district, thus in effect setting up another antinomy. Havighurst offers some general rules for working toward a satisfactory balance of power and responsibility between a large central office and each local school.[19] Summarized in part, his suggestions are:

1. Increased educational options would be made available to parents and students by providing for open attendance among an array of neighborhood schools and superior "magnet" schools; the latter would be accessible to every student.

2. Substantial responsibility would be delegated to local community groups; each principal would be required to organize a school–

community advisory council which would be allotted funds for development activities.

3. Central administrations would maintain pools of professional and nonprofessional personnel and retain, initially at least, control over the appointment of professional employees; if continuing study warranted, however, even the power to appoint teachers and administrators might be transferred to local school councils.

4. The central administrative office would continue to control capital outlays and to record and audit all transactions of local councils.

5. School districts would increase their cooperation across metropolitan areas; state and federal funds would be allocated so as to foster such cooperation.

"Achieving a constructive alliance between localized power and decision-making and areawide power and decision-making," Havighurst believes, "is the main task of educators in the large cities and metropolitan areas during the 1970's."

Reforms Unreported

Because of our focus on the burdens of urban education and on the methodological and practical obstacles to urban school reform, it has not been possible to describe the hundreds of innovative projects conducted in recent years. These have included reforms in curricula and classroom practices, in the preparation of teachers and other personnel, and, with increasing frequency, in the design of new organizational structures. Evaluations of these projects are found in special urban education issues of many educational journals.

From the "aggregational" perspective favored by the authors, the most promising proposals are concerned with organizational reform and with improving the climate of schools. To evaluate such projects, however, would require quite a different kind of book.

In Retrospect

On the whole, I think that neither the primitive societies nor the ancient civilized societies show us, except rarely, the phenomenon of conscious reform in their institutions. It is not easy for men to adopt the explicit position that it is their work to make over human living. Ancient reformers speak as if they were restoring the purity of the past.

Yet in a time of great crisis the minds of men imagine a future that is different from the past. Reform has two parts: a vision of an altered future, and a program for reaching it. It is the vision, the dream, that comes easier to a people. It takes longer in the human career for people to formulate and adopt programs of reforming action.[1]

ROBERT REDFIELD

So with the American dream of equality of opportunity which gave shape to the American Revolution and to much subsequent political and social change in other nations. The U.S. Constitution itself is a kind of "program of reforming action," a vital instrument for guiding and controlling political and social activity throughout the past two hundred years. In the visions of Noah Webster, Horace Mann, and other nineteenth-century educational reformers, universal education was the main program for extending political and social equality; the common school was the expression of their

279

vision. The twentieth century saw schooling for all become a reality; but the current plight of urban education is a mark of our failure to realize the dream of equal opportunity.

It is easier, as Robert Redfield suggests, for people to share an ideal than to carry out the reforms necessary to realize it. In our treatment of urban education, the guiding ideals have remained largely implicit; nor have we dwelt much on specific reform programs. Instead, we have tried to describe those aspects of schools as urban institutions of which reformers most need to be cognizant.

The dreams and the reforms of the nineteenth century were the outgrowth of an agrarian society in which there was a prevailing moral consensus. In it, educational reformers discovered a common framework for defining their goals. But the trend toward urbanization has brought with it new and complex problems—above all, the secularization and cultural pluralism that have dissolved the moral consensus typical of an agrarian community.

Urban schools can no longer transmit either a cohesive moral view or the special body of knowledge associated with a common cultural heritage. Their instructional role must now be to facilitate the learning process, with less privilege to dictate the specific content of what is learned. They can help students to form their own values and to sort out alternatives and possibilities. And they can help in discovering what urban society is and how it works.

The implicit purpose of the school as defined by Solon Kimball and James E. McClellan is "to bring the child from the world of the family and induct him into the corporate world, but to do this without destroying his willingness and ability to re-establish his own nuclear family . . . Only by dying can an American escape the drive for movement and change; this leaves only two alternatives for one who would live as a member of this new social order: either he can be carried along as a passive passenger, or he can be himself a moving force in determining his own destiny. The difference will be the degree to which he *knows* what the system is."[2] Students, parents, educators and noneducators are all involved in that transforming process. For all of us, the responsibility is inescapable.

Notes

Preface

1. Lawrence A. Cremin, *The Transformation of the School: Progressivism in American Education, 1876–1957* (New York: Knopf, 1961).

2. Sol Cohen, *Progressives and Urban School Reform: The Public Education Association of New York City: 1895–1954* (New York: Teachers College, Columbia University, 1963).

3. Colin Greer, *Cobweb Attitudes* (New York: Teachers College Press, 1970).

4. The fifty cities are: Akron, Atlanta, Baltimore, Birmingham, Boston, Buffalo, Chicago, Cincinnati, Cleveland, Columbus, Dallas, Dayton, Denver, Detroit, El Paso, Fort Worth, Honolulu, Houston, Indianapolis, Jersey City, Kansas City, Long Beach, Los Angeles, Louisville, Memphis, Miami, Milwaukee, Minneapolis, New Orleans, New York, Newark, Norfolk, Oakland, Oklahoma City, Omaha, Philadelphia, Phoenix, Pittsburgh, Portland, Rochester, St. Louis, St. Paul, San Antonio, San Diego, San Francisco, Seattle, Tampa, Toledo, Tulsa, and the District of Columbia.

5. Abraham Bernstein, *The Education of Urban Populations* (New York: Random House, 1967).

Chapter 1

1. "Newsfront: Hazlett on Job Hazards," *Phi Delta Kappan*, L (October 1968), 135.

2. Adapted from Bernard J. McCormick, "Toward the Education Park: Pittsburgh," *The Schoolhouse in the City*, ed. Alvin Toffler (New York: Praeger, 1968), 200–201.

3. "Dr. Henley's Cry for Help," *The Washington Post* (December 8, 1969).

4. Adapted from Perry McMahon, "Board Disruptions Barred by Judge," *The Pittsburgh Press* (February 20, 1969).

5. "Public Schools: Academic Sickness in New York," *Time* (March 24, 1967), 35, 36.

6. Adapted from Nadeane Walker, "Dallas Busing Plan Ignites City-Wide Opposition," *The National Observer* (June 19, 1971).

7. "Raid at School Nets Seven Narcotics Sellers," *The Los Angeles Times* (October 10, 1969).

8. Fred M. Hechinger, "N. Y. U. Adopting a School for Brooklyn Slum Study," *The New York Times* (July 17, 1966).

9. Homer Bigart, "N. Y. U. Clinic Stalled in Trying To Improve School," *The New York Times* (November 26, 1967).

10. Adapted from "Sands Junior High in Brooklyn Is Found Facing an Explosion by Students," *The New York Times* (February 23, 1969).

11. Adapted from an Associated Press release datelined Portland, Oregon, September 16, 1971.

12. Adapted from Richard J. H. Johnston, "Insurance on Schools Becomes Hard To Obtain After Disorders," *The New York Times* (October 12, 1969).

13. Adapted from an Associated Press release datelined Boston, Massachusetts, September 22, 1971.

14. "19 Teacher Demands on Board Listed," *The Pittsburgh Press* (January 14, 1969).

15. "Newsfront: A New Tactic," *Phi Delta Kappan*, L (June 1968), 609.

16. "A Public School Classroom," *HGSEA Bulletin* (Summer 1969), 1, 3.

17. " 'Great Schools' Plan Abandoned," *Phi Delta Kappan*, LII (November 1970), 189.

18. "Replacements Hard To Find," *Christian Science Monitor* (February 3, 1969).

19. "Newsfront: Inner-City Grads Unemployed," *Phi Delta Kappan*, LI (December 1969), 224.

Chapter 2

1. Nat Hentoff, *Our Children Are Dying* (New York: Viking Press, 1966); James Herndon, *The Way It Spozed To Be* (New York: Simon and Schuster, 1968); Herbert Kohl, *36 Children* (New York: New American Library, 1967); Jonathan Kozol, *Death at an Early Age* (Boston: Houghton Mifflin, 1967).

2. Robert J. Havighurst, "Requirements for a New Criticism," *Phi Delta Kappan*, XL (September 1968), 21.

3. *Ibid.*, 20.

4. Melvin M. Webber, "The Post-City Age," *Daedalus*, XCVII (Fall 1968), 1091–92.

5. Raymond Callahan, *Education and the Cult of Efficiency* (Chicago: The University of Chicago Press, 1962).

6. Lawrence A. Cremin, *The Transformation of the School: Progressivism in American Education, 1876–1957* (New York: Knopf, 1961), 20–21.

7. Sol Cohen, *Progressives and Urban School Reform* (New York: Teachers College, Columbia University, 1963).

8. Cremin, 17.

9. *Ibid.*, 19.

10. *Ibid.*, 18.

11. David K. Cohen and Marvin Lazerson, "Education and the Industrial Order," a paper read at the annual meeting of the American Educational Research Association in Minneapolis, Minnesota, March 6, 1970.

12. Dana F. White, "Education in the Turn-of-the-Century City: The Search for Control," *Urban Education*, IV (July 1969), 170.

13. Edgar Friedenburg, *The Vanishing Adolescent* (Boston: Beacon Press, 1959).

14. Kenneth E. Boulding, "General Systems Theory—The Skeleton of Science," *Management Science*, II (1956), 205.

15. *Ibid.*

16. Talcott Parsons, *Structure and Process in Modern Societies* (Glencoe: Free Press, 1960); Talcott Parsons *et al.*, *Working Papers in the Theory of Action* (Glencoe: Free Press, 1953).

17. Daniel Levine and Robert J. Havighurst, "Social Systems of a Metropolitan Area," *Metropolitanism: Its Challenge to Education*, ed. Robert J. Havighurst, The Sixty-seventh Yearbook of the National Society for the Study of Education (Chicago: University of Chicago Press, 1968), 52–53.

18. James Thompson, *Organizations in Action* (New York: McGraw-Hill, 1967), 163.

19. *Ibid.*, 10.

Chapter 3

1. Lewis Mumford, *The City in History* (New York: Harcourt, Brace, and World, 1961), 82–83.

2. Jane Jacobs, *The Economy of Cities* (New York: Random House, Vintage Books Edition, 1970), 36.

3. Hannah Arendt, *The Human Condition* (Chicago: University of Chicago Press, 1958), 33.

4. Mumford, 103.

5. John W. Dyckman, "Civic Order in an Urbanized World," *Daedalus*, XCV (Summer, 1966), 797.

6. James M. Gavin and Arthur Hadley, "The Crisis of the Cities: The Battle We Can Win," *Saturday Review* (February 24, 1968), 30.

7. A Standard Metropolitan Statistical Area (SMSA) is defined by the U. S. Bureau of the Census as "a county or group of contiguous counties which contains at least one city of 50,000 inhabitants or more, or 'twin cities' with a combined population of at least 50,000. In addition to the county or

counties containing such a city or cities, contiguous counties are included in an SMSA, if according to certain criteria, they are socially and economically integrated with the central city." The Bureau of the Census recognized approximately 250 SMSA's in the 1970 census, including 231 defined in 1967 and additional ones defined in 1970.

8. Harvey Cox, *The Secular City* (New York: Macmillan, 1965), 85.

9. *Ibid.*, 85.

10. Jean Gottman, *Megalopolis: The Urbanized Northeastern Seaboard of the United States* (Cambridge, Mass.: M.I.T. Press, 1961).

11. John B. Calhoun, "The Social Use of Space," unpublished manuscript (Bethesda, Md.: National Institutes of Health, 1962).

12. Robert Penn Warren, *All the King's Men* (New York: Harcourt, Brace, 1946), 188–89.

13. Cox, 1–2.

14. *Ibid.*, 147.

15. George D. Spindler, "Education in a Transforming Culture," *Harvard Educational Review*, XXV (Summer 1955), 149.

16. Urie Bronfenbrenner, "The Changing American Child," *Journal of Social Issues*, XVII (1, 1961), 6.

17. Harold Howe in August 1967 at a conference on urban school planning, sponsored by the Stanford School Planning Laboratory and the Educational Facilities Laboratories of New York.

18. Cox, 33–51.

19. Louis Wirth, "Urbanism as a Way of Life," *Cities and Society*, eds. Paul K. Hott and Albert J. Reiss (New York: The Free Press, 1957), 54.

20. Cox, 52–73.

21. For an extended and detailed description of the plight of American cities, see the well-publicized *Report of the National Advisory Commission on Civil Disorders*, published in 1968 by the U. S. Government Printing Office. For an updating of the so-called Kerner Report, see the 1971 report by the National Urban Coalition entitled *The State of the Cities*. This assessment of progress since 1968 indicates that conditions generally worsened between 1967 and 1971. "Housing is still the national scandal it was then. . . . Schools are more tedious and turbulent. . . . The rates of crime and unemployment and disease and heroin addictions are higher. . . . Welfare rolls are larger. And, with few exceptions, the relations between minority communities and the police are just as hostile." Coalition members concluded, "The most disturbing point most of those we spoke with made was that they had no faith at all in 'the system'—the government and the private wielders of power—as a protector or a provider."

22. Families and unrelated individuals are classified as being above or below the poverty level by using the poverty index adopted by a Federal Interagency Committee in 1969. Income cutoffs are adjusted to take into account such factors as family size, sex, age of family head, number of children, and farm–nonfarm residence. These poverty cutoff levels are updated each year to

reflect changes in the Consumer Price Index. In 1969 the poverty threshold for a nonfarm family of four was $3,743; in 1959 it was only $2,973.

23. U. S. Department of Commerce, Bureau of the Census, *The Social and Economic Status of Negroes in the United States, 1970*, Current Population Reports, Series P-23, No. 38 (Washington, D.C..: U. S. Government Printing Office, 1971), 1.

Chapter 4

1. Sam D. Sieber, "Organizational Influences on Innovative Roles," *Knowledge Production and Utilization in Educational Administration*, eds. Terry L. Eidell and Joanne M. Kitchell (Eugene, Oregon: The Center for the Advanced Study of Educational Administration, 1968), 122.

2. New York City Public Schools, *Facts and Figures: 1968/69*.

3. Robert J. Havighurst, "Metropolitan Development and the Educational System," *The School Review*, LXIX (Autumn 1961), 252.

4. Basil G. Zimmer and Amos H. Hawley, *Metropolitan Area Schools: Resistance to District Reorganization* (Beverly Hills: Sage Publications, 1968), 42.

5. Thomas R. Dye, "Urban School Segregation: A Comparative Analysis," *Urban Affairs Quarterly*, IV (December 1968), 143.

6. William G. Buss, Jr., "The Law and Education of the Urban Negro," *Educating an Urban Population*, ed. Marilyn Gittell (Beverly Hills: Sage Publications, 1967), 80.

7. Dye, 144.

8. U. S. Congress, *Civil Rights Act*, Public Law 352, 88th Congress, 2nd Session, 1964, 247.

9. U. S. Department of Health, Education, and Welfare, *Equality of Educational Opportunity*, Summary Report, Documents Catalogue Number FS 5.238:38000 (Washington, D.C.: U. S. Government Printing Office, 1968), 3.

10. Thomas Pettigrew, "School Integration in Current Perspective," *The Urban Review*, III (January 1969), 4.

11. U. S. Commission on Civil Rights, *Racial Isolation in the Public Schools*, Introduction to Summary Report, CCR Clearinghouse Publication No. 7, March 1967.

12. *Ibid.*, 1.

13. David Rogers, "Obstacles to School Desegregation in New York City," *Educating an Urban Population*, ed. Marilyn Gittell (Beverly Hills: Sage Publications, 1967), 157–58.

14. Robert J. Havighurst, *The Public Schools of Chicago* (Chicago: The Board of Education of The City of Chicago, 1964), 35.

15. *Ibid.*, 25.

Chapter 5

1. James S. Coleman, "Equal Schools or Equal Students," *The Public Interest*, IV (Summer 1966), 73–74.

2. Urie Bronfenbrenner, "The Split-Level American Family," *Saturday Review* (October 7, 1967), 60.

3. Frederick Shaw, "Educating Culturally Deprived Youth in Urban Centers," *Phi Delta Kappan*, XLV (November 1963), 93.

4. Carl E. Thornblad, "A Summary of the Fiscal Impact of a Concentration of Low Income Families on the Public Schools—A Study of Public Housing and Public Education in Chicago in 1962," based on a study conducted by the National Opinion Research Center and submitted during a Hearing before the General Subcommittee on Education of the Committee of Education and Labor, House of Representatives, Ninety-first Congress, First Session, on H. R. 1285 (Washington, D.C., March 4, 1969), 6.

5. For related studies, see Edward Frankel and George Forlano, "Pupil Mobility and Variation in IQ Trends," New York City Board of Education, Bureau of Educational Research, 1964 (mimeo.); Joseph Justman, "Stability of Academic Aptitude and Reading Test Scores on Mobile and Non-Mobile Disadvantaged Children," presented at the Fourth Work Conference on Curriculum and Teaching in Depressed Urban Areas, Teachers College, Columbia University, June 21-July 2, 1965; Blanche R. Kasindorf, "The Effects of Pupil Transiency on Pupil Functioning," New York City Board of Education, Bureau of Educational Program Research and Statistics, Publication No. 202, 1963.

6. Paul A. Witty and Paul J. Kinsella, "A Report on Televiewing in 1961," *Elementary English* (January 1962), 26.

7. Wilbur Schramm, "Mass Media and Educational Policy," *Social Forces Influencing American Education*, ed. Nelson B. Henry, The Sixtieth Yearbook of the National Society for the Study of Education (Chicago: University of Chicago Press, 1961), 208.

8. Sprague Vonier, "Television—The Urban Outlook," *Television Quarterly*, III (Winter 1964), 25.

9. These data are based on special studies of American Negroes and of metropolitan–nonmetropolitan distinctions, conducted by the U. S. Bureau of the Census in the 1960's and as part of the 1970 census.

10. Alan K. Campbell and Philip Meranto, "The Metropolitan Education Dilemma," *Educating an Urban Population*, ed. Marilyn Gittell (Beverly Hills: Sage Publications, 1967), 23–24.

11. Richard L. Derr, "Urban Educational Problems: Models and Strategies," *Educating an Urban Population*, ed. Marilyn Gittell (Beverly Hills: Sage Publications, 1967); Patricia Sexton, *Education and Income: Inequalities in Our Public Schools* (New York: Viking Press, 1962); H. Thomas James, J. Alan Thomas, and Harold J. Dyck, *Wealth, Expenditures and Decision-Making for Education* (Stanford, Calif.: Stanford University Press, 1963); Jesse Burkhead, *Input and Output in Large City High Schools* (Syracuse, N. Y.: Syracuse University Press, 1967); James S. Coleman *et al.*, *Equality of Educational Opportunity* (Washington, D.C.: U. S. Government Printing Office, 1966).

12. Bronfenbrenner, 61.

13. Carl Dolce, "The Inner City—A Superintendent's View," *Saturday Review* (January 11, 1969), 36.

14. Samuel Shepard, Jr., "The Disadvantaged Child," *The Schoolhouse in the City*, ed. Alvin Toffler (New York: Praeger, 1968), 82.

15. "Where Teachers Teach," *NEA Research Bulletin*, LXVI (May 1968), 47.

16. *Pennsylvania State Education Reporter*, XXXIV (April 13, 1966), 48.

17. In 1969–70, only 19 per cent of the nation's urban teachers taught in buildings less than ten years old; the comparable figure for suburban teachers was 34 per cent. By contrast, 48 per cent of all urban teachers, but less than 21 per cent of all suburban teachers worked in buildings more than thirty years old. *NEA Research Bulletin* (October 1972), 82.

18. Howard K. Holland and Armand J. Galfo, *An Analysis of Research Concerning Class Size*, Research Contribution to Educational Planning, Number II (Richmond, Va.: State Department of Education, Division of Educational Research, November 1964).

19. William P. McLure, *Fiscal Policies of the Great Cities in the United States* (Chicago: The Research Council of the Great Cities Program for School Improvement, 1961).

20. Michael D. Usdan, "Some Issues Confronting School Administrators in Large City School Systems," *Educational Administration Quarterly*, III (Autumn 1967), 231.

21. Frank Riessman, *The Culturally Deprived Child* (New York: Harper and Row, 1962).

22. Robert J. Havighurst, *Education in Metropolitan Areas* (Boston: Allyn and Bacon, 1966).

23. A. Harry Passow, *Education in Depressed Areas* (New York: Columbia University Press, 1964).

24. Kenneth B. Clark, *Dark Ghetto* (New York: Harper and Row, 1965).

25. James S. Coleman *et al.*, *Equality of Educational Opportunity* (Washington, D.C.: U. S. Government Printing Office, 1966).

26. Stephen F. Gold, "School—Community Relations in Urban Ghettos," *The Record*, LXIX (November 1967), 149–50.

27. Holland and Galfo, *An Analysis of Research Concerning Class Size*.

28. *Ibid.*

29. "Teacher Strikes, 1960–61 to 1969–70," *NEA Research Bulletin* (October 1970), 69.

30. "Why Some School Boards Are Little More Than Employment Agencies," *Education Summary* (August 20, 1971), 5.

31. George D. Spindler, "Education in a Transforming Culture," *Harvard Educational Review*, XXV (Summer 1955), 150.

32. "Why Some School Boards Are Little . . ."

33. Luvern L. Cunningham and Raphael O. Nystrand, "Toward Greater Relevance in Preparation Programs for Urban School Administrators," *Educational Administration Quarterly*, V (Winter 1969), 8.

34. Elwood P. Cubberley, *Public School Administration* (Boston: Houghton

Mifflin, 1916), 132; as quoted in Raymond E. Callahan, "Changing Conceptions of the Superintendency in Public Education, 1865–1964" (Cambridge, Mass.: The New England School Development Council, 1964), 13.

35. Chester I. Barnard, *The Functions of the Executive* (Cambridge, Mass.: Harvard University Press, 1938).

36. F. J. Roethlisberger and W. J. Dickson, *Management and the Worker* (Cambridge, Mass.: Harvard University Press, 1939).

37. Cunningham and Nystrand, 10.

38. *Ibid.*, 6.

39. Keith Goldhammer, John E. Suttle, William D. Aldridge, and Gerald L. Becker, *Issues and Problems in Contemporary Educational Administration* (Eugene, Oregon: Center for the Advanced Study of Educational Administration, 1967), 5.

40. *Ibid.*, 53.

41. Robert L. Crain and David Street, "School Desegregation and School Decision-Making," *Educating an Urban Population*, ed. Marilyn Gittell (Beverly Hills: Sage Publications, 1967), 142–43.

Chapter 6

1. Daniel Levine and Robert J. Havighurst, "Social Systems of a Metropolitan Area," *Metropolitanism: Its Challenge to Education*, ed. Robert J. Havighurst, The Sixty-seventh Yearbook of the National Society for the Study of Education (Chicago: University of Chicago Press, 1968), 52–53.

2. John I. Goodlad, "The Schools vs. Education," *Saturday Review* (April 19, 1969), 61.

3. Robert J. Havighurst, "Chicago's Educational Needs—1966," *Educating an Urban Population*, ed. Marilyn Gittell (Beverly Hills: Sage Publications 1967), 45–46.

4. *Ibid.*, 46.

5. Robert H. Salisbury, "Schools and Politics in the Big City," *Harvard Educational Review*, XXXVII (Summer 1967), 413.

6. *Ibid.*, 412.

7. Bernard Bard, "New York City Principals: On the Razor's Edge," *Saturday Review* (January 24, 1970), 72.

8. Salisbury, 410.

9. Robert Presthus, *The Organizational Society* (New York: Vintage Books, 1962), 27–58.

10. *Ibid.*, 40.

11. U. S. Office of Education, "Targeted Program in Research and Development: The Organization and Administration of Elementary and Secondary Schools," In draft form, June 1970 (mimeographed), 76.

12. Goodlad, 61.

13. Buford Rhea, "The Large High School in Its Social Context," *The Bulletin of the NASSP*, CCCXXXI (November 1968), 37.

14. George B. Thomas, "Tension: A Tool for Reform," *Saturday Review* (July 19, 1969), 50.

15. Goodlad, 60.

16. Edward C. Banfield, *Unheavenly City: The Nature and the Future of Our Urban Crisis* (Boston: Little, Brown, 1970).

17. U. S. Office of Education, "Targeted Program . . . ," 73.

18. Bard, 59.

19. Michael B. Katz, *The Irony of Early School Reform: Educational Innovation in Mid-Nineteenth Century Massachusetts* (Cambridge: Harvard University Press, 1969).

20. *Ibid.*, 58.

21. Martin Mayer, "What's Wrong with Big-City Schools," *The Saturday Evening Post* (September 1967), 21.

22. John H. Fischer, "Urban Schools: Issues in Responsiveness and Control," *Decentralization and Racial Integration*, eds. Carroll F. Johnson and Michael D. Usdan, a Report of the proceedings of a Special Training Institute on Problems of School Desegregation, July 10–12, 1968 (New York: Teachers College, Columbia University, 1968), 24.

23. U. S. Office of Education, "Targeted Program . . . ," 84.

Chapter 7

1. H. Thomas James, James A. Kelly, and Walter I. Garms, *Determinants of Educational Expenditures in Large Cities of the United States*, Cooperative Research Project No. 2389, Office of Education, U. S. Department of Health, Education, and Welfare, 1966, 17.

2. For a more comprehensive treatment of the fiscal conflict between city and suburban schools, the reader is referred to Seymour Sacks, *City Schools/ Suburban Schools* (Syracuse: Syracuse University Press, 1972). Focusing on the thirty-seven largest metropolitan areas in the United States, Sacks documents and describes in considerable detail the critical disparities between large city and suburban school finances, their historical development, present status, and prospects for the future. His analysis is the product of over a decade of study at The Maxwell School, Syracuse University, of the economics, finance, and governance of public education, especially that in large cities.

3. Alan K. Campbell and Seymour Sacks, *Metropolitan America: Fiscal Patterns and Governmental Systems* (New York: The Free Press, 1967).

4. Penrose B. Jackson, *Trends in Elementary and Secondary Education Expenditures: Central City and Suburban Comparisons: 1965–1968*, U. S. Office of Education, Office of Program Planning and Evaluation, June 1969.

5. *Serrano v. Priest*, 96 California Reporter 601 (1971).

6. Quoted in "The Locally Assessed Property Tax," *Education Summary* (September 17, 1971), 2.

7. Ben E. Graves, "The Decaying Schoolhouse," *The Schoolhouse in the City*, ed. Alvin Toffler (New York: Praeger, 1968), 64.

8. "Age of School Buildings Where Teachers Teach," NEA *Research Bulletin* (October 1970), 82.

9. Graves, 61–62.

10. *The Schoolhouse in the City*, a report from Educational Facilities Laboratory (New York: 1966), 1–2.

11. Michael D. Usdan, "Some Issues Confronting School Administrators in Large City School Systems," *Educational Administration Quarterly*, III (Autumn 1967), 231–32.

12. George B. Brain, "Pressures on the Urban School," *The Schoolhouse in the City*, ed. Alvin Toffler (New York: Praeger, 1968), 41.

13. William P. McLure, *Some Determinants of Educational Costs in Eleven Great Cities* (Chicago: The Research Council of the Great Cities Program for School Improvement, 1963).

14. Usdan, 231.

15. Carl E. Thornblad, "A Summary of the Fiscal Impact of a Concentration of Low Income Families on the Public Schools—A Study of Public Housing and Public Education in Chicago in 1962," based on a study conducted by the National Opinion Research Center and submitted during a hearing before the General Subcommittee on Education of the Committee on Education and Labor, House of Representatives, Ninety-first Congress, First Session, on H. R. 1285 (Washington, D.C., March 4, 1969), 5.

16. Alan K. Campbell, "Inequities of School Finance," *Saturday Review* (January 11, 1969), 46.

17. *Ibid.*

18. Harold Howe II, "The City as a Teacher," *The Schoolhouse in the City*, ed. Alvin Toffler (New York: Praeger, 1968), 13.

19. Seymour Sacks, *Fiscal Balance in the American Federal System*, a report prepared for the Advisory Commission on Intergovernmental Relations, 1968.

20. David K. Cohen, "The Economics of Inequality," *Saturday Review* (April 19, 1969), 64.

21. Campbell, 46.

22. Howe, 17.

23. Campbell, 44.

24. U. S. Department of Commerce, Bureau of the Census, *Census of Business*, 1958.

25. Oscar H. Steiner, "Slums Are a Luxury We Cannot Afford," *The Reporter* (November 14, 1957), 27.

26. *The Impact of Urbanization on Education*, Summary Report of the Conference on the Impact of Urbanization on Education, Office of Education, May 28–29, 1962 (Washington, D.C.: U. S. Government Printing Office, 1962).

27. James *et al.*, 13.

28. *Ibid.*, 14.

29. *Ibid.*, 16.

30. Quoted in Howe, "The City as a Teacher," 18.

31. Seymour Sacks and David C. Ranney, "Suburban Education: A Fiscal Analysis," *Educating an Urban Population*, ed. Marilyn Gittell (Beverly Hills: Sage Publications, 1967), 66.

32. James *et al.*, 12.

33. Seymour Sacks, *City Schools/Suburban Schools: A History of Fiscal Conflict* (Syracuse: Syracuse University Press, 1972), 177.

34. Mark R. Shedd, "Nationalize the Big-City Schools!" Harvard Graduate School of Education Association *Bulletin*, XVI (Spring, 1972), 16.

Chapter 8

1. U. S. Riot Commission, *Report of the National Advisory Commission on Civil Disorders*, An Advance Copy of the Report (New York: The New York Times Company, 1968), 390.

2. *Ibid.*, 391.

3. Daniel U. Levine and Robert J. Havighurst, "Negro Population Growth and Enrollment in the Public Schools: A Case Study and Its Implications," *Education and Urban Society*, I (November 1968), 24–25.

4. Raymond Vernon, *The Changing Economic Function of the Central City* (New York: Committee for Economic Development, 1960).

5. Jeanne R. Lowe, "Race, Jobs, and Cities: What Business Can Do," *Saturday Review* (January 11, 1969), 29.

6. Based upon reports issued by the U. S. Departments of Labor, Commerce, and Health, Education and Welfare.

7. "Moynihan's Memo," *The National Observer* (March 9, 1970).

8. Seymour Sudman, Norman M. Bradburn, and Galen Gockel, "The Extent and Characteristics of Racially Integrated Housing in the United States," *The Journal of Business of the University of Chicago*, XLII (January 1969), 52–65.

9. Lowe, 27.

10. *Ibid.*, 30.

11. *Ibid.*, 27.

12. Melvin M. Webber, "The Post-City Age," *Daedalus*, XCVII (Fall 1968), 1097.

13. U. S. Department of Commerce, Bureau of the Budget, *Standard Metropolitan Statistical Areas* (Washington, D.C.: U. S. Government Printing Office, 1964).

14. David W. Minar, "Interactions of School and Local Non-School Government in Metropolitan Areas," *Metropolitanism: Its Challenge to Education*, ed. Robert J. Havighurst, The Sixty-seventh Yearbook of the National Society for the Study of Education (Chicago: University of Chicago Press, 1968), 199.

15. *Ibid.*, 199.

16. *Ibid.*, 200.

17. *Ibid.*, 200–201.

18. John C. Bollens and Henry J. Schmandt, *The Metropolis: Its People, Politics, and Economic Life* (New York: Harper and Row, 1965), 209–10.

19. John A. Rehfuss, "Metropolitan Government: Four Views," *Urban Affairs Quarterly*, III (June 1968), 94.

20. Citizens' Advisory Committee to the Joint Legislature Committee on Urban Area Government, *City and Suburb—Community or Chaos* (Seattle: Joint Committee on Urban Area Government, 1962), 4–6.

21. Daniel R. Grant, "The Metropolitan Government Approach: Should, Can, and Will It Prevail," *Urban Affairs Quarterly*, III (March 1968), 104–5.

22. Rehfuss, 101.

23. Robert J. Havighurst, *Metropolitanism: Its Challenges to Education*, The Sixty-seventh Yearbook of the National Society for the Study of Education (Chicago: University of Chicago Press, 1968), 4.

24. Scott Greer and David W. Minar, "The Political Side of Urban Development and Redevelopment," *The New Urbanization*, ed. Scott Greer, Dennis L. McElrath, David W. Minar, and Peter Orleans (New York: St. Martin's Press, 1968), 301.

25. Grant, 109.

26. Grant, 110.

Chapter 9

1. Morris Janowitz, *Institution Building in Urban Education* (New York: Russell Sage Foundation, 1969).

2. *Ibid.*, 51.

3. Although apparently carried on without specific reference to the Janowitz model, organizational changes at the Dr. Martin Luther King School in Syracuse, New York, nicely illustrate the principles of the model. They are reported by William W. Wayson in "Organizing Urban Schools for Responsible Education," *Phi Delta Kappan*, LII (February 1971), 344–47.

4. Louis C. Schaw, *Bonds of Work* (San Francisco: Jossey Bass, 1968), 2.

5. Melvin M. Webber, "The Post-City Age," *Daedalus*, XCVII (Fall 1968), 1091–1110.

6. James S. Coleman *et al.*, *Equality of Educational Opportunity* (Washington, D.C.: U. S. Government Printing Office, 1966).

7. David K. Cohen, "The Price of Community Control," *Theory Into Practice*, VIII (November 1969), 231–41.

8. Daniel U. Levine, "Concepts of Bureaucracy in Urban School Reform," *Phi Delta Kappan*, LII (February 1971), 329–33.

9. Ivar Berg, *Education and Jobs: The Great Training Robbery* (New York: Praeger, 1970), 191.

10. Edward C. Banfield, *Unheavenly City: The Nature and the Future of Our Urban Crisis* (Boston: Little, Brown, 1970), 135.

11. Marcia Freedman, "Poor People and the Distribution of Job Opportunities," *Journal of Social Issues*, XXVI (Summer 1970), 35–46.

12. Eli Ginzberg, "Vocational Education Is Not the Answer," *Phi Delta Kappan*, LII (February 1971), 369–71.

13. David K. Cohen, "The Economics of Inequality," *Saturday Review* (April 19, 1969), 64.

14. Cohen, "The Price of Community Control," 233.

15. Harold Howe II, "Anatomy of A Revolution," *Saturday Review* (November 20, 1971), 84–88, 95.

16. Mario Fantini, *The Reform of Urban Schools* (Washington, D.C.: National Education Association, Center for the Study of Instruction, 1970).

17. One particularly promising design for opening up a school is the "multiunit" or "unitized school" concept being developed and tested by the Wisconsin Research and Development Center for Cognitive Learning, one of ten federally supported educational Research and Development Centers.

18. Robert J. Meeker and Daniel M. Wyler, "A New School for the Cities," *Education and an Urban Society*, III (February 1971), 129–243.

19. Robert J. Havighurst, "The Reorganization of Education in Metropolitan Areas," *Phi Delta Kappan*, LII (February 1971), 354–58.

In Retrospect

1. Robert Redfield, *The Primitive World and Its Transformations* (Ithaca, New York: Cornell University Press, 1953), 123, 124.

2. Solon T. Kimball and James E. McClellan, Jr., *Education and the New America* (New York: Random House, 1962), 258.

Index

Aggregation and specialization models of institutional change, 247-50

Agriculture and the growth of cities, 48-49

Arendt, Hannah, 50-51

Assessment of student achievement, 250-51

Authority structure in schools, 34-36, 258, 265, 275

Banfield, Edward C., 247, 267

Bard, Bernard, 152-53

Berg, Ivar, 266-67

Bernstein, Abraham, xiv

Black capitalism, 228

Bollens, John C., 238

Boulding, Kenneth, 37, 38

Bradburn, Norman M., 223-26

Brain, George B., 184

Bronfenbrenner, Urie, 67

Bureaucracy in urban schools, 154-60, 163, 260

Business ideology in school administration, 33-34, 159

Buss, William G. Jr., 101

Bussing to achieve racial integration, 17-18, 97-98, 257-58

Calhoun, John B., 65

Callahan, Raymond, 29, 33-34, 159

Campbell, Alan K., 115, 177, 189, 192, 195

Career education, 269-70

City:
  compared with the village, 47-50
  in history, 47-49
  as a transformer of man and society, 45-47

Clark, Kenneth, 124

Cohen, David K., 192, 257, 272-73

Cohen, Sol, ix, 30

Coleman, James, 125, 272

Compensatory education, 150, 259, 271-72

Counts, George, 154

Cox, Harvey, 65, 66, 69, 70

Crain, Robert, 142

Cremin, Lawrence, ix, 29-31

Cronin, Joseph, 137

Cubberly, Elwood P., 139

Cult of efficiency in school administration, 33-34

Cunningham, Luvern, 140

Decentralization of school districts, 260-61, 275

Desegregation of schools, 8-9, 17-18, 96-98, 257-58

Dolce, Carl, 116

Drugs in schools, 9-10
Dye, Thomas R., 97

Educational level of Negroes, 221-23
Educational planning and urban
    schools, 166-67
Employment:
    of inner-city school graduates, 22
    of nonwhites, 219-23
    prospects in urban centers, 212-19
    and schooling, 265-71
Equality of educational opportunity,
    148-51, 271-74, 279-80
Evaluation of school programs, 250-
    51
Expenditures in urban schools, 168-
    80

Fantini, Mario, 275
Fiscal constraints faced by urban
    schools:
    the burdens of public housing, 186-
    89
    the costs of constructing and main-
    taining facilities, 181-84
    the costs of special programs, 185-
    86
    declining revenues, 16-17, 187-98
    inequities in state aid provided to
    suburbs and cities, 199-203
    a loss of human capital, 198-99
    the mounting costs of insurance,
    15-16
    "municipal overburden," 189-90
    personnel costs, 184-85
    the stagnant tax base in most cities,
    192-202
    a "taxpayers' revolt," 16-17
Fischer, John H., 165
Flexner, Abraham, 29
"Four-walls" school, 147
Freedman, Marcia, 268
Friedenberg, Edgar, 36

Galbraith, John Kenneth, 148
Galfo, Armand J., 119
Garms, Walter I., 169, 196-97, 199,
    201
Gavin, James M., 55-56

Ginzberg, Eli, 269
Gockel, Galen, 223-26
Gold, Stephen F., 125-26
Goldhammer, Keith, 141-42
Goodlad, John, 146, 159, 161
Goodman, Paul, 24
Gottman, Jean, 64
Grant, Daniel R., 239, 242, 244
Graves, Ben E., 181-82
Great High Schools Plan in Pitts-
    burgh, 21, 256-57
Greenbaum, William, 137
Greer, Colin, ix
Greer, Scott, 241

Hadley, Arthur, 55-56
Harris, William Torrey, 31, 32, 34,
    35
Havighurst, Robert, 23-24, 38-39, 89,
    146-47, 210-12, 240, 249, 277-
    78
Hawley, Amos H., 95
Hentoff, Nat, 24
Herndon, James, 24
Historical perspective on urban
    schools, 26-37
Holland, Howard K., 119
Howe, Harold, 69, 190, 194, 273

Immigrants to cities, then and now,
    72-74
Industrialism:
    and its influence on the design of
    schools, 32-33
    and the specialization of work, 50-
    53
    and urban expansion, 53-56

Jackson, Penrose B., 178
Jacobs, Jane, 48, 49
James, H. Thomas, 169, 196-97, 199-
    201
Janowitz, Morris, 247-48

Katz, Michael, 163
Kelly, James A., 169, 196-97, 199-
    201
Kimball, Solon, 280

Kinsella, Paul A., 114
Kohl, Herbert, 24
Kozol, Jonathan, 24

Lazerson, Martin, 32
Levine, Daniel U., 38-39, 210-12, 260
Lowe, Jeanne R., 215

Magnitude of big-city schools, 83-88
Mann, Horace, 28, 31, 32
Marland, Sidney, 256-57
Mass media and effects on urban children, 114-15
Mayer, Martin, 164
McClellan, James E., 280
McLure, William P., 119, 186
Meeker, Robert J., 277
Meranto, Philip, 115
Metropolitanism, 234-44
Minar, David W., 236-37, 241
Moynihan, Daniel, 220, 247
Mumford, Lewis, 46-48, 51, 53

New York City Public Schools, 86-88
Nonpublic schools and their influence on urban schools, 4, 90-96
Nystrand, Raphael O., 140

"Open" classrooms and schools, 274-77

Parsons, Talcott, 38, 41
Passow, A. Harry, 124
Pettigrew, Thomas, 105
Political separation of schools as a myth, 29-30, 151-54
Population:
    density in cities, 56-58, 253-54
    distribution of Negroes in metropolitan areas, 74-80
    distribution of the poor in metropolitan areas, 78-81
    migration to cities, 54-60
    migration of minority groups, 72-78
    movement to suburbs, 5, 60-64, 76
Presthus, Robert, 154-57

Racial segregation in urban school enrollments:
    the degree of, 102-9
    efforts to reduce, xii, xiv, 255-58
    the influence of legislation upon, 98-102
    one outcome of urbanization, 89-90
    trends in, 208-12
Ranney, David C., 200
Redfield, Robert, 279-80
Reform in urban schools:
    early efforts to achieve, 29-32
    methodology of, 246, 251-52
    organizational innovations as examples of, 274-78
    resistance to, 160-67
    strategies for, 246-50
Rehfuss, John A., 239
Residential segregation by race, 223-26
Rhea, Buford, 160
Riessman, Frank, 123
Rogers, David, 108
Role and goals of urban schools, 145-48
Rugg, Harold, 154

Sacks, Seymour, 177, 190, 200, 203
Salisbury, Robert H., 148-49, 153-54
Schaw, Lewis, 251
Schmandt, Henry J., 230
School administrators, 138-42
School as an agency of social control, 30-32
School-university collaboration, 10-12
Secularization and the pluralism of values, 65-68, 149-50
Shaw, Frederick, 113
Shedd, Mark, 203
Shepard, Samuel, 116-17
Sieber, Sam, 82
Social engineering in school design and operation, 35-36
Social system perspective on urban schools, xi, xii, 26, 37-42, 143-44
Socioeconomic stratification in urban school enrollments, 109-10, 208-12

Specialization of work:
    in bureaucracies, 157
    its effects on the growth of cities,
        50-52
    its psychological effects, 51, 52
    for students, 52
Spencer, Herbert, 34-35
Spindler, George D., 67, 137
Steiner, Oscar H., 195
Street, David, 141-42
Student achievement, 250-51, 259
Student dropout, 246
Student enrollment in big-city schools,
        82-87, 102-110, 207-12
Student unrest, 7-8, 12-15
Sudman, Seymour, 223-26
Supreme Court decision in *Serrano vs.
    Priest*, 178-80, 202

Teachers in urban schools:
    characteristics of, 120-22
    placement of, 117-24
    relations with parents, 124-26
    salaries and working conditions of,
        126-33, 184-85
    unionization and militancy of, 7-8,
        18-19
Thomas, George B., 161
Thompson, James, 40, 41
Thornblad, Carl E., 186-87
Transforming men and societies:
    role of the city in, 45-50
    role of urban schools in, 280

Unitary community as a myth, 148-
    51
Urban children:
    and educational disadvantage, 115-
        17, 255
    as influenced by mass media, 113-
        14
"Urban community" school, 147
Urban ghettos, 227-31, 254-55
Urban neighborhoods, 111-13
Urban reconstruction, 231-33
Urban school boards of education,
    133-38
Urbanization:
    and industrialism, 53-56
    and racial and socioeconomic im-
        balance, 89-90
    and secularization, 65-71
    and social problems, 71-72
    and urban school reform, 252-55
Usdan, Michael, 119-20, 184, 186

Vandalism in urban schools, 5, 14-16
Vernon, Raymond, 215
Vonier, Sprague, 114

Warren, Robert Penn, 65, 243
Webber, Melvin, 25, 26, 234, 253
White, Dana, 34
"White flight" to the suburbs, 76-77
Wirth, Louis, 70
Witty, Paul A., 114
Wyler, Daniel N., 277

Zimmer, Basil, 95